Unequal Contest
Bill Langer and His Political Enemies

By

Robert Vogel

Edited by Janet Daley

Unequal Contest: Bill Langer and His Political Enemies
Copyright © 2004 by Robert Vogel

First edition published in 2004 by **Crain Grosinger Publishing**, Mandan, North Dakota

Author: Robert Vogel
Edited by Janet Daley
Project Editor: Paula Crain Grosinger, RN
Senior Editor: Brian D. Grosinger, JD

Except for the purpose of fair review, no part of this publication may be reproduced or transmitted in any form or by any means, electronic or mechanical, without written permission from the publisher.

International Standard Book Number 0-9720054-3-9

Printed in the United States of America by Sentinel Printing Inc. St. Cloud, Minnesota

Acknowledgments

Many people have assisted me in the research, writing, and editing of this book. My thanks to Dan Rylance for his generous sharing of research material, to Dr. Charles Barber, who read early versions of the manuscript and made substantive suggestions about its revision and documentation, and to Janet Daley, the editor who shaped and polished the text.

*The publisher would like to thank the following for their assistance with the production of **Unequal Contest**:*

*Beth Smith - Aberdeen, South Dakota
June Veit - Bismarck, North Dakota
The State Historical Society of North Dakota*

It is a noteworthy coincidence that a book about a man who began his legal career as a Morton County, North Dakota prosecutor should be published ninety years later by a firm owned by a Morton County prosecutor and located in Mandan, North Dakota.

To the memory of Bill Langer, the Nonpartisan League, and especially to the memory of my father, Frank Vogel.

Frank Vogel

Table of Contents

Foreword i

Preface ii

1 William Langer and His Legacy 1

2 Langer's Enemies and the Origins of the
  North Dakota Trials 9

3 The First Conspiracy Trial:
  May 22–June 10, 1934 36

4 Reversal by the Eighth Circuit Court of Appeals:
  March–May 1935 71

5 The Affidavit of Prejudice and Perjury Trial:
  December 3-6, 1935 80

6 The Second and Third Conspiracy Trials:
  October 29–November 16 and December 10-19, 1935 89

7 The Senate Investigation:
  January 3–November 2, 1941 102

8 The Senate Hearings and Decision:
  November 3, 1941–March 27, 1942 131

Conclusion 139

Appendix A: Langer and the Historians 156

About the Author 177

About the Editor 179

Endnotes 180

Index 203

Foreword

Although with the passing of time the memory of Bill Langer has dimmed a little, he still stands bigger than life. Those who are aware of his conflicts and accomplishments are in awe. His principles of justice and fairness are timeless. Bill Langer withstood devastating political and personal attacks while forwarding the cause of the underprivileged. In spite of adversity he never lost sight of the goal.

The author, Robert Vogel, is also bigger than life. He has worn many hats in his career: state prosecutor, federal prosecutor, state supreme court justice, trial lawyer and university professor. Regardless of the hat he was wearing he consistently worked for the betterment of others and fought for those who needed help. He has carried on the legacy of Bill Langer.

On a more personal note, it was Bob and his firm that gave me my first job in the legal profession. In that capacity I too benefited from his dedication to helping others. Years later, I still rely on the lessons he taught me and strive to forward the same principles. I cannot repay a debt of this nature, and I'm sure the many other trial lawyers Bob has mentored over the years would agree.

Bill Langer always rose to the challenge when it came to helping those in need. Bob Vogel has also consistently stood up for those who need it most. They are shining examples that should be emulated by all of us. It is with pride that I have the honor of playing this small role in this publication.

Brian D. Grosinger
Senior Editor

Author's Preface

Writing this book has been both an intellectual enterprise and a deeply personal experience for me. I have a profound conviction that journalists and historians, intentionally or unintentionally, have misinterpreted or falsified some events in North Dakota's history, and an important case in point is the legal wrangling involving William Langer. In the seventy years since his political career and that of his closest advisors were attacked and subjected to scrutiny in the courtroom, and later in the United States Senate, those events have not received the objective and critical examination they deserve. My belief is that in fairness to the people involved, they deserve a more objective history than they have received so far from the bitter partisans of the day whose record of the events appeared in the major city newspapers, as well as from historians who have only skimmed the surface of the dynamics of the trial.

I realize, of course, that what I have written, since I was a participant in some events and the son of one of the main actors in others, will be regarded by some as self-serving and to the extent I refer to my father, Frank Vogel, an act of filial piety. On the other hand, while there are, no doubt, better lawyers in North Dakota, and certainly better historians and politicians, I know of no one in the state who has as much background and experience in all three fields as I have. I may be one of the few persons alive who has spent the long hours required to read all of the records of the four trials Bill Langer and his codefendants went through and of the effort to unseat Langer from the Senate.

Certainly many historians have known little or nothing of law or politics; the politicians almost without exception are much more interested in making history than writing it; and lawyers, while often interested in politics, generally lack an interest in writing history. In default of someone else better qualified, I think I am well qualified to offer my commentary on the law, history, and politics of my native state, and the interaction of the three of them during my lifetime, from 1918 to the present.

I knew many, if not most, of the people named in this account. Of course, I was most closely connected with Frank Vogel, my father, but I also knew Bill Langer, Alvin Strutz, Oscar Erickson, Usher Burdick, Francis Murphy, James Mulloy, and C. R. Verry. I even sued Verry once for a client. I was at least acquainted in person and by reputation, with Judge Christianson, George Shafer, Harry Lashkowitz, John Sullivan, John Williams, R. A. Kinzer, and most of the other North Dakota lawyers and politicians who are mentioned.

I not only knew P. W. ("Pete") Lanier, Sr., but, after a brief hiatus when Ralph Maxwell was acting U.S. attorney, succeeded him in that position. I was a government witness in a case he tried, and in it had the experience of being cross-examined by J. K. Murray, whom I also knew quite well, having opposed him in five trials, all memorable. I heard Langer, Lemke, Nye, Vogel, Strutz, Erickson, Usher Burdick, and even A. C. Townley, in his later years, speak to public crowds. As a teenage boy, I walked down to the courthouse in Bismarck after school to watch P. W. Lanier in his role as prosecutor against Bill Langer and my father and the other defendants in 1935.

While some may think that an active presence at events creates a bias, I think there is a greater advantage to having been present at many of the events and knowing many of the people involved in the story being told. I have attended Nonpartisan League meetings in one-room country schools and county courthouses, attended League picnics, and I can recall the dim lights and musty smell of the old Silver Ballroom of the Patterson Hotel in Bismarck where the colorful and democratic NPL state conventions were held. These personal experiences give me a feel for the personalities and politics that no amount of research alone can give. It helps to have been there.

In addition, I have read the transcripts of all four trials, the Senate investigators' interviews (4,000 pages of what they called "affidavits", their highly slanted reports, the Senate majority and minority reports, the debate in the Senate, the private political records of Harry Hopkins, director of FERA, the records of prosecuting attorney P. W. Lanier, the records of the Clerk of United States District Court and the Eighth Circuit Court of Appeals, the entire correspondence and memoranda of the Department of Justice relating to the four trials. I have also been the grateful recipient of typewritten notes of Daniel P. Rylance on his exploration of records of the Federal Emergency Relief Administration and other agencies, as well as many books and articles relating to the trials and the attempts to unseat Bill Langer in the U.S. Senate. While I have had ready access to the voluminous Langer Papers at the Chester Fritz Library at the University of North Dakota, I do not pretend to have read them all (they take about a sixth of a mile of shelf space).

After spending more than fifty years in the field of law, including prosecuting as state's attorney and U.S. attorney, defending a great many criminal cases, and trying hundreds, perhaps thousands of civil cases, as well as having been a justice of the Supreme Court of North Dakota and a professor of law at the University of North Dakota School of Law, I have a strong interest in our justice system and its fairness. I recognize and deplore the abuse of that system when it is used for political purposes and make no apology for exposing that abuse of the system when it happens, as it did in the trials of William Langer.

Unequal Contest
Bill Langer and
His Political Enemies

Chapter 1
William Langer and His Legacy

"I'm the most predictable damn fellow in the Senate! I'm always on the side of the underdog."
— William Langer[1]

"Senator William Langer, of North Dakota, was the last blown-in-the-bottle Populist . . .The newspapers always rated him as unpredictable. I always knew exactly how, and why, he would vote. Whenever people were in trouble, with their backs against the wall, Bill would be on their side, swinging both arms and pouring out a stream of violent language."
— Senator Paul Douglas, Illinois [D][2]

William Langer was the most loved and most hated political figure in North Dakota for several generations—the most maligned and the most praised, the devil incarnate and the patron saint of the oppressed. From 1914 to 1959 he was state's attorney, attorney general, governor and United States senator, and a highly successful trial lawyer when not in office. In his political career, he won ten elections and lost three.[3]

Bill Langer's career as one of North Dakota's most colorful politicians and a leader of the Nonpartisan League (NPL)[4] has often been misinterpreted by his opponents, particularly journalists, within North Dakota and in the East. As an example, the *Saturday Evening Post* described him in 1954 as "the most baffling man in the Senate."[5] One cannot discuss either Langer's successes or his challenges without also examining the role of the Nonpartisan League, arguably one of the most remarkable agrarian reform movements of the twentieth century in this country. Historian Scott Ellsworth described the NPL as:

the most successful democratic mass movement in twentieth century American history. Born in 1915, the NPL came to embody the democratic political and economic aspirations of hundreds of thousands of American farmers and laborers in nearly twenty Western and Midwestern states. In its home state of North Dakota, the League captured control of the state government, and retained it long enough to successfully implement its program of economic reforms, including the creation of a state-owned terminal grain elevator, flour mill, and bank.[6]

Within four years of its inception in 1915, the Nonpartisan League had taken over North Dakota state government. The NPL established a state-owned bank, a state-owned mill and elevator, a state bonding fund, a state-run bank deposit insurance fund, and a state-run hail insurance fund. It put in place state controls on private sector banks, railroads, and the grain business. The NPL movement spread into a dozen other states and three Canadian provinces, and, at its height, had close to 200,000 members, 70 percent of whom were located in North and South Dakota, Minnesota, and Montana.[7]

The League's symbol was neither the Republican elephant nor the Democratic donkey, but the NPL goat, the "Goat that Can't be Got." After a Republican legislator allegedly told farmers in 1915 to "go home and slop the hogs and leave the legislating to us," they cited this contemptuous statement as their rallying cry.[8] Their motto became, "We'll Stick, We'll Win," and they usually did both, but not without cost, both personal and political.[9] The League's leaders were abused and assaulted. In several states, especially Minnesota, organizers were run out of town, and even tarred and feathered. Some supporters had their places of business or homes painted yellow by nocturnal vandals during World War I. Others were accused of being Bolsheviks and allegedly supporting the teaching of "Free Love" in the schools, simply because a non-circulating book with those two words was discovered in the North Dakota State Library.[10] A. C. Townley and Joseph Gilbert, two of the League's most prominent organizers, were prosecuted and convicted of sedition by the state of Minnesota for advocating the "drafting of wealth," through the use of income and excess profit taxes to pay for World War I, rather than the issuing of war bonds which returning veterans would have to help pay off.[11]

Members of the Nonpartisan League believed in democracy. From 1922 on, in order to frustrate the control of national party bosses, they held simultaneous, or near-simultaneous, meetings in each of the 2,200 North Dakota precincts to elect delegates to the fifty-three county meetings, where delegates to the state convention were elected by secret ballot. The state convention endorsed candidates and decided which political party's ballot column they would run them in. The idea was that no political boss could control that number of precinct or county conventions at one time. During much of its existence, the League controlled the Republican Party in North Dakota. In the thirty years after 1918, it held the governorship for fifteen, the attorney general's office for seventeen, and controlled one or both houses of the legislature and many elected offices most of the time.[12]

In 1932, when the League regained full control of the state government in the midst of the Depression, its new leaders felt the full fury of both opportunistic and conservative opposition to their movement, supported by the editors of the major daily papers in the state, the *Bismarck Tribune*, the *Fargo Forum*, the *Grand Forks Herald*, and the *Minot Daily News*. That opposition was focused on William Langer.

Born near Casselton, North Dakota, on September 30, 1886, William Langer was the son of farmers of German heritage. A bright student, Langer graduated from the University of North Dakota School of Law and passed the North Dakota bar when he was still too young to practice law. He received a second degree from Columbia University in New York City, where, as class valedictorian, he was voted "Most Likely to Succeed" and also "Noisiest." Returning to North Dakota, he practiced law in Mandan and served as assistant state's attorney of Morton County at age twenty-five, a "boy attorney."[13] According to historian Elwyn Robinson, Langer was "a brilliant, ambitious young attorney:

William Langer as a young lawyer in Mandan, North Dakota.
State Historical Society of North Dakota
A4292

3

six feet tall and weighing some two hundred pounds, aggressive, handsome, and self-confident." He described him as a "picture of easy, confident strength," with "his powerful frame, his high forehead and searching eyes. With a warmhearted spirit, he had a talent for friendship and apparently a sort of instinct for the popular medium of human emotions and loyalties in which a politician works."[14] His political courage was tested early in his career. After being elected state's attorney of Morton County in 1914, Langer spent his first days in office bringing a lawsuit against several of the biggest corporations doing business in the state. The case ultimately involved 2,038 grain elevators, more than 1,000 lumber yards, and 260 tank oil stations.[15]

From the beginning of North Dakota's statehood, land and buildings on railway right-of-way leased from the railroads had not been considered real estate subject to taxation and had not been assessed for taxes. Thus neither the railroad nor the owners of buildings on railroad land were paying taxes on the value of the buildings. Langer, as Morton County state's attorney, brought a lawsuit to tax all of the grain elevators, lumberyards, warehouses, oil stations, and other buildings on railroad rights of way, not only in Morton County but throughout the whole state. After a trial and appeal, he won, forcing the big corporations to return to the tax rolls property worth about thirty million dollars and to pay back taxes of about one and a quarter million dollars, an amount equivalent to twenty-two million dollars in year 2002 dollars. In doing so, he took on the state's top corporate lawyers—including a future federal judge, Andrew A. Miller—and beat them all, as the North Dakota Supreme Court upheld Langer's opinion on December 13, 1915.[16]

Early conflict with Andrew Miller was indelibly sealed when Attorney General Langer helped Bismarck citizens show that Miller's company was supplying the city with contaminated water.
State Historical Society of North Dakota A1302-1

From 1917 to 1921, Langer served as attorney general of the state, running as an NPL candidate on the Republican ticket. When he lost his first attempt to become governor of North Dakota in the 1920 election and another to become attorney general in 1928 by a small margin, Langer went into private law practice, becoming a successful criminal defense and civil plaintiff's lawyer.[17] Then, in 1932, he ran for governor again and won, in the biggest landslide in North Dakota's history. Bill Langer's future looked bright.

As governor, however, he faced a devastating drought and massive unemployment. The Great Depression, added to an earlier farm depression, had created a desperate situation. Supreme Court Judge A. M. Christianson, head of the relief committee in North Dakota, testified that the committee had a caseload at one time of 34,553 families, or about 150,000 individuals—nearly a quarter of the population of the state. Pierce Atwater, a field representative for Harry Hopkins, head of the Federal Emergency Relief Administration, Interior Department, estimated families on relief in North Dakota in 1935 to be 40 percent of the population.[18]

Tax collections were drying up, local governments were deep in debt, and people clamored for state jobs, any jobs. The Langer papers in the Chester Fritz Library of the University of North Dakota contain about five thousand job applications sent to Langer while he was governor in the 1930s.[19] One of William Langer's closest advisors was my father, Frank Vogel, who had much to do with patronage in the Langer administrations. He once commented on the political fallout of dispensing state jobs, saying, "For every opening there were ten applicants, and when you chose one you ended up with nine enemies and one ingrate."[20]

During and after Langer's inauguration month of January 1933, violence was erupting in other states in protest to foreclosures, hunger, and unemployment. In North Dakota, Langer and the League-controlled legislature went immediately into action, reducing state appropriations by 52 percent in 1933, an accomplishment unprecedented at that time and unmatched since. The only aspect of government that was not reduced was elementary and secondary education. The state-owned Bank of North Dakota and Mill and Elevator were called in to assist farmers and reduce distress, and Governor Langer declared a moratorium on farm foreclosures and an embargo on exporting wheat. The embargo was effective in raising wheat prices for a time although held unconstitutional later. The prompt action of Langer and the Nonpartisan League legislature spared North Dakota the violence that was going on in other states, saved a lot of

North Dakota's new "skyscraper capitol" was built during the Depression, after a fire destroyed the first capitol building in 1930.
State Historical Society of North Dakota 1075-64

farms, and protected the credit of the State of North Dakota.[21]

The cut in appropriations, however, also made enemies—state employees who lost jobs, college professors who had their pay cut, corporate recipients of state contracts that were cancelled, and many others. These enemies joined the long list Langer had already accumulated: out-of-state bankers, millers, and railroads, long accustomed to treating North Dakota as a province to be exploited, now forced to pay taxes and accept regulation; as well as all the larger daily newspapers and a substantial number of local political opponents.

Because he was so adamantly opposed by the state's daily newspapers, Langer organized a weekly paper, the *Leader*, to support the Nonpartisan League and answer its critics, with the aid of contributions from state employees, a common practice legal at the time and later. A year into his administration, his enemies struck. Halfway through his first term as governor, Langer and several other North Dakota state officials were convicted of conspiracy to impede the operation of federal law, in other words, attempting to defraud the federal government. The scenario that prompted the charge was that an individual soliciting contributions to the *Leader* had gone into a downtown Bismarck office where state employees were working and tried to raise funds for the paper. Some of the employees, working in an office bearing the sign "State Emergency Relief," were administering a federal program and were being paid by federal funds. Representatives of a Democratic Party in power in the presidency and both houses of Congress interpreted such solicitations of state employees on behalf of a Republican governor, who was administering federal funds, to be illegal.[22] The solicitor, Harold McDonald, had obtained a total of $179.50 in contributions from a few of them. The government's claim was that McDonald's action constituted a conspiracy by Langer and others to impede the operation of Acts of Congress providing for welfare. Also charged were a second solicitor, Oscar J. Chaput (also listed as business manager of the *Leader*); Frank Vogel, who was highway commissioner at that time, Oscar E. Erickson, commissioner of insurance (and publisher of the *Leader*); Gideon A. Hample, a highway department employee; R. A. Kinzer, executive secretary of the State Emergency Relief Committee; his son Joseph Kinzer; and Paul J. Yeater. The charges were criminal ones, but the motivations behind them were strictly political.[23]

Langer had been sued before, and always won. But this case was different. It was tried before Federal Judge Andrew A. Miller, who had been Langer's personal, professional, and political enemy for almost thirty years. In addition to having represented some of the defendants in Langer's 1914 lawsuit to collect unpaid corporate and railroad taxes, Miller had also been one of the owners of a water company that Langer proved had spread typhoid fever in Bismarck, after which the company was bought by the city at a price much lower than the owners wanted. This resulted in a financial loss to Miller and his two co-owners, one of whom was Alex McKenzie, formerly the longtime political boss of North Dakota.[24] More animosity arose when Andrew Miller ran for the United States Senate in 1914, and Langer publicly campaigned against him. Miller lost the election. Before he was appointed United States District Judge by President Harding in 1922, Miller had represented out-of-state banks and corporations in foreclosing on farms and businesses in North Dakota. When he attempted to order foreclosure sales on North Dakota farmers from the bench in 1933, he found his will thwarted by Governor Langer's moratorium order and willingness to use the national guard to enforce it.[25]

An epic confrontation was in the making, which resulted in four criminal trials. The first trial, before the hostile Judge Miller and a handpicked jury, was timed so as to prevent Langer from campaigning during the crucial Republican primary campaign in 1934. The trial resulted in a conviction on June 17, ten days before the primary election date.[26] At that election, the voters of North Dakota let their opinion of the conviction be known by giving Langer the biggest landslide in the history of the state, with him receiving many more votes than his two opponents combined.[27] Though Langer and his codefendants were removed from office, contrary to popular impression, they never spent an hour in jail. Nevertheless, political victory for their enemies had been achieved. Although the convictions were reversed on appeal, Langer and the other officials' terms of office ended before they could be reinstated.[28] Even after a reversal by the appellate court, the federal government pursued a prosecution, which many called persecution, for three more trials. The second one ended in a directed verdict against the federal government. The third ended in a hung jury, and, finally, the fourth ended in an acquittal. These exonerations were not just victories for Bill Langer, but for the NPL as well.[29]

While the story of the 1934–36 confrontation and its consequences for the participants and to the state of North Dakota is a gripping one, it does not end there. The culmination of the attacks on Langer came when he was elected to the United States Senate in 1940; a motley group of his enemies challenged his right to be seated on moral grounds. He was conditionally seated, and then the U.S. Senate Committee on Privileges and Elections began hearings on the charges in November 1941. Their efforts involved examining his entire legal and political career and giving a platform to all the enemies Langer had made in politics and law during that career.

The details of Langer's vigorous defense of himself and his codefendants and the machinations of his detractors is a fascinating story on many levels, not the least of which are the legal missteps taken inside and outside of the courtroom. As an attorney with more than fifty years of experience, defending clients, prosecuting criminals, and sitting on the North Dakota Supreme Court as a justice, I will examine the conduct and misconduct of those who would have William Langer's legacy besmirched for posterity. In doing so, my hope is that this book will correct the misinterpretations of his political reputation and restore him and his codefendants to their proper place in history's records.

Chapter 2
Langer's Enemies and the Origins of the North Dakota Trials

"I started to veto appropriations right and left, and finally cut $5,000,000 from $10,000,000. Of course, every cut meant that people lost jobs, and that caused hard feelings. So I made a lot of enemies."

— William Langer, in testimony before U.S. Senate Committee on Privileges and Elections[30]

When William Langer became governor in January 1933, he already had many adversaries. That year, he and the League-controlled legislature quickly made new enemies by reducing state appropriations. His inauguration came in the depths of the Great Depression, when about one-third of North Dakota's people were on relief (what we now call welfare), and a lot of taxes were unpaid. Many cities and counties had exhausted their resources and were paying wages and other bills with warrants pledging future revenues, if and when received. Of course, merchants and banks were reluctant to accept such paper in place of money and often devalued the warrants 10 percent or more when they did accept them.

Governor Langer and the NPL-dominated legislature made the hard choices in this era of drought and depression. No cuts were made in elementary and secondary education, but drastic cuts were made in appropriations for other state offices and agencies, including higher education. In the end, Langer and the legislature cut state appropriations by more than half. This unprecedented feat did not endear Langer and the NPL to state employees or private contractors dependent on state government for their income. Particularly unforgiving were the newspaper editors in the state who had vested interests—politically, personally, and economically—before and after the election, in opposing Langer.

Confronting his opponents and attacking the major media became a part of Bill Langer's overall campaign style that he maintained the rest of his political life. Watching him in action was something this author will never forget and which I described in an earlier essay:

> Bill Langer was a master at 'working a crowd.' He drew large crowds, which he usually kept waiting, because he planned to meet an impossible schedule of perhaps 6 or 8 meetings a day. No matter how fast his drivers drove, he could not get to all the meetings on time. He was often two hours late, but the crowds waited for him. My brother Dave [Vogel] drove for him one campaign, and told about being so exhausted he slept standing up, propped against the walls in a corner of a crowded hall that had no chair for him to sit on.
>
> If Bill Langer was speaking in a German speaking community, he would throw in a few words of German, a joke or a pun or some remark about a political enemy known to the crowd—probably an enemy who did not speak German. He always loved to refer to local people in his speeches. He told stories about local politicians, including friendly ones. And he got lots of laughs.
>
> In fact, he got laughs in all talks, to all crowds, keeping the crowds in stitches a good share of the time. He especially liked to make fun of newspaper people, knowing full well that the press was solidly against him, and that he had nothing to lose from raking them over the coals. He certainly did not kowtow to the press, as so many politicians do.
>
> One year he told the audiences he was running a contest to see which of the four biggest daily newspapers was the biggest liar. Usually the [closest] local newspaper [of the four] would be reported as being in the lead.
>
> Another time he said he was running a contest to decide who was the ugliest man in North Dakota, and said that the leader was the Associated Press reporter who was following him around the state to report on his meetings . . . He was sublimely disinterested in buttering up the media. He often said he didn't care what the press said about him, as long as they spelled his name right.
>
> He had a big voice (but often strained from too much speaking, and sounding as if he had gravel in his throat), a quick wit, a gift for simplifying issues, and the ability to put any issue into black and white, without any confusion from shades

of gray. He also had a genuine interest in ordinary people, and the people of North Dakota recognized that fact.

In spite of the entertainment aspect of his speeches, he worked a lot of facts into them. He named his adversaries, challenged them to contradict him, and occasionally invited people from the audience to come to the platform.[31]

With his history of making enemies, Langer had realized that he—and, by extension, the Nonpartisan League—needed a medium that could be used to answer negative charges and promote the League program. None of the large, daily papers supported the League, and radio stations (in the years before cable television) exercised a strict censorship over what they allowed to be broadcast.[32] For the most part, censorship was exercised by lawyers for the stations, who were often also attorneys for large corporations. The only uncensored station in the state was KFJM, owned by the University of North Dakota at Grand Forks—a station that covered only the northeast corner of the state. In 1936, during Langer's second term as governor, he would foil an attempt by private interests to purchase the station and make it an affiliate of the Columbia Broadcasting Company.[33]

Although some in the resurgent NPL leadership of the 1930s, including Frank Vogel, were uncertain that the financing of an independent media source in the reestablishment of the NPL newspaper, the *Leader*, was the wisest step in the long run, William Langer thought otherwise. He was convinced that none of the major media could be won over to the NPL point-of-view, and that the best thing to do would be to answer their distortions of the NPL program and his record in kind and to attack them from a media source that they could not control. The rejuvenated Nonpartisan League needed a paper of its own, just as the NPL had earlier, a newspaper first called the *Nonpartisan Leader*.

Langer first tried to reestablish the *Leader* in 1928 while he was still in private practice and reorganizing the League. He personally financed the effort by selling subscriptions through agents paid on commission. When his effort did not succeed, he refunded all money paid in, a total of more than twenty thousand dollars.[34] William Langer was, by North Dakota standards, a wealthy man. In addition to family resources, which included an inheritance of land near Casselton and his wife's considerable resources, he had carried on a very successful private practice as a trial lawyer in the 1920s. He thus could afford relatively large outlays of money, without expecting any immediate return, except on principles of reciprocity which his NPL colleagues readily understood.

In testimony presented to a fact-finding committee of the North Dakota House of Representatives, which convened in August 1934 after Bill Langer's first trial and conviction, Fred J. Argast, a farmer from Moffitt, said that in 1928, he and the two other elected members of the Executive Committee of the Nonpartisan League—Roy Frazier from the Third District, and Carl Anderson from the First District—assumed their responsibilities under the onus of a factional fight that had the previous chairman of the NPL refusing to turn over any records of the organization.[35] They were thus obliged to built up a mailing list from scratch, "select an organization in every County in the State, and select a Campaign Manager," and all of this on a fully depleted treasury."[36] Argast had recommended William Langer to become head of the NPL, and Carl Anderson recommended William Lemke, but the three of them soon decided on Langer because they knew "Bill Langer was the only man we had we could fall back on that had any money to put into this that would accept their proposition." Argast testified, "we called an Executive meeting in Bismarck, and drew up a contract, and hired him [Langer] as our attorney, and gave him the power of attorney to reorganize the League, and use his best judgment how to do it." Langer's secretary, Mrs. Ethel Mills, typed up the contract, and "the three members of the Executive committee signed it, authorizing him to go ahead with his work."[37]

On the matter of finances, Langer was to be paid for his efforts from the first money the Nonpartisan League acquired through membership drives, but such was not the case for the next four years. The NPL accumulated debts to Langer throughout those four years for his legal work on their behalf well in excess of twenty thousand dollars. Numerous audits by the Executive Committee of the NPL confirmed the existence of this debt, which Langer and the three committee members established as a compromise figure of nineteen thousand dollars the NPL owed him.[38]

There were two differences between Langer's plan in 1933 and fund-raising techniques of other state administrations, both Democratic and Republican—past, present, and future. The first was that the proceeds of Langer's fund-raising went to a newspaper, the *Leader*, rather than a campaign fund, and a smaller amount to repay the debt the Executive Committee had agreed to for his work in 1928–32. The second was that contributors could get their money back by selling a one-dollar subscription to the *Leader* for each one dollar contributed. The plan worked well, and soon the *Leader* had the biggest circulation—more than 100,000 subscribers—of any weekly in the state and a higher circulation than some dailies. Not surprisingly, the daily press deplored and condemned Langer's fund-raising idea and reported that state employees were being fired for not contributing. Those same false charges were made in Langer's trials to come, but they were all dismissed.

Langer and the four major daily newspapers (*Fargo Forum*, *Bismarck Tribune*, *Grand Forks Herald*, and *Minot Daily News*) had become bitter adversaries early in his career. One of the most influential papers in the state was the *Bismarck Tribune*, edited by Kenneth Simons. The paper had been neutral in the primary election in 1932 between Langer and Frank Hyland, the Independent Voters Association (IVA) or regular Republican, candidate for governor, even commending Langer at one point for promising to reduce state appropriations by one million dollars.[39] In fact, just before the primary election, the *Tribune* announced on its front page that it did not attempt to tell people how to vote, that it would be presumptuous to do so.

One may well wonder, then, what had happened to change the *Tribune*'s position between the primary election, when it declared its intentions to not tell people how to vote, and the general election in November, when it put a flyer in every mailbox and on many front porches in the state telling the voters to vote against Langer—the lawyer who cheated old ladies out of their money.

Bill Langer suggested that he knew why. One of the features in his plans to cut a million dollars from state appropriations was the establishment of a state printing plant, which would do all of the state's printing. During the fall campaign, he told the voters that the *Bismarck Tribune* had received $232,000 (about $3.2 million in 2002 dollars) from the State of North Dakota for printing, legal fees, and bookbinding during the previous biennium with George Shafer as governor. He quoted S. S. McDonald, a printer and later a member of the Railroad Commission (now the Public Service Commission), who had worked at the *Tribune*, as saying that with a fifty thousand-dollar appropriation, and a small room, North Dakota could have as fine a printing plant as other states had and save a lot of money as well.[40]

Saving the State of North Dakota money may have been good for the taxpayers, but it was certainly a blow to the interests of the *Tribune*. This plan alone would be enough to explain the sudden hostility of an otherwise neutral observer. While it may have been the triggering reason for the actions of the *Tribune*, there may also have been lingering animosity from the earlier water plant fight in Bismarck and Langer's opposition to political boss Alex McKenzie dating back to 1914. Checkbook journalism and political dirty tricks did not start in the 1980s; they have long been a part of the country's political history.

Once Langer's budget-cutting proposals began to hit close to home, the *Tribune* began an all-out attack on Langer, using the circumstances of what became known as the "Johnson case" to cast him in a negative light.[41] Ten days before the 1932 general election, Langer was sued by Esther Johnson, a widow from Donnybrook, North Dakota, who accused him of accepting a two thousand dollar fee from her to get her son Floyd pardoned for the crime of murder and then failing to do anything to earn the fee. The facts were much different, according to Frank Vogel's recollection.

As Frank Vogel recalled, in 1930, two years before Langer became governor, Floyd Johnson's mother retained Langer to represent her son in an attempt to get his life sentence for first-degree murder reduced so that he could ultimately be paroled (not pardoned, as was often stated.). A parole releases a prisoner, usually under supervision of a parole officer, before his term is completed while a pardon can wipe out the crime and the corresponding punishment from that time forward.

Langer checked the records at the Ward County Courthouse. He found that Floyd Johnson had pleaded guilty, without an attorney, to first-degree murder. There was no doubt that he had killed a friend. Johnson admitted it. Even the prosecutor believed that the crime was committed under the influence of drugs, something then considered an ameliorating factor, not an aggravating factor as now.

Langer contended there was no premeditation, a requirement for a conviction of first-degree murder. He believed Johnson was guilty of second-degree murder, at most. Langer also found that Johnson was not given the opportunity to consult an attorney or even talk to his parents before he was taken to court where he pleaded guilty. Langer concluded that the maximum degree of guilt should have been second-degree murder, which carried with it a possibility of parole after seventeen years in prison, instead of first-degree murder with a sentence of life imprisonment and no parole possible for at least half Floyd's life expectancy, perhaps thirty years.

Langer knew that a pardon was out of the question because Johnson had admitted killing his friend. He also knew that even a parole would be difficult to obtain because the law then required a unanimous decision by the five-person Parole Board, which was highly unlikely to happen. Langer had served on the Board and knew that very often one member of the board would prevent the granting of a parole. That person was not named, but Langer hinted that it was the chief justice of the North Dakota Supreme Court. He told Mrs. Johnson it would be difficult, expensive, and time-consuming to get any relief for her son, but he was willing to attempt it. To get relief, he told her, he would have to try to get the law changed so that a majority or a vote of four of the five members of the board could grant a parole, or he would have to get the legislature to change, or the Supreme Court to declare unconstitutional, the law that prevented parole until half of the imposed sentence had been served or half of the prisoner's life expectancy had been served. In other words, he agreed to prepare bills for the legislature to try to lobby for a change in the law so as to make it possible for Floyd Johnson to be paroled much earlier than he could otherwise be for the crime he had pleaded guilty of committing, and to try to get an amendment, or a declaration of unconstitutionality, of the law that fixed a minimum number of years to expire before parole could be granted.

Langer testified that he had checked the records, prepared a bill for the next legislative session, and appeared before a legislative committee in support of it. The committee, however, did not recommend it, and it did not pass. Langer said he then encouraged another lawyer to challenge the constitutionality of the statutes in the conviction of a Joe Milo; however, the other attorney decided not to do so for fear that a new trial might result in a longer sentence. Langer also had his former secretary, Ethel Mills, continue to work on the Johnson case after he became governor.

Mrs. Mills testified that the chances of a parole would have been fairly good, except that Floyd Johnson got in trouble while in the penitentiary. Johnson admitted that while he was acting as a prison trusty (an inmate allowed to engage in some activity outside the prison walls) in the warden's home, he had sexual relations with a woman prisoner, also a trusty working there, and she bore his child. The warden at the time of the birth of the child, Dell Patterson, confirmed that Johnson admitted being the father. The parole board would not be likely to parole a prisoner who had admitted fathering an illegitimate child while serving a life term after pleading guilty to a murder charge.

While waiting for action to be taken at the legislature, Mrs. Johnson gave no thought to suing Langer until she was approached by an ex-deputy sheriff of Ward County, who told her that she should sue Langer and that her expenses would be taken care of if she did.

He suggested Ben Bradford as an attorney. Bradford properly insisted on talking to her before taking the case and agreed to take the case after doing so.

Within a matter of days, a representative of the *Bismarck Tribune* called on Mrs. Johnson. Her daughter identified the person as Ken Simons, editor of the *Tribune*. Two of the people who later filed charges against Langer before the U.S. Senate, C. R. Verry and D. D. Riley, tried but failed to get an affidavit from her. She did, however, give the *Tribune* permission to get copies of her checks to Langer from her attorney, and Bradford gave the copies to the *Tribune*.

Bradford filed the lawsuit against Langer in Minot on October 29, 1932. Simultaneously, the *Tribune* published a full-page story of the suit, accompanied by copies of the complaint and documents, including the two checks signed by Esther Johnson and endorsed by William Langer, along with pictures of the widow and her farmstead, and a cartoon of Langer pushing a check across the table for her signature, while she was clutching her throat. The *Tribune* obviously had prepared the story well before the complaint was officially filed. In addition to the story in the regular edition of the paper, with headlines, "Loss of Money Fills to Brim Woman's Cup of Sorrow," the *Tribune* also put out a special edition with a long story about the case: Langer's having defrauded a widow out of her money by promising a pardon to her son in the penitentiary.[42] Not satisfied with sending the story to its subscribers, the *Tribune* printed up a special full-page flyer, a total of 89,000 copies, according to one employee, which was delivered by mail to post office-box holders throughout the state and put on people's front porches in the major cities.

The trial was scheduled for after the election, and some pretrial maneuvering took place. The day after Langer filed his answer to the Johnson complaint, the trial was set for the December term. Langer demanded a prompt trial before he took office in January. On December 6, Judge George McKenna of Napoleon was appointed to preside, after Johnson's attorney, Bradford, filed an affidavit of prejudice against Judge R. G. McFarland, who, as the district court judge, had been scheduled to preside at the December term. On the fourteenth, Langer again demanded an early trial, saying, "I do not want the slightest delay in this lawsuit but I want to expose to the broadest daylights the politicians who instigated this case, and the lengths they went to, to induce Mrs. Johnson to bring this action."[43] On November 16, he invited all the members of the State Bar Board (which had the power to conduct proceedings to disbar or discipline lawyers and make recommendations to the Supreme Court) to attend the trial and ask questions, promising that the defense would not object to their doing so. The Bar Board declined. The *Tribune*'s editorial noted, "Mr. Langer's invitation to the Bar Board was nothing more than a bid for public sympathy or cheap political bluff."[44]

The district court convened on December 21, 1932, with Judge Gudmunder Grimson of Rugby then named to preside. Before any actual testimony was heard, Mrs. Johnson's son-in-law, Clarence Hultin, brought written instructions to Ben Bradford to drop the legal action. The testimony differs as to whether Mrs. Johnson was even in Bismarck at the time. In reporting that the widow had dropped her suit the next day, the *Tribune* quoted the instructions from Johnson: "I have been wrongfully influenced by the political enemies of William Langer and that an injustice has been done him thereby, I desire to dismiss this action."[45] No money was paid to settle the case, but Langer protested that he wanted to tell in court what had happened. He was not allowed to do so.

One important detail never revealed in the *Tribune*'s reporting of the Johnson case—not revealed until years thereafter, and then rarely publicized—was that the *Bismarck Tribune* financed the lawsuit against Langer. This fact came out in the testimony of Mrs. Johnson herself, her attorney Ben Bradford, and her daughter, Edith Hultin, all of whom were interviewed by two Senate investigators, Elbert Smith and Sam Hood, Jr., in 1941.[46] After Langer was elected to the U.S. Senate in 1940, his political enemies lodged a complaint to prevent him from being seated. The Senate Committee on Privileges and Elections sent Smith and Hood to North Dakota where they interviewed more than 160 witnesses. Their report included selected transcripts of some of those interviews, which were called "affidavits," but, in truth, they fit no known description of an affidavit: they were not read by the witness, sworn to be correct, or signed or approved by the witness after being given. They were merely edited transcripts of dialogues between witnesses sworn to tell the truth and interviewers, with no opportunity given those interviewed to examine the transcript or make corrections or sign or refuse to sign the transcript. It is deceptive to describe them as affidavits, and I therefore have put the word in quotation marks whenever I refer to them. In his "affidavit," Ben Bradford testified that the *Tribune* paid part of his fee, and Mrs. Johnson paid the rest, some $179. In Mrs. Johnson's "affidavit," she said that Langer told her "there was some flaw in the law that he would have to change before he could work on it and it would take a lot of work." Obviously, the law could not be changed until the legislature met. Bradford, while claiming

Langer's fee was too high, also corroborated Mrs. Johnson's account. He said that Mrs. Johnson told him Langer said to her that, as the law stood, there was not much he could do for her or Floyd, but he proposed to get the law changed so he could get a pardon or parole. Bradford also confirmed that Langer agreed to work on the matter for a fee of two thousand dollars, which Mrs. Johnson paid in two checks on different dates, with two thousand more to be paid if he were successful. Mrs. Johnson's testimony is in agreement with Langer's version of the event, a fact generally disregarded by those who used the Johnson case to criticize Langer, particularly by his opponents in the many campaigns in which the case became an issue. Nor did the Senate investigators give these facts to the United States Senate but instead only mentioned that Langer was accused of taking money from a widow by promising her son a pardon in return. They had the full story from the "affidavits" of those who had participated in the case but chose not to tell it, which can only be considered as a deliberate deception of the U.S. Senate. So far as this author has been able to determine, the *Tribune* never admitted its role in the Johnson case.

At a later date, Mrs. Johnson retained another lawyer, Ed Sinkler, to seek a reduction of the sentence and a reduced parole date. He was successful in doing exactly what Langer had promised to do, for which the latter was sued. No one involved had any criticism of Mrs. Johnson, whom they all agreed was a fine woman, perhaps only somewhat misled. Unfortunately for Langer's political reputation, this subsequent resolution of the Johnson case was not added to testimony that reached the U.S. Senate in 1941.

Though the Senate investigators already knew the facts of the case when they were conducting their interviews, they nevertheless repeatedly asked their interviewees if they had any knowledge about Langer's involvement in "an incident in which he allegedly secured a check or checks of $2,000 from a widow . . . for the purpose of ostensibly securing the release of her son and subsequently doing nothing toward accomplishing that objective?"[47] Such a question was bound to result in a different answer from one that included input from Mrs. Johnson, who had already told the investigators that Langer's effort on her behalf was to try to get the law changed. They also knew that Floyd Johnson himself had decided he did not want to have the case against Langer tried and that the prospects of a parole had become dismal in view of Johnson's admission that he had committed adultery and fathered a child while a trusty in the State penitentiary. The investigators also ignored input from prosecuting attorney, O. B. Herigstad, who said that Langer had interviewed him. They were only interested in the publicly notorious questions about Langer but they showed no interest in the "checkbook journalism" of the *Bismarck Tribune*.

If there is one valid criticism of William Langer in all of this, it is that he might have refunded some of the fee that he received. On the other hand, the two thousand dollars was not contingent on his winning a parole for Floyd Johnson, and it is difficult to criticize a lawyer, who has pursued a case in good faith, for not refunding a fee after the client sues him. Langer had a policy of not settling lawsuits against him but going to trial, and no doubt thought that if he had refunded the money, it could be viewed as an admission that he had done something wrong in the Johnson case. The refund would then become the issue in campaigns against him.

The Johnson case had another result, which the *Bismarck Tribune* could not have anticipated. Bill Langer was so angered by the *Tribune*'s manner of publicizing the case—even though he did not then know of the newspaper's greater culpability in financing the lawsuit against him—that he changed his speaking schedule for the last week of the general election campaign of 1932 and spent that week in Burleigh County, asking the voters to vote against the *Bismarck Tribune* for county newspaper. The thing had gotten personal.

Part of Langer's indignation about the Johnson case was that someone had taken the trouble to send his elderly parents three separate copies, each by registered mail, of the *Bismarck Tribune* issue that headlined the charges against him. At the height of his popularity in the gubernatorial election, Langer filled the halls in every small town in Burleigh County for his speeches, to which the *Tribune* publisher, George D. Mann, was invited. Mann did not come, but Ken Simons, editor of the paper, came to one meeting and got into a fistfight with a Charlie Boise, a man about twice his age. According to Langer, Boise beat Simons.

The predictable result of the 1932 election was an even more hostile press towards Langer and the League. The Nonpartisan League faithful, moreover, had a reciprocal animosity toward the press. Matt Mulholland, chairman of the Nonpartisan League Executive Committee, said to the Senate investigators, "That *Fargo Forum*! . . . If Christ came down to earth, they wouldn't let him live three days any more!"[48]

One of North Dakota's longest-serving politicians, Usher Burdick, was a staunch supporter of William Langer and quite courageous in his own way. Burdick served in the North Dakota legislature, was Speaker of the House and lieutenant governor, and won election to the U.S. House of Representatives ten times (1935–45; 1949–59), but, unlike Langer, he was best known as a conciliator, befitting someone whose career in North Dakota politics lasted from 1907 to 1960. Burdick was of the opinion that the decision to publish the *Leader* was one of Langer's biggest political misjudgments, and a crucial factor behind the effort in 1932 to convict him of conspiracy. Although Burdick agreed that the *Leader* filled a real need and was perfectly legal, it stepped on the toes of the major dailies in North Dakota and the Twin Cities in such a way as to truly hurt their circulation.[49] The *Leader* maintained a reading public of more than 100,000 during these years, and thus assured Langer a hostile media, due to this unwanted competition. Langer knew this, of course, but he was a fighter, first and foremost. The first issue of the *Leader*, published on July 14, 1933, sent out the first volley: "Driven to it by the vicious propaganda and the unfair attacks of those opposed to the administration because of political differences, the *Leader* comes into being as the state organ of the progressive movement in North Dakota."[50]

Profit margins for a newspaper in a sparsely populated area like western North Dakota cannot have been large, and the proposed publication of a new competitor for advertising revenue like the *Leader* cannot have been welcome to any major newspaper in the state. This was especially damaging in Bismarck, the center of the state's political activity. In addition, the pocketbook interests of the owners of the *Bismarck Tribune* were likely to suffer, if some of Langer's proposed tax-saving plans were to bear fruit in 1933. Add to this his campaign against the *Tribune* in Burleigh County in October 1932, and the antagonism becomes understandable, even if not excusable in the form that it took in the Johnson case. Usher Burdick's point is well taken.

There is evidence that the animus of the *Bismarck Tribune* toward Candidate Langer was as much driven by economic motives as by political or personal ones. The day before the 1932 election, a front-page article in the *Tribune* said that Langer, among other failings, had maligned a former NPL candidate for governor, T. H. H. Thoreson, showed a lack of guts, was a showoff, and had problems telling the truth.[51] The *Tribune* did not mention Langer's meetings around Burleigh County during the last week of the campaign. Instead, it campaigned obliquely for its retention as the official newspaper for political notices. Each day of that week it ran a front-page "box" extolling its unbiased coverage, its courage in challenging wrongdoing, its willingness to stand up for what was right, and its local ownership and news coverage.

In the primary election a few months previously, the *Tribune* had received about 4,400 votes for Burleigh County's official newspaper compared to 2,000 votes for the *Bismarck Capital*. After Langer spent the last week of the fall campaign in Burleigh County, the *Tribune* lost the election bid, 4,890 to 2,877. When the returns came in showing the *Bismarck Tribune's* defeat, its issue of November 9 carried a short two-paragraph, one-column-wide story on page one with the headline, "*Tribune* Defeated for Official Paper." An editorial blamed its loss on a "slanderous and mendacious campaign" and false attacks against it without specifying what the slander and mendacity and falsity were.[52]

Langer's gubernatorial fortunes did not suffer, however. In spite of having spent the last week of the campaign in one county on this highly parochial matter, Langer nevertheless won the governorship handily.[53] The next day, November 10, the *Tribune's* editorial said that Langer was "egotistical, unstable, vindictive and abusive." All of the other League victors (the entire ticket) were praised but warned to beware of their NPL colleague, Langer. The following day the *Tribune* also attributed Langer's victory to his fellow candidates, rather than to his own efforts. The heading was "Langer is Carried into Governorship by Party's Victory." While it is true that Langer's majority was smaller than most of the other League candidates, he still garnered a substantial 25,000-vote majority. It is also true that the campaign was fought mainly over Langer's policies and those of his opponent, H. C. DePuy, a highly respected Democrat.[54]

The League swept the legislative races, winning at least 82 of the 113 House seats.[55] Apparently, the Johnson case was not the weapon it was expected to be in defeating the head of the League ticket. The voters were seeking answers from the NPL as well as Franklin Delano Roosevelt.

The Politics of Relief

The original federal complaint against Langer, which sparked the whole series of prosecutions, was as much or more about lack of patronage than of illegal activity. The complaint came from an A. M. Anderson, whose letterhead showed he ran a collection business in Valley City. In a letter dated July 6, 1933, and sent to President "Frank" Roosevelt, Anderson identified himself as a Democrat and complained generally about the Langer moratorium on farm mortgage foreclosures, which he said was sustained by military force, and about the way Langer was using poor relief in the state. Anderson went on to write, "In this state there is no Federal relief fund—it is a Governor Langer relief fund, and all the employees connected with it are Republicans and each one has to donate 7% of their monthly salary to the Governor's next campaign fund." He continued, "We are hoping to elect a Democratic Governor here next fall, and I wish you would help us to the extent of taking this Federal relief bureau away from the Republicans and getting Democrats instead. This will take a certain amount of cash away from their next campaign fund."[56]

Roosevelt's aide, Louis McHenry Howe, sent a copy of Anderson's letter to the Federal Emergency Relief Administration (FERA), headed by Harry Hopkins, and someone from the FERA office sent a copy on to R. A. Kinzer. On July 22, 1933, Kinzer sent a three-page reply to President Roosevelt, and Howe sent it to the Department of Interior, where it apparently incensed Hopkins, who was himself no innocent when it came to politics.[57]

In the letter, Kinzer explained some facts about North Dakota politics. He pointed out that the North Dakota Democrats normally got very few votes before Roosevelt ran and that they had generally cooperated with the right-wing Republicans in opposing the majority Nonpartisan League candidates who ran in the Republican column. He pointed out that most of Roosevelt's votes had come from the Leaguers, who had also elected Langer, their candidate for governor, by a big majority. He said he did not know the affiliation of people in his office but had asked many who they voted for, and most of them, though accused by Anderson of being Republican, had voted for Roosevelt. He also pointed out that federal money could not be used for Langer's campaign because it was controlled by, and audited by, the state relief committee headed by North Dakota Supreme Court Justice A. M. Christianson, who was highly respected by all parties and factions. Kinzer described Anderson, the author of the original complaint, as well known to him and of a "chronic disposition." He said that Anderson had applied to him for a job, when he mistakenly thought Kinzer was going to be chief game warden, and that Anderson did not stand in well with the Democrats of his own city. Later, Sherrard Ewing, a representative of the federal committee and acting on behalf of FERA under orders from Hopkins, asked the state committee to remove Kinzer from his position, which it did.[58]

The reason Kinzer's removal had been sought was that he had written his letter directly to President Franklin Roosevelt, which apparently had made Hopkins, a close friend of the president, very unhappy.[59] Kinzer's letter, instead of offending them, should have educated the authorities in Washington, but these Potomac politicians were obviously uninformed about North Dakota politics and chose not to follow Kinzer's advice. They bear much of the responsibility for carrying forward the ultimately abortive effort to prosecute Langer and others.

After North Dakota Democrats lodged many more complaints about lack of patronage, the Interior Department began an investigation on January 26, 1934, about one year after Langer had begun the elective governorship. During the same time, P. W. Lanier had lost a race for Congress by a more than two-to-one margin, but had been rewarded with the appointive position of U.S. district attorney, a position from which he managed the prosecutions of Langer and his codefendants.

In January 1933, Langer was in a Bismarck hospital, from where he took the oath of office and spent the first two months of his first term as governor, recovering from one of his several collapses from a diabetic condition. Nevertheless, within a few days of taking office, the governor had appointed the state committee to administer federal welfare aid in North Dakota, mainly in the form of grants to counties. He intended to, and did, appoint a committee in which all political groups were represented. In spite of all the uproar about the solicitation of funds from employees of that state committee, not a single change—aside from the firing of its executive secretary at Harry Hopkins's insistence—was made in the makeup of the committee during Langer's term of office. The committee was uniformly praised by every one of the Interior Department field representatives who worked with them. One of them, T. J. Edmonds, described the committee in these words:

> The State Committee is well assorted. Judge Christianson is a Republican of the old Theodore Roosevelt progressive sort, Thompson a Democrat, Mrs. Craig a Non-Partisan leaguer, but not of the same faction as the Governor; Stangler of the famous Bank of North Dakota, a Republican and, I believe, rather friendly to the Governor; and Nichols a Non-partisan Leaguer. Thompson, the Democrat, is the most active member of the Committee next to the Judge, and Thompson has no complaint about the state CWA [Civil Works Administration, a relief agency].[60]

Like Kinzer, Edmonds tried to dissuade Hopkins from changing the relief set up in North Dakota.

Another Interior field man, Pierce Atwater, described Judge Christianson as "a man who would be an outstanding citizen in anybody's state." Atwater was critical of P. W. Lanier, the U.S. Attorney, and S. J. Doyle, U.S. Marshal, who he said were trying to gain control of the committee so as to get patronage.[61] A third field man, Sherrard Ewing, was also supportive of the committee, and later testified for the defense in the first trial. Judge A. M. Christianson was a justice of the North Dakota Supreme Court, not a supporter of Langer; Minnie D. Craig was the first female Speaker of a State House of Representatives in the United States; Robert Stangler was a highly respected banker who managed both the Bank of North Dakota and the State Mill at various times; Lee Nichols had been the county auditor of Morton County since 1915; and Arthur E. Thompson was state superintendent of public instruction and a Democrat. All lived in or near Bismarck, as the Interior Department had requested; none of the members were paid for services, except Mrs. Craig who also acted as a field worker; and all of them spent a lot of time and money on committee work.[62]

Langer's enemies were not daunted by the committee's makeup or its adherence to policy. They seized upon an incident that occurred only because state offices had been relocated all over Bismarck when the original state capitol had burned on December 28, 1930, and the new capitol building was not completed. A solicitor for the *Leader* had gone into an office in downtown Bismarck that displayed a sign "State Emergency Relief" and obtained contributions totaling $179.50 from six of more than a hundred employees. It turned out that these employees were paid with federal funds. Prior rulings by the federal government had established that once money had been turned over to the state to be used for welfare purposes (as the money involved here had been), it belonged to the state. There are many sources for these facts, including the opinion of the Eighth Circuit Court of Appeals in *Langer v. U.S.*[63] Internal correspondence in the Justice Department files shows that Assistant Attorney General Joseph Keenan had given the department's opinion in an Ohio case (*U.S. v. Byers*), where Democrats had solicited federal employees, that the money was no longer federal after being turned over to the states, and that he had always held this opinion and still did, even after the first Langer trial.[64] But despite ruling for Democratic state patronage in Ohio, Keenan was nevertheless willing to have the litigation against Republicans in North Dakota continue as a "test case." In a Justice Department memorandum to the attorney general, Keenan wrote:

> Due to the urgent request of Secretary [of the Interior] Ickes that vigorous prosecution be instituted, we transmitted the necessary documents to the United States Attorney. From the evidence presented to this Department, submission to the Grand Jury was warranted, although no one in this Department has any firm conviction as to the case being susceptible to successful prosecution. The United States Attorney, however, appears to have such opinion.[65]

The Interior Department was headed by Harold Ickes, no novice in political infighting. He wrote at least five letters to the Justice Department to urge quick and heavy action. He also gave advance notice to the two senators from North Dakota, Gerald P. Nye and Lynn J. Frazier, on the day before the indictment was returned, telling them that it was coming.[66] On the day of the indictment Senator Nye gave a speech in the Senate, lamenting that a terrible crime had been committed. Nye spoke of embarrassment and regret but found the evidence persuasive and said, "Let the ax fall where it will, even though it shall involve indictment and trial of one rewarded by election to so high an office as that of Governor of the State."[67]

Despite legal precedents that indicated otherwise, an indictment appeared, charging that Governor Langer, Highway Commissioner Frank Vogel, Insurance Commissioner Oscar E. Erickson, R. A. Kinzer, Joseph Kinzer, Harold McDonald, Oscar Chaput, Paul J. Yeater, and Gideon Hample, had conspired to impede the operations of federal laws appropriating money for welfare purposes. And so the Langer trials began.

Patronage and its Discontents

Such is the animus that can be produced by disappointed office seekers, but the energy expended on such long political wars would seem to stem from other motivations as well. It is clear the Democratic patronage seekers in North Dakota did not want a nonpolitical administration of welfare, which was the case under the commission approved by Governor Langer. One Democratic politician, who dissented from his fellow Democrats was R. B. Murphy—former national committeeman for North Dakota—who supported the makeup and actions of the state relief committee. He told the Washington departments concerned that there was no contact between Langer and the relief committee and predicted that prosecuting Langer and others would be a "a colossal political blunder," since it would appear to be political persecution, which, indeed, it was.[68] The North Dakota House of Representatives committee hearings in 1934, in fact, show that Langer did not interfere in any way with the dispensing of federal relief through the state but was content to sign off on the committee's decisions, as was his statutory obligation. Lee Nichols had been appointed to the relief committee by Governor Langer in January 1933 and served until its functions were taken over by Judge Christianson as state administrator of relief. In his testimony, he was asked why Governor Langer had not become active in the work of the relief committee. Nichols said Langer had told him that "He didn't want to be bothered about it; he had troubles enough of his own. He appointed the Committee for that." The next question was, "Now, in the matter of hiring employees, or fixing salaries of the employees, did the Governor have anything to do with that?" Nichols responded, "Nothing in any way whatsoever."[69]

In contrast to the interparty harmony exhibited by Langer's handling of state relief efforts, the intraparty correspondence of local Democrats shows they were sharply critical of each other, with National Committeeman Murphy referring to newly appointed U.S. Attorney Lanier as a "poseur."[70] Thomas Moodie, the man who would be governor, and was—for about a month before he was removed because he had not resided in North Dakota the required five years—was particularly caustic about his fellow Democrats. After losing the governorship in the courts, Moodie was rewarded by being made head of the Works Progress Administration (WPA) in North Dakota under Harry Hopkins. This did not appear to make him a contented soul, however. In a letter to Postmaster General James Farley, chief dispenser of patronage in the Roosevelt administration, which was then sent on to President Roosevelt's secretary, Louis Howe, Moodie called the Democratic organization in North Dakota "an ancient and doddering organization which thinks only in terms of the plums of patronage and not of the principles which are so vital to our people at this time."[71] Another letter from Moodie, which was also forwarded by Farley to Howe, said that the state Democrats had tried to control patronage in the WPA by demanding that he employ "impossible types of people . . . who would be no credit to the administration and in many cases were rankly unqualified."[72] While insisting on his own undying loyalty to the president, Moodie called the state Democratic organization "both puerile and silly." Moodie also mentioned in several letters that a majority of North Dakotans supported both William Langer for governor on the Republican ticket and crossed party lines to vote for President Roosevelt, a Democrat.[73]

John C. Eaton, the Democratic national committeeman, however, did not share Moodie's opinion of who was loyal and a good Democrat. He wrote Farley (and again it was forwarded to Howe), that Moodie had done "many things not beneficial to the party organization"—and that in the appointments he makes "consideration is mainly given to the wishes of Senator Nye," and that there was great dissatisfaction in the party at the number of "Old Time Republicans" who were receiving preference from the Federal Land Bank, the Regional Agricultural Credit Corporation, and the WPA setup. In particular, Eaton was highly indignant that George Shafer, former Republican governor, was receiving "the cream of the legal business sent from the Federal Land Bank."[74]

Such bickering among Democrats might indicate that their will to engage in a concerted political frame-up of a Republican governor might have been lacking, but most of them were more than willing to aid and abet the powerful forces that were gathering in Washington and the U.S. Attorney's office in Fargo. Many of the leading Democrats in North Dakota disagreed with R. B. Murphy and favored going ahead with the trials.[75]

The authorities in Washington obviously paid more attention to the complaints of patronage seekers than to the advice of Murphy and the local Interior field men (Ewing, Edmonds, and Atwater), all of whom praised the State Relief Committee.[76] Aubrey Williams, a high official of Interior, warned the field men that they were being deceived in their admiration of the State Relief Fund administration. When the field men mildly questioned the plan to relieve Langer of his statutory duty of signing requisitions and endorsing checks, they were told that Washington had other reports that Judge Christianson was being taken in by the Republicans and might be building up his own political machine and planning to run for office. This was out-and-out slander. Anyone in North Dakota who knew (or argued appeals before) Judge Christianson, as this writer did, would find ludicrous the idea that Christianson could be manipulated or that he was running for any office other than Supreme Court judge—a position he held for thirty-two years, longer than anyone else in the history of North Dakota. It was Christianson's even-handedness toward Democrats and Republicans alike, that stood in the way of dealing with William Langer. No such scruples barred the ambitions of United States Attorney P. W. Lanier.

Powless W. Lanier, Sr.

A former attorney general for North Dakota, Alvin Strutz, once characterized P. W. Lanier as "the only man I knew who could strut sitting down."[77] When he prosecuted a case Lanier never spoke of himself as an individual lawyer, he wrapped himself in the U.S. flag and became "the government," as in, "The Government opposes the motion of the lawyer for the defendant."[78] Long after the prosecutions of the 1930s, and during the attempt to bar Langer from the Senate, Lanier spoke to a Senate investigator to the effect that there were a lot of worse (presumably in a criminal sense) politicians in North Dakota than Langer was, a surprising admission from one who had been the driving force of the conspiracy trials, pursuing Langer with such relentless vigor.[79] Even more surprising, perhaps, is the report from the U.S. Senate on February 17, 1942: "By Mr. Langer, from the Committee on the Judiciary: Powless W. Lanier, to be United States Attorney for the District of North Dakota."[80] On the next day, P. W. Lanier was confirmed.[81] Lanier's reappointment came when the attempt to unseat Langer had not yet been voted on by the full Senate, but the majority and minority reports had been released, and the vote by the Senate was about a month away.

P. W. Lanier was born in 1885 and passed the bar in Tennessee, his home state. He came to Fargo and was admitted to practice there on November 6, 1923. A Democrat in a Republican-dominated state, he ran unsuccessfully for the U.S. Senate against Gerald Nye in 1932, shortly before his appointment as U.S. attorney, and also unsuccessfully for Congress against Usher Burdick and Otto Krueger in 1954, shortly after he was replaced as U.S. attorney, when the Eisenhower Administration ended twenty years of Democratic appointments to that position. He was in a law partnership with Harry Lashkowitz in Fargo throughout his term as

P. W. Lanier was the lead prosecutor in the trials against Langer and his codefendants in 1934 and 1935.
State Historical Society of North Dakota
C3599

U.S. attorney, since there was no requirement that it be a full-time position until President Eisenhower's administration.

Lanier stuck to his Tennessee accent in North Dakota as tenaciously as native son Lawrence Welk would stick to his German-Russian one on television, but this did not hinder the career of one of the few practicing attorneys in North Dakota who was also a Democrat. He was thus in line to be appointed for the inevitable federal patronage when Franklin D. Roosevelt became president, receiving his appointment as U.S. attorney on July 21, 1933.[82]

Eight months later, in a preliminary step, Hopkins removed Langer, by telegram, on March 1, 1934, from his figurehead position as head of the relief committee. The telegram said, and the press trumpeted, that this was done because of political interference with the committee's work. This act was followed immediately by Senator Nye's speech in the U.S. Senate demanding that Langer be indicted. While the *Bismarck Tribune* was reporting that such charges made "the stomach retch," the NPL state convention endorsed Langer for reelection. Shortly thereafter Harold Ickes, secretary of the interior, urgently recommended prosecution of Langer and others in a letter to the U.S. attorney general.[83]

Once the report of the Department of Interior reached the desk of the United States Attorney P. W. Lanier, it acquired a new life. Lanier's first letter to the Department of Justice on the case, a few days before a scheduled grand jury, said there were rumors that the grand jury was going to hear a case on Langer, but he had no official reports and he needed them at once. When he received them, he demanded that the investigator report to him so he could explain what further investigation was needed. As more reports were submitted, he complained that they were "striking in their incompleteness" and demanded more. From that point on, he got several apologetic letters from the investigators, saying that witnesses flatly refused to say that the *Leader* solicitor had been hired by Langer (they ultimately found one who would say it), and that other witnesses, who said Langer should be prosecuted if guilty, refused to go along with statements that would be proof of guilt, and that the statements they were sending were the best the investigators could get. The investigators also gathered evidence of solicitation of state employees not funded by federal money—a practice the Court of Appeals later said was not forbidden by law. On April 10, 1934, a special grand jury met for three days and returned a conspiracy indictment against Langer and others. Meanwhile, Lanier wrote the first of many letters to the Internal Revenue Service to investigate the tax returns of

Langer, his fellow indictees, and the *Leader*. Judge Andrew A. Miller, a long-time enemy of Langer, conducted the first trial before a jury that was selected in such a way as to be in violation of applicable law and was not representative of the State of North Dakota.[84]

Judge Andrew A. Miller

William Langer and Andrew A. Miller had known each other for a long time, but not as friends. They each made a lot of enemies over their lifetimes, including each other. Miller was born in Denmark, studied law in an office in Iowa, and moved to Bismarck where he joined the law firm of Zuger and Miller. The firm represented Alex McKenzie, North Dakota's political boss for many years, as well as many corporate clients, including some of the losing defendants, such as Standard Oil Company, in Langer's big tax case as the Morton County state's attorney in 1915.[85] Great corporations, which can have perpetual existence, can also have very long memories. Langer's testimony before the U.S. Senate details some of the things that he gave them to remember about the case of the *Northern Pacific Railway Company versus Morton County*. He said:

> I had discovered that what we choose to call the more prominent people had been escaping taxes. I decided to sue the Standard Oil Co., the Occident Elevator Co., the Northern Pacific Railway Co., and the Dietz Lumber Co. for not paying their taxes, and they were the biggest folks in North Dakota; as big as the biggest, anyhow.
>
> So I began by suing the Occident Elevator at New Salem for $190.73, claiming that they had not paid any taxes on their railroad right of way since they had placed their elevator there, and that it immediately became taxable as soon as they built there, even though the railroad paid taxes at a certain amount per mile. I sued Dietz for $53.07 and Standard Oil for $46.31, and I enjoined the railroad because they owned the right of way. Well, this action was defended by Judge Andrew Miller, who, at that time, I believe was still Attorney General [of North Dakota] [Murphy says, no, he went out in 1913. Langer says: I know, but I brought the action before I became State's Attorney, a few months before. He went out and Mr. Linde came in.] Anyway, he was in the lawsuit, a member of Miller and Zuger. We tried it before Judge Nuessle on a change of venue from Judge Nuchols. I won against all but the elevator company. The Judge held that the elevator company, of necessity, had to be on a railroad right

of way. I appealed, and the three losing defendants cross-appealed to the Supreme Court, and by then, of course, they had all woke up to the fact that 30 million dollars of property was involved.

So we had this lawsuit involving 2,038 elevators, over 1,000 lumber yards, and 260 oil tank stations. The decision of the Supreme Court is at 32 N.D. 635. That is where my troubles started. Incidently, I won against all four, and they had to pay out in cash, for the 6 years they had escaped paying taxes, about $1,250,000 and they have kept on paying since. Of course I could not go back farther than 6 years because of the statutes of limitation.

The Miller who was on the other side was the Federal Judge who presided at my first trial.[86]

The next confrontation between Langer and Miller arose from an epidemic of typhoid fever in Bismarck in 1916. A citizens' group suspected, quite reasonably, that the city water supply was the cause of the epidemic. The water was supplied by the Bismarck Water Supply Company, owned by Alex McKenzie, C. B. Little, a prominent banker, and Andrew A. Miller. Aided by Langer, who was then attorney general and a member of the State Board of Health, the citizens' group hired experts who reported that the water was not only not fit to drink, it was not even fit to take a bath in. An examination of the plant from February 1916 through March 1917 by a United States public health sanitary engineer, showed that sixty-three tests of the water during a six-month period proved that the contamination by E. Coli bacteria was 15 to 200 times higher than allowed by federal standards. He concluded that the water "is contaminated, containing organisms of the E. Coli group in large amounts at all times," that "the typhoid fever death rate is higher than should be the case in a city of pure water supply located as far North as Bismarck," that "Gastro-intestinal diseases are of common occurrence, and all indications point to the water supply as the source of infection," and that "treatment with liquid chlorine would produce a safe, though not especially palatable, water supply." A similar report from the state public health laboratories at the University of North Dakota said that "the water is polluted very greatly with sewage matter and should not be used for drinking purposes."[87]

Tests of water in Grand Forks, Fargo, and other cities showed that their water supply was within the tolerable limit of 2 E. Coli per 100 cubic centimeters (cc) of water during the same period when tests in Bismarck were showing levels of from 30 to 400 E. Coli per 100 cc. Most tests in the other cities showed no E. Coli at all. After litigation and a public election to condemn the water company, the company was finally purchased by the city for much less than the owners demanded. During the attempt to remove him from the Senate, Langer told the Senate that Miller's loss in the value of his water stock was thirty thousand dollars (about $422,000 in 2002 dollars).[88]

Miller had been a North Dakota assistant attorney general from 1906 to 1908, when he ran against the man who hired him, Attorney General McCue, and defeated him. Miller ran as a Progressive Republican endorsee, while Thomas F. McCue was endorsed by the regular, or "Stalwart" Republicans. Miller was criticized severely at the time for being a "traitor to the cause." After being reelected twice, he resigned to run for the United States Senate in 1914. Langer actively campaigned against Miller, criticizing him for conflicts of interest in continuing to represent corporate clients, including railroads, while attorney general.[89]

Miller lost the election, but President Harding appointed him a U.S. district judge for North Dakota in 1922. A temporary second judgeship had been created because Judge Charles Amidon's health was poor, but Harding's appointment brought "an immediate torrent of protest, as he [Miller] was felt to be a political 'hack' completely unqualified for the position." A meeting of Progressives invited U.S. Senator McCumber to attend a meeting about the appointment, and while he agreed to "appear to read a prepared statement he would under no conditions submit to questioning."[90]

The *Grand Forks Herald* opposed the nomination, pointing out that Miller had been attorney and lobbyist for Alexander McKenzie, and that he had represented McKenzie's interests in the long fight waged by the citizens of Bismarck for lower water rates. On the other hand, the *Bismarck Tribune* warmly approved the nomination. To add to the controversy, a group of lawyers, legislators and state court judges formed a Citizens Clean Courts Committee to oppose the nomination.[91] Miller's lawyer during the disputed Senate hearings on the appointment was James M. Hanley, later one of the lawyers for Langer in the conspiracy trials of 1934. Miller was confirmed by the Senate, and Senator Porter McCumber was defeated for reelection later in the same year by Lynn J. Frazier in the June Republican primary.

After a split with the Nonpartisan League in 1920, Langer ran for governor in 1920 with the support of the NPL's opposition, the Independent Voters Association, or IVAs. It took Langer until 1928 to get back in the good graces of the League. He ran then for attorney general with League endorsement and lost by a small margin. During this time, 1921 to 1932, Langer was in a successful private law practice and sometimes appeared in Judge Miller's court. They still were not friendly, with Langer publicly criticizing some of the judge's rulings and public statements.[92]

BY THEIR FRUITS YE SHALL KNOW THEM
Matt: 7:17:20

I stand squarely upon my record.

Under my administration, taxes have been reduced from over $10,007,000 per biennium to $4,500,000, the greatest reduction of any state in the Union. North Dakota bonds were selling at $.62 on the dollar when I took office. Today they are $1.03. My enemies say this is due to federal refinancing of farm mortgages. But if this is true, why are not the bonds of neighboring states, like Minnesota, Montana and South Dakota, up also?

I have reduced the payroll $78,000.00 per month, and will reduce it more.

I have removed some of the burden of taxes from farm and city homeowners and placed it upon the backs of those drawing large incomes.

Utility corporations have had their taxes raised from five percent to twelve percent.

The once-weakened Bank of North Dakota today has $22,000,000.00 in liquid assets. It could pay up all of its obligations today and have several million dollars left over.

The S t a t e Mill and Elevator has ground more flour and shown greater profit than ever before in its history.

Waging the embargo fight alone, I raised the price of wheat from 49 cents a bushel to 72 cents. I propose to continue the fight and raise the price still higher.

I caused the enactment of legislation which saved the state $40,000.00 and private citizens unknown thousands of dollars, in the use of electricity.

Under my administration, excellent care has been taken of the feeble-minded, the deaf and dumb, and the blind; and a hundred and three crippled children have been rehabilitated so that they can become self-supporting citizens of the future. The heads of the institutions for the care of these unfortunates have been left in charge. That is my answer to the cry of politics and payrollers.

The issue in this campaign is whether the railroad companies who are refusing to pay over a million dollars in taxes this year; the utility companies who are refusing to pay a half million; the express companies who likewise have their taxes in court; the chain banks, the sale of whose stock has been stopped in this state; and other outside interests in Minneapolis, Chicago and New York are going to run North Dakota, or whether we are going to keep on running it.

Those outside big business interests, blinded with greed and avarice, drunk with power, do not like this administration. The laborers, the farmers and small business men, the state bankers who are opposed to the chain banks, like it.

As long as I am Governor, the moratorium will remain in full force until we have good crops and good prices. The common people will remain secure in their property and homes. I will continue to fight the corrupt interests.

WILLIAM LANGER.

Langer's campaign statement in the 1934 gubernatorial election offered encouragement to farmers suffering from drought and the Great Depression, promising "the moratorium will remain in full force until we have good crops and good prices."

State Historical Society of North Dakota 1060-2

When Langer ran for governor in 1932, he and the whole League ticket were elected in a landslide. As governor, he declared an embargo on the export of wheat from North Dakota, an act that was held unconstitutional, but the price of wheat, especially durum, rose for a time, to the great benefit of North Dakota farmers. Langer also declared a moratorium on farm foreclosures. Other governors in the drought-stricken Midwest sent the National Guard to protect sheriffs conducting foreclosure sales; Langer sent the National Guard out some sixty times to prevent the sheriff from conducting such sales. Sometimes he did so at the request of a sheriff who anticipated trouble if he went ahead with the foreclosure sale.[93]

When Judge Miller ordered foreclosure of a farm in Richland County, friends and neighbors and the debtor offered the U.S. Marshal the total of the payments then due, but the creditor refused to accept it and insisted on the sale. A group of farmers, relying on Governor Langer's moratorium, went to the farm and locked the federal marshal in a shed or outhouse until he was persuaded to accept the money. Judge Miller was extremely angry.[94]

Judicial ethics say a judge should not act in a case in which there is even an appearance of bias or partiality. In view of this long-standing antagonistic relationship between Langer and Miller, one might assume Judge Miller would disqualify himself from acting as judge in the first trial of William Langer. He did not, then or later. Even after the first trial and the filing of an affidavit of prejudice against him—which at that time usually resulted, and still does, in a judge's withdrawal—and in spite of his admission to Senate investigators in 1940 that he thought the defendants guilty, he did not withdraw.[95]

Instead, he tried to avoid being replaced for the subsequent trials. The Court of Appeals had to order that another judge take his place for the second and later trials. Even though he was disqualified from acting in the case, he instructed U.S. Attorney Lanier to look into prosecuting the defendants for perjury for what they said in the affidavit of prejudice, and he called the grand jury into session to bring the indictment.[96] Lanier followed the instructions and prosecuted Langer, Vogel, and Kinzer for perjury in filing an affidavit of prejudice, something unprecedented in the English-speaking judicial tradition and apparently never done again.

Judge Miller also tried to influence the new judge, Judge A. Lee Wyman of South Dakota, in the handling of the trial, to the point that Judge Wyman told him to stop interfering.[97] When the trial was over and the defendants acquitted, internal memoranda of the Justice Department show that Judge Miller was "furious" about the affidavit of prejudice and insisted that the lawyers who filed it against him ought to be disbarred.[98] Actually, any lawyer has the right to file such a document, if he or she has grounds, and has a duty to do it if the bias of the judge will, in the lawyer's opinion and that of his client, prevent a fair trial. For challenging Judge Miller, the defense lawyers involved deserved praise, not disciplinary or criminal action.

From the point of view of the NPL, farmers who had voted for both William Langer and FDR in 1932, the faces of the New Deal Democrats dispatched from Washington, D.C., to North Dakota in 1934 were beginning to resemble those of earlier oppressors dispatched from the Twin Cities by Alex McKenzie. The situation was actually more precarious in 1934, however. In 1919, when the powerful corporate forces of the private sector squared off against the NPL, the farmers could count upon a champion of their state at the federal level, Charles Amidon, a federal district judge who was not averse to civil rights or the right of legislatures to experiment with regulatory measures. It was he who decided that the League industrial program was constitutional in *Green v. Frazier*, a decision affirmed by the United States Supreme Court in 1920.[99]

Charles Amidon's judicial colleague in 1922 and eventual successor in 1937, Andrew Miller, was hostile to his predecessor's legal philosophy, adamantly opposed to the NPL in general, and to William Langer in particular. With the additional hostility of the Roosevelt administration in 1933, the federal government, at precisely the time it became a source of refuge against the malefactors of great wealth in the rest of the United States, had become a "clear and present danger" in North Dakota, not just to Governor Langer, but also to the Nonpartisan League and the farmers who supported it. What ensued in the conspiracy trials to follow was as potentially tragic as it was dramatic and, at times, farcical.

Chapter 3
The First Conspiracy Trial
May 22–June 10, 1934

"So that there will be no mistake about it, I want to charge after seeing those 72 names, that that jury was absolutely hand-picked. I do not want any doubt about that in any Senator's mind at all. It just could not happen that those men, some of whom had just got through suing me, some of the men I had just got through suing—it just could not happen that so many of them were in the jury box.

— William Langer[100]

"When he [Judge Andrew A. Miller] wanted a man convicted, he practically handled that whole thing himself, and when he did not want a conviction, I could not get by him, and his method of charging the jury, while in print it was all right—if you would see him deliver the charge, you would say it was all wrong."

— Usher Burdick[101]

"I think that any lawyer that defends Langer in this case is getting hot money."

— Judge Andrew Miller[102]

The Charges in the Indictment

The indictment against Governor Langer and his codefendants alleged a conspiracy to defraud the United States by corruptly administering acts of Congress: one regarding the Reconstruction Finance Corporation and public employment; another allowing cooperation with the states in promoting employment under the Federal Emergency Relief Act; and the third relating to employment under the National Industrial Recovery Act. These, of course, were three of the mightiest pillars of the New Deal edifice, which were bitterly opposed by die-hard members of the Republican Party and those who maintained that the world of Wall Street was not ready for reform. The U.S. Supreme Court rejected some of these major acts in 1936. In 1934, however, U.S. Prosecutor Lanier was asking the jury in Bismarck, North Dakota, to believe that the $179.50 solicited by Harold McDonald from employees in the State Welfare Office represented a clear and present danger to that legislation's intent for North Dakota. The specific charge in the U.S. government indictment was "Violation of Section 37 of the Federal Penal Code."[103]

The federal indictment alleged that the defendants promoted their political interests by soliciting and demanding a percentage of the pay of employees paid by federal funds in order to pay off deficits of the Nonpartisan League, to sell subscriptions to the *Leader*, and as job insurance. It alleged a total of twenty-seven "overt acts" committed to support the conspiracy, twenty of which were abandoned and withdrawn by the United States attorney at the end of the trial. The only overt acts not withdrawn were those numbered 13, 18, and

*Three men pose with a copy of the **Leader** bearing the headline, "League Ticket Sweeps N. D. Election: Langer Beats Welford by 3,000 Votes," November 12, 1936.*

State Historical Society of North Dakota C1421

23–27. Overt Act 13 of the indictment alleged that "some of the defendants, the exact defendants being to the Grand Jurors unknown, deposited a large sum of money to the account of 'The Leader' in the Bank of North Dakota, which money had been received by reason of the solicitations mentioned in this indictment."[104]

Overt Act 18 alleged that R. A. Kinzer had reduced the monthly salary of an employee in the State Relief Office, Edith Scott, from ninety to eight-five dollars in August 1933, "because she had failed and neglected to contribute five per cent of her yearly salary for subscriptions to 'The Leader,' the political newspaper in the State of North Dakota, which supported the administration of the defendant William Langer, the said Edith Scott being then and there a person working at Bismarck, North Dakota, and receiving money for her services by reason of the operation of the Federal Emergency Relief Acts . . ."[105]

Overt Act 23 alleged that between June 5, 1933, and March 5, 1934, Langer withdrew cash from the *Leader* account at the Bank of North Dakota "and deposited to his personal account in the Dakota National Bank and Trust Company of Bismarck, North Dakota, various sums of money amounting to approximately $15,006.73, a portion of which said money had been contributed by the persons mentioned and described in this indictment."[106]

Overt Act 24 alleged that in May 1933, Harold McDonald solicited 5 percent of the salaries of federal relief employees in Bismarck, including "W. J. Pfenning; Phrene Junge; O. T. Forde; and Ed. Ryckman and Rose Zlevor, for subscriptions to the 'Leader,' a political newspaper to support the administration of the defendant WILLIAM LANGER in the State of North Dakota." Overt Act 25 was similar, citing the solicitation in July 1933 of L. M. French and Stella Brandby. Overt Act 26 alleged that McDonald solicited Edith Scott in August 1933. Overt Act 27 alleged that Kinzer received 5 percent of the salaries of those named in those counts who contributed: "During the months of June, July and August, 1933, at Bismarck . . . the defendant R.A. Kinzer received five percent of the monthly salaries of W. J. Pfenning; Phrene Junge; O. T. Forde; and Ed Ryckman and Rose Zlevor, etc. . . ."[107]

The Use and Abuse of Conspiracy in the Law

A conspiracy in the law is an agreement of two or more persons to commit a criminal or otherwise unlawful act. It is a federal crime to conspire to violate any federal law prohibiting an activity, even though no penalty is prescribed for such a violation. During the earlier period of the English common law, a conspiracy was said to be committed simply by making such an agreement, but the concept was so abused in England that modern-day statutes also require an "overt act" in aid of the conspiracy. This was not much of an improvement, however. One can be found guilty even if no criminal act is committed—just planning or talking about it, plus one "overt act" is enough to convict. Many acts that are not criminal if done by one person can be criminal if done by more than one who "conspire" together. Obviously, charges of conspiracy are subject to abuse by unscrupulous or overly ambitious prosecutors and judges.

When the labor movement arose in Great Britain and the United States, employers had great success in obstructing strikes by claiming successfully that although any one employee could quit work, a combination of two or more who quit constituted a criminal conspiracy. In 1875, England exempted unions from the conspiracy statute, but it took the United States until 1932 in the Wagner Act to limit the power of the federal courts to forbid union activity. In the meantime, Eugene Debs and many others had been prosecuted and convicted on conspiracy charges in federal courts.

Abuses of the statutes often occur because of the special rules of evidence that are sometimes applied, such as the rule that the acts of one "conspirator" are binding on the others, whether the others know of them or not; that statements of one are binding on the others, even if they involve allegations of misconduct by the others or even if they involve a violation of the rules against hearsay evidence. And all defendants can be held guilty of any substantive crime committed by only one of their number.[108] Other possible abuses of the conspiracy law are that an eager prosecutor can tack on a conspiracy charge to other charges in the hope that a jury will seize upon it as ground for conviction even if other charges are unproved; one defendant can (in return for being given immunity or a lenient sentence) say he was part of a conspiracy and committed an "overt act," and thereby obtain the conviction of others even though they had no knowledge of his actions.

Through many years, dissenting opinions in the Supreme Court have complained of the abuses involved in the use of conspiracy statutes, but no majority has agreed. One such dissent can be found in *Krulewitch v. United States*, 336 U.S. 400 (1949). Some courts do, however, require that the elements of the charge of conspiracy be strictly complied with, as Judge Wyman did in the final Langer case, where he required that the jury find that the defendants had agreed to solicitation of federal employees in order to find the defendants guilty, instead of merely finding, as Judge Miller had said they could, that the defendants agreed to solicit money for a newspaper and the act of one of them in soliciting federal employees could be held to be the responsibility of all.

Miller's charges notwithstanding, it is important to remember that the employees whom the prosecution claimed to be "federal employees" were actually engaged in their employment in an office called "State Emergency Relief Office." There was no prohibition in 1933–34, or for some time thereafter, of solicitation of funds for political purposes from state employees. All factions of all parties in North Dakota engaged in this practice in varying degrees. Second, although many witnesses from the highway department (headed by Frank Vogel) testified, none of the remaining overt acts related to the highway department—they all related to the State Emergency Relief Office and the disposition of funds solicited for the *Leader*. If one is to draw political conclusions from this, rather than legal ones, it is clear that the only real target in the indictment was the elected governor of North Dakota, William Langer.

Jury Selection

Langer's first trial provided examples of more than one miscarriage of justice, beginning at the earliest stages with a tainted method of creating the jury pool, the unfair processing of jury selection by Judge Andrew Miller and the prosecuting attorney, P. W. Lanier, and, for the first and only time in the living memory of twentieth-century trial lawyers in North Dakota, Judge Miller's refusal to let defense attorneys see names on the jury panel before the start of the trial. The defense attorneys finally got the list just before the jury selection began, and only later could they check into the backgrounds of the jurors.

Investigating the background of jurors is something that lawyers regularly do so as to avoid unexpected prejudices and relationships of jurors that may be harmful to their clients. The attorney prosecuting Langer, P. W. Lanier, had certainly felt free to do so in his tenure as federal prosecutor.[109] When Langer's lawyers were finally able to check the backgrounds of the jurors in his case—after the jury was already selected and sworn in—they were aghast at how many jurors were anti-League and anti-Langer, how heavily weighted the jury panel was with city residents, and how few of the jurors were from rural areas, where the Nonpartisan League was strongest and where most North Dakotans resided. Testimony showed that the vast majority of the jurors were from towns and cities, very few were rural residents, and very few, if any, were members of the Nonpartisan League, even though the League had large majorities in the previous election. The defense moved to quash the jury panel and draw a new jury according to proper procedure.[110]

At the pretrial hearing in May 1934 to hear the motion, Frank Talcott, deputy clerk, who usually acted in place of the elderly Clerk of the District Court J. A. Montgomery, was obliged to testify.[111] Talcott said the counties were divided up between Montgomery, a Democrat, and Jury Commissioner Wynn Hooper, a Republican, both of whom had been appointed or reappointed by Miller.[112] In the counties he was responsible for, Hooper would secure names "from men who he has confidence will send in the right names, and in the balance of the counties the names are secured in some instances from men in whom Mr. Montgomery has confidence, and in a very few instances from men whom I know."[113] Obviously, such a selection method is subject to manipulation, and is not a random selection, as most jurisdictions require. It is not surprising that the "men in whom he [Montgomery] had confidence" would share the prejudices of the those who picked them, and that those who did the picking would share the prejudices of Judge Miller, who appointed them.

The jury for the first Langer trial was also drawn in violation of a federal law requiring that juries in federal court be drawn in the same way as those drawn in the state in which the federal court was sitting. North Dakota law required that juries be drawn at random from tax or voting lists, a requirement Judge Miller ignored. North Dakota law also

Judge Andrew Miller presided at Langer's first trial and, when accused of malfeasance, charged Langer and his codefendants with perjury, an unprecedented judicial response.

State Historical Society of North Dakota A1302

required that women be eligible for jury duty. No woman had ever been called for a federal court jury at the time of the first Langer trial, and none was called in that trial.[114]

Immediately after Talcott's testimony and without the presentation of any evidence to contradict it, Judge Miller ruled against the defense motion challenging the array—in other words, attacking the method of selection of the jury. He gave no reason for denial at the time, but later, after the defense made a motion to adopt the system used in state courts, Miller said that the jury was drawn as it always had been in federal court in North Dakota, that subpoenas had been issued to federal witnesses, and there would be additional expense and delay if the motion were granted. He then said, without discussing the evidence produced by the defense, that the system used would be "as fair as any other."[115] Judge Miller did not refer to the figures the defense presented to show bias but agreed with Attorney Lanier's statements acknowledging them, and then proceeded to deny the motion and ordered the trial to proceed.[116] From the point of view of the defense, a miscarriage of justice had already take place at the grand jury level.

Evidence to support the irregularities of the jury selection is available from a variety of sources. The testimony of Usher Burdick on two separate occasions, once for the North Dakota House of Representatives fact-finding committee in 1934 and a second time for a U.S. Senate committee hearing in 1941, is quite telling. Usher L. Burdick, elected to Congress in 1934, had been an assistant U.S. attorney in Fargo to Hoover appointee Peter B. Garberg from 1929 to 1932 and had tried most of the government cases before Federal Judge Miller, owing to Judge Charles Amidon's semi-retirement. Prior to that he had served for seventeen years as Williams County state's attorney in Williston. The rest of his twenty-nine years of legal practice had been in "the defense of criminal actions."[117] Although he had consistently identified himself with underdogs in North Dakota, most notably Native Americans, Usher Burdick had also pursued successful legal and banking careers that earned the respect, if not the affection, of the well-to-do. When Usher Burdick spoke, people on all sides of the issues in North Dakota listened.

In his testimony in August 1934, Burdick noted that the two men in charge of choosing names for the jury pool, Clerk J. A. Montgomery and Jury Commissioner Wynn Hooper, were outspoken enemies of Langer. He also pointed out that he knew how the system worked, "because I worked it." He described it for the House members:

... under the Federal statute a jury is drawn in the following manner, whether it is a Grand Jury, or a petit Jury: the Clerk of the United States District court or his deputy, and the Court Commissioner, collect names from any source, according to their particular wishes, and place the names in a box ... the two keep on, then, alternating, until they have drawn for a Grand Jury, say, seventy-five names, and for a Petit Jury a hundred names.

Any Federal Attorney, or United States Marshall can submit names for either Jury, by writing the name of a citizen on a piece of paper, and handing it to the Clerk of the United States District Court, with the request that that citizen's name be put in the box. Usually the United States Marshal supplies names which are selected by the Clerk of the District Court.

After the names are all in the box, then the formal drawing takes place in a public place, in the Federal Building, and the names are drawn out of the box which were previously put in by the Clerk or his deputy and the Commissioner; and the only names that they can formally draw out of the box are the names they have put in the box; so the drawing is a farce. For a petit jury they draw from sixty to seventy-five names out of a box into which they have inserted two hundred names; and they can draw out no name which they have previously not put into the box.[118]

As Burdick's House testimony continued, one of Langer's attorneys, J. M. Hanley, asked him if the jury system presently in use would assure "that the jury that is selected, and whose names are put in the box, shall be representative, and come from all portions of the State, and represent different occupations and different political organizations?" Burdick's answer was negative: "It depends upon what the case is, entirely." Continuing testimony by Burdick revealed the full extent of how Judge Miller and Prosecutor Lanier used jury selection to predetermine a guilty verdict against Governor Langer. He told the House hearing that it was "a positive cinch" that those who put the names in the box for the jury pool could "select the individuals from a certain political faith or class, if they so desire; and that jurors for the federal court—invariably taken from the Conservative class."

The difference between federal court and state court procedures with regard to the jury was huge for a defense lawyer, but a federal judge like Judge Miller's predecessor, Charles Amidon, had permitted the more-even handed procedures of the state level to prevail. As

Burdick explained in the House hearing, "In Federal Court counsel for the defendant can not inquire of a juror at all. The entire examination is conducted by the Court itself; but in the State Courts counsel may go into the question of credibility, fairness, prejudice, or any other matter that might make a prospective juror unfit to sit in a case." Burdick verified from his own experience that not all federal judges enforced the rule as Judge Miller had. He testified, "I have never been permitted to inquire directly from jurors as to their qualifications in Judge Miller's Court; but I was permitted to do so during the term of his predecessor, Judge Amidon."

Burdick also affirmed the unusual nature of Judge Miller's refusal to make public the jury list: "I would say that it is unusual, and extremely unfair to the defendant." The litany of unfairness continued in Burdick's testimony, next addressing the activity of U.S. Marshal Gunvaldson of Fargo. The marshal, who had also been the editor of a Norwegian-language newspaper, the *Normanden*, and strongly opposed the Nonpartisan League, had spoken freely and repeatedly of his animosity toward the governor to Burdick and in front of others. Burdick quoted Gunvaldson as telling him at the Patterson Hotel in Bismarck that "he was 'going to get' Langer, if it was the last thing he ever did; and added in one conversation the following: 'you know how I can do it'; and my answer was, 'Yes I know how you can do it, all right; but it is a thing that you shouldn't do.'"

The House committee also took the testimony of a third party, H. C. Schumacher, who had witnessed the conversations between Burdick and Gunvaldson. Schumacher said that while the grand jury was in session, Gunvaldson had gone to Burdick's office, where Schumacher recalled him pounding on the table and saying about Langer, "We're going to get that son of a bitch." Schumacher testified that he had known about Gunvaldson's enmity for William Langer for years. He reported that two years before, when Langer was running for governor, the marshal was "absolutely hostile" and had said Langer was a "double-crosser." He supported Usher Burdick's testimony about other evidence of Gunvaldson's prejudices, quoting him as saying after Langer's indictment, "We got so damn much stuff on him [Langer], if he ever goes to trial, they'll be convicted; every damn one of them." His recollection of the conversation at the Patterson Hotel was that Gunvaldson had warned Burdick not to run on the same ticket as Langer. Schumacher quoted Gunvaldson as saying, "'The reason is, Langer is going to be indicted, or going to get into trouble about this five percent.' That is what he said. He said, 'They're going to get the whole damn outfit,' he said, 'and it wouldn't stop with Langer.'"[119]

The second time Usher Burdick provided sworn testimony was at hearings in front of the United States Senate Committee on Privileges and Elections, held November 3–18, 1941.[120] Langer had been elected to the U.S. Senate in 1940, defeating William Lemke and Charles Vogel in a three-way race. Eight of his political enemies had presented a petition to prevent Langer's assuming his seat in the Senate, which eventually led to a Senate investigation and these hearings. In addition to U.S. Congressman Burdick, Francis Murphy, the lead defense attorney for William Langer in all trials after the first one, and someone who had probably tried as many cases as any lawyer in Miller's court, and J. M. Hanley, a former North Dakota district judge [1915–20] and legislator, Democratic candidate for governor, an army colonel, and a major in the army reserve, also testified.[121] Hanley had been Judge Miller's lawyer in the latter's confirmation hearings before the U.S. Senate earlier in the 1920s and still considered himself a friend of the judge, but he was critical of the jury selection nevertheless.[122]

They all agreed that the federal jury selection system was subject to abuse, was abused in the Langer cases and others, and did not comply with the law. First, they noted the unprecedented refusal to release the names of the jurors, something Judge Miller and his predecessor, Judge Amidon, had ordinarily done, and which their successors continued after this trial. Second, they pointed out that the federal judge also appointed the two people in charge of the naming of jurors from the pool of several hundred names kept on file for that purpose: the clerk of district court and the jury commissioner. Under federal law, the two must be of opposing political parties, and in this case one was Democrat and one Republican. Neither had any affiliation with the Nonpartisan League, which was for all practical purposes a third party (although it filed its candidates in the Republican column of the ballot) and was, in fact, the strongest of the three. Both regular Republicans and Democrats generally opposed the League and the clerk of court and jury commission certainly did.

In his testimony before the U.S. Senate committee, Congressman Burdick noted that if a federal judge wanted a defendant convicted, it was relatively easy to do so. The drawing itself was fair, but the pool of names was not necessarily so. The names were kept in a book; anyone could hand in a name and it went into the book. Burdick noted, "There is not a single name in the book but what they know all about, and you can frame up on anybody."[123] He explained how the jury selection was done in 1934, in practice, noting that the marshal was the "big man," and whenever he was out around the state, he inquired about good people for the jury. Burdick said he once told the U.S. Marshal that he knew some cattlemen whom he would like to see on the jury and gave him four or five names; when the court was convened, there they were.[124]

At one time, names came from the postmasters, but by the time of the Langer trials, the hundred names on the petit jury list and seventy-five on the grand jury list came entirely from the U.S. Marshal, Ole Gunvaldson. As he had testified in 1934, Burdick noted that the marshal was a bitter personal enemy of Langer, an assertion confirmed by Gunvaldson's own correspondence.[125] Burdick said that he didn't know that Marshal Gunvaldson had plugged the jury box but that he could have done so if he so desired. As a matter of fact, Burdick told the Senate hearing, "I could have plugged it if they had left it to me."[126] He repeated Gunvaldson's repeated prediction: ". . . we are going to get the son of a bitch [Langer]." Burdick said he did not know that Miller had impounded the jury list, but when asked if that was a usual procedure, he answered, "Not for Judge Miller." Burdick noted that the defendants had ten peremptory challenges in the Langer trial and had used nine of them. He said it was "a practice among experienced lawyers to always save one challenge for the reason that they may draw one worse than what they have; and with this jury picked, and with 75 names on the panel, the arbitrary striking of ten names would not give the defendants proper protection, in view of the way the names were selected, as heretofore testified to."

He testified about how difficult it was to get a juror excused for cause when the judge is the only one allowed to question the jury, not the defense counsel. Burdick noted, "The practice is that when a prospective juror shows a tendency to disqualification, the court usually asks him this question: 'In spite of what you have just said, do you feel that you can render a fair and impartial verdict between the Government and the defendant, based upon the evidence and the instructions of the Court?' The answer is invariably, 'Yes, I can.'" When asked if that would be the prospective juror's answer, even if he were truly prejudiced, Burdick's answer was yes.[127]

At the Senate hearing, James Hanley corroborated Burdick's testimony as to the unfairness of Judge Miller's handling of jury selection. One protection against prejudiced jurors available to defendants in federal court was the peremptory challenge, which gives the defendant the right to excuse a juror without giving a reason for the dismissal. Hanley reported that in the first trial, the defense got down to their last peremptory challenge [ten for a total of six defendants] and a juror named Lester Hulett was called. The defense had to decide whether to reject him, using their last peremptory challenge, and take the chance of getting a worse one drawn, or take him and trust to luck. Choosing Hulett, as they eventually decided to do, turned out to have very negative results for the governor, but the dilemma of having to choose such a hostile juror over the possibility of a worse one, was determined by Judge Miller's unprecedented process of jury selection. Hanley also noted that the judge's comments to the jury at the beginning of the Langer case were longer and more emphatic than in the ordinary case, which may have been due to the importance of the case, but the judge was particularly emphatic more in certain portions than in others.

Hanley said his relations with Miller had always been cordial and pleasant and that he had personally gone to the judge before the trial and asked to see the jury list. Miller told him he had decided not to release the names before the jurors reported at the beginning of the trial, and he did not, the first and only time in Hanley's experience he ever heard of such a ruling. None of the jurors, Hanley testified, was known to the defense lawyers, and "the judge would not let us question them. If we suggested a subject, he would sometimes examine them."[128]

Francis Murphy, a prominent trial lawyer in Fargo who handled Langer's appeal after the first case and was lead counsel in all the other cases, also testified at the Senate hearing. He had practiced law in North Dakota for a good many years in both state and federal courts and had his observations to share about Judge Miller.[129] Murphy noted the statutory jury list of three hundred names, as prescribed by law for federal trials, were selected, not indifferently from lists of voters or tax lists as in state court, but rather, as the clerk or the jury commissioner of the opposite political party might desire. Murphy said he had at times suggested that the system employed by Court Clerk Montgomery and Jury Commissioner Hooper was a haphazard method of selection and he did not like it, since by federal law, every qualified juror in North Dakota could potentially sit as a juror in federal court. Unfortunately for Langer and others who ran afoul of prejudiced federal judges, this federal system of jury selection remained on the books until 1948, when a system much closer to the North Dakota state random selection was put into place.[130] Like Burdick and other witnesses, Murphy also noted that women, who were qualified jurors under the laws of North Dakota, had never been put on a jury in federal court in North Dakota.

Murphy filed a petition, well in advance of the trial, asking that the jury list be set aside, and a new list be made, in accordance with

Members of the federal court jury pictured here in May 1934 found sufficient evidence to bind William Langer and eight other defendants over for trial on the charge of misuse of federal relief funds.
State Historical Society of North Dakota   D635

statute. In that petition he pointed out that, according to federal law, the jury list should include three hundred names. The judge then was supposed to order a jury panel of fifty to seventy names.[131] The defense's first objection was that the original method of making up the list was incorrect, as testified by the deputy clerk himself. The clerk's method was to write to a friend and crony of his in Minot, for example, who shared his outlook on life, and ask him to send him a list of names of people he knew who would make good jurors. His contact would inevitably send in five or six names of friends and cronies of his. That is how, in the judgment of the defense, it came to be that the jury box was made up of people of the same attitudes, without charging any design on the part of anyone to back it up at all.

The second objection was that the selected jurors did not have to come from different counties; in fact, all fifty could come from one county. The clerk, of course, was in charge. He was appointed by the judge; he remained in office during the pleasure of the judge; he could be removed at the pleasure of the judge. Murphy explained that the judge, as was always the practice in federal court, examined potential jurors. If the lawyers wanted to ask a juror a specific question, they had to submit it to the judge in writing and he would decide whether to ask it or not.[132]

In the 1941 Senate hearings, Langer himself described Judge Miller's conduct of jury selection. Langer noted that the jury list was impounded in the first trial, rather than following the custom of releasing the names on the lists of both grand jurors and trial jurors in advance, and the newspapers then publishing them. In his many years of practicing law in state and federal courts in North Dakota, he had never heard of a variance of this until his own trial, nor since that time. In fact, just before he left North Dakota for Washington to begin his first term in the Senate, Langer noted that a complete list of grand jurors had been published in the paper.[133]

Langer had wired Judge Miller from New Rockford before the trial and asked him for a list of jurors. The telegram was never answered. Francis Murphy was asked if such a request was customary; Langer answered that requests were never required and that he had often gotten the jury names from the newspaper.

As the trial began, only eight of the defendants were in court, the judge having sent a doctor to check on the ninth defendant, Oscar Erickson, who was ill. He had been in the hospital since April 27, and the court-appointed physician testified that Erickson could not appear for "an indefinite length of time." His trial was delayed.[134] When Langer and his defense team finally saw the list of jurors, they were dumbfounded. Of the seventy or so names on the panel, there was not one recognizable friend or acquaintance of his. As the trial proceeded, the defendants tried to check on the jurors during noon hours and evenings. One problem for the defense was that many of the jury pool shared the names of Olson and Nelson and other Scandinavian names, and sometimes with the same first and last names as others in the same community. Langer and his lawyers had difficulty getting any information to determine the possibility of prejudice against the defendants.

When Bill Langer was questioned at the Senate hearing, he, like Burdick, noted that Judge Amidon would let lawyers ask questions of the jury.[135] Scott W. Lucas, the Democratic senator from Illinois (Senate service, 1939–51) and hostile to Langer, asked if Langer was charging the federal authorities with willfully and knowingly putting on the jury seventy-two enemies of his. Langer replied in the affirmative.[136] He said that the system of jury selection was responsible for the fact that he had no friends among the seventy-two prospective jurors, and the defense naturally objected to the names that went in. In fact, they challenged the entire jury panel because of the way that names went in. Many times since the trial, Langer had challenged a man named Al Fruh, a deputy marshal at the time, for walking down the streets of towns and going into businesses and asking for a hundred dollars for subscriptions to a newspaper that was fighting Langer, just a few weeks before the trial, and having every person who gave him that amount put on the jury panel. Langer said he had been told by friends that one of the jurors in the first trial, Hulett, had donated one hundred dollars just two or three weeks before the trial.

Senator Lucas asked him who did the selecting. Langer replied that Fruh was newly appointed and he did not want to judge him, but a campaign was on in 1934 and the opportunity was there to send in names of the opposite party. When the senator responded that Langer was making a serious charge, Langer replied that it was so serious that he asked the legislature to investigate, and even the state senate, which was overwhelmingly opposed to him in 1935, agreed to memorialize Congress to change the method of drawing jurors in federal court in North Dakota.[137] Langer added that even P. W. Lanier, Sr., the prosecutor, volunteered to him that he was surprised that Langer had so few friends on the trial panel, and that he figured there were only six of Langer's friends out of the pool.[138] Langer said that one of the jurors, J. T. Brady, had actually sued him, when Langer was governor, over a law involving sale of automobiles, and another juror, Lester Hulett, manager of a credit corporation in Mandan, had filed a complaint against him. Hulett was in charge of a credit agency that loaned money to farmers, but which required each borrower to buy stock in his corporation in the amount of 10 percent of the loan. Although the cost of the stock was to be repaid when the farmer paid off the loan to Hulett, investigations showed that those repayments were not being made. Langer called a hearing to investigate the Hulett matter, during which he asked Hulett what his salary was. Hulett replied that it was three hundred dollars a month, and Langer said that hereafter he would take one hundred twenty-five dollars a month of that and use it to repay the farmers. Hulett was very bitter about this, and within a short time he was on the jury—one of the better jurors, the lawyers thought at the time.

In support of Langer's statements, Murphy offered in evidence and read an affidavit of James Mulloy—the same man who had earlier testified against Langer in the Senate hearings. Mulloy, who was present, admitted it was his affidavit and placed it about the time of the motion for new trial. It stated that he knew that Hulett was embittered. Mulloy said he was told by the widow of another juror, Otto Roder, that her husband told her that Hulett was the juror who led the fight to convict Langer and his codefendants. Mulloy was in the courtroom when Hulett refused to disqualify himself and Judge Miller refused to remove him. He agreed that attorneys for defendant Langer had called the facts in the affidavit to Judge Miller's attention.[139] Mulloy also stated that after the election, the company Hulett had headed, which had been suspended from conducting business, was given permission to resume business, allowing the farmers of North Dakota to be swindled out of hundreds of thousands of dollars. Langer noted that the Securities Commission, consisted of himself as governor, Attorney General P. J. Sathre, and former senator Gronna.[140]

Many years after the Senate hearing, Langer told this author of another explanation of the incredible antagonism of the jury panel at the first trial (and perhaps the subsequent trials). Langer said that he had talked to a deputy clerk of the United States District Court at Fargo, perhaps Talcott, who described the method used to assure a pro-government jury. Talcott said that all the jurors were rated by whether they would be pro-government and anti-Langer, and the names of those favorable to the prosecution were written on stiffer and slightly longer slips of papers than the others. The clerk or deputy who reached into the jury wheel for names of jurors to be examined could thus pick up slips bearing names of jurors and retain the stiffer slips between his or her fingers, while the more flexible and shorter slips would fall out. In that way, no name would be called unless the person had been determined in advance to be anti-Langer.[141] Faced with a judge who was his enemy and a jury that was handpicked from his personal and political enemies, Langer and the other defendants proceeded to trial.

The Conduct of the Trial

Judge Miller conducted the trial as might have been expected from his pretrial rulings. At the outset, in the presence of all potential jurors, the defense had asked for a delay due to the illness and hospitalization of Oscar E. Erickson, a defendant as well as an important witness. Judge Miller, in denying the request, said "either one of two things exists: either the defendants are innocent or else they are cheap, petty chiselers who are no more important than anyone else."[142] That comment set the tone for the trial.

In addition to William Langer, Sherrard Ewing, Edith Scott,

Harold McDonald, and Frank Vogel, other defense witnesses were R. A. Kinzer, Joseph Kinzer, Oscar Chaput, George E. Wallace (a former tax commissioner), E. H. Brant, and Dave Hamilton, a district manager of the highway department. The five members of the State Relief Committee appointed by Langer—Judge Christianson, Lee Nichols, Minnie D. Craig, Arthur E. Thompson, and Robert M. Stangler—all gave no testimony that could be considered damaging to the defendants and some of their testimony was quite favorable. None of the committee members implicated any defendant with anything untoward done within the committee. In fact, they all indicated that Langer behaved quite properly and corroborated the procedure for handling funds, as earlier testimony had been offered.

The following is an abbreviated summary of the testimony of various witnesses, taken from the record of the first trial, as agreed to by the attorneys for both sides and part of the appeal record in the Court of Appeals.[143]

William Langer's Testimony[144]

Organizing the *Leader* was Langer's idea. "The Leaguers needed a voice to contradict the daily press, which was united against us, and to tell our side of matters in dispute," he said. When Langer took office in January 1933, he was in the hospital. Inexplicably, outgoing Governor George Shafer had not applied for federal relief money for January and February of that year. Federal law required the governor to appoint a relief committee to get federal funds, and Langer did. The federal government wanted a nonpolitical committee, and he appointed one. He appointed Supreme Court Judge Adolph M. Christianson as chair, who was affiliated with the faction of the Republican Party in opposition to the NPL, the Independent Voters Association [IVA], although he was elected to the court on a no-party ballot and served from 1915 to 1954. Christianson was a wonderfully, thoroughly honest man; he spoke Norwegian and knew the law. Langer also appointed Robert Stangler, who spoke German and was also a member of the IVA.

German-Americans and Norwegian-Americans constituted the overwhelming ethnic percentage of North Dakota's population, so it is clear that Langer was attuned to the spirit of representation called for in New Deal relief initiatives. As for gender representation, Langer appointed Minnie Craig, Speaker of the House [the first woman in the United States to accomplish that feat], a member of Langer's NPL, and the outstanding female politician in North Dakota at the time.

Democrats were not excluded, although, as a party, they were a distant third in balloting behind the NPL and the IVA. Arthur E. Thompson, a Democrat elected on the No-Party ballot as superintendent of public instruction was appointed, as well as Lee Nichols, county auditor of Morton County. They all lived close to Bismarck, as the field representative of the Interior Department, which was administering the federal relief program, Sherrard Ewing, said they should be. Langer wanted a committee that would take complete charge and would be as efficient as it could be.

All of these members of the Federal Relief Committee testified for the defense in the first trial, but anyone who thinks that these people would do as they were told by Langer [or anyone else] did not know them as North Dakotans knew them. They were fiercely independent. In fact, Judge Christianson was one of the four judges on the North Dakota Supreme Court whose ruling removed Langer from office in 1935 because of his felony conviction in the first trial (one judge voted against the removal). Arthur Thompson was anti-Langer—one of seven officials who refused endorsement on a Langer ticket in 1936 (and the only one of the seven to survive in

*Subscribers to the **Leader**, the Nonpartisan League newspaper, received stock certificates as shares in the nonprofit corporation, like this one to Frank R. Vogel from June 1949.* From the Robert Vogel Collection

office after the election). Robert Stangler was considered by all political groups as a competent and nonpolitical banker, and Minnie Craig, as Speaker of the House, was considered fair by all parties.

According to his own testimony, Langer signed the requests for federal funds that the committee gave him and forwarded them to Washington, and he endorsed over to them the checks that came back. He had nothing to do with their work, except he was once asked to comment on a potential employee, and he asked John Williams (who replaced Joseph Kinzer as secretary of the committee) to hire Senator Nye's brother, and he did. This, despite the fact that Gerald Nye, one of Langer's bitterest enemies in North Dakota, had been working hard behind the scenes to bring about Langer's downfall in the first trial.

The NPL never planned to solicit anyone to purchase subscriptions who was not a state employee. As soon as Langer heard that federal relief employees had been solicited, he got in touch with three members of the committee and tried to reach Judge Christianson in order to put a stop to it, and, to his knowledge, that warning was sufficient to end it. Langer said he did not know of a single instance of anyone losing a job for not contributing.

As to his bank account (which had been subpoenaed and put in evidence), Langer had fifty-two thousand dollars in accounts receivable from his law practice when he became governor, and some of that was paid after he took office.[145] When not in public office, Bill Langer was the most successful trial lawyer in North Dakota. In addition, he had farm land and received rentals, and stored the harvested grain and used money from the account to buy futures to protect the price of his crop. Hedging the price of his grain was the basis for the headlines in the *Bismarck Tribune* and elsewhere that Langer used *Leader* money to gamble on the grain market. Hedging is often recommended to farmers by federal agricultural officials and bankers and is not gambling but, rather, is a method of protecting the price of the grain. There is nothing illegal about it.[146] Langer testified that the *Leader* and League owed him more money than the nineteen thousand dollars transferred to him as repayment for money he had spent in reorganizing the League from 1928 onward and that the NPL Executive Committee had agreed to repay the money.[147] It was Langer who had provided all the funding to reorganize the League after the 1928 election. He bought two cars for solicitors and paid all expenses. The total he expended, which the NPL Executive Committee, consisting of Roy Frazier, Fred Argast, and Carl Anderson, agreed to repay from their funds or the profits of the *Leader*, was more than twenty-one thousand dollars. Not everyone knew of this, but the NPL Executive Committee and Oscar Erickson did.[148]

The NPL Executive Committee had wanted to establish a newspaper in 1928, too, but decided that they could not, and Langer refunded all the money for that purpose, except to a few people who asked that the League keep the money. Langer also paid for the sales tax campaign (to oppose the repeal by referral of the tax passed in 1932 to raise money for schools and for state bond interest), and he was reimbursed for some of that. Langer alone had devised the plan for the *Leader* and had begged Oscar Erickson to take charge because he was the Republican state chairman and a trusted friend. The one time that Langer took money that came from the *Leader* account was at the request of the executive committee. He testified, "Since the *Leader* owed me more money than I received, I was asked to take the money to avoid a threatened garnishment of the *Leader* account."[149] During his cross-examination, U.S. Attorney Lanier insisted that Langer's testimony about the debt was a recent invention, and that there was no such debt. In his opening statement, Lanier had told the jury, "We will show that at least some $14,000 were diverted from the *Leader* account to the account of Governor Langer," thereby inferring that Langer had taken money to which he had no right.[150] The prosecution then put in evidence records that Langer had, indeed, received such money. The defense objected to the opening statement and to the records, but the judge overruled their objection.

In response, in order to corroborate Langer's testimony on this very important—perhaps crucial—point, the defendants put on the witness stand Carl Anderson, a former member of the NPL Executive Committee. When the government objected to his testimony, Judge Miller said that Anderson was "immaterial" and refused to let him testify. The defense then made an "Offer of Proof," which is a statement by an attorney to the judge, in the absence of the jury, as to what the witnesses will say if allowed to testify. This is done so that there is no doubt as to what the testimony will be, and the trial judge, and any appellate court, can decide whether the testimony is admissible or not. The offer of proof was, in the opinion of many practicing lawyers, then and now, erroneously rejected by Judge Miller.

The defense then offered P. J. Aarhus, who had led the effort to create an earlier newspaper paid for by Langer at a cost of more than twenty-five thousand dollars. The Executive Committee of the NPL had also agreed to repay Langer for this sizable outlay of funds. The judge likewise rejected his testimony, as well as all such offers to prove the same facts by other witnesses, though the offers of proof were in perfect form. The judge's rulings permitted the U.S. government to create the inference that there was no basis for the payment to Langer except the government version of the facts, which P. W. Lanier claimed showed a conspiracy to defraud and that Langer's statement had no corroboration. Rulings like these caused Usher Burdick to conclude Langer was a victim of a judicial and political conspiracy and that he had been railroaded by political enemies and a biased judge.[151] There can be no doubt that this corroborating testimony was admissible, and it was reversible error for Judge Miller to reject it. But everyone involved in the May–June 1934 trial knew that a reversal could well come too late to save Langer's governorship in that year or the next.

Judge A. M. Christianson

Judge Christianson, chair of the State Relief Board, explained how the board functioned: "Governor Langer appointed a five-person committee to handle relief matters, and he told us to handle the matters in any way we saw fit."[152] The committee prepared the requests for money and the governor signed them without change. When the money came, in the form of checks, Langer sent them to the committee. Christianson noted that the only other contact the board had with him was one time when he objected to hiring a person he was opposed to (Langer testified he was asked to comment on the hiring), and once Christianson had gone to the penitentiary where the governor was attending a meeting of the Pardon Board to get his signature on a telegram for more funds.[153]

Members of the committee were not paid, and Judge Christianson spent his own money for gas and tires. Hiring and firing was handled by the secretary, E. H. Brant, and later Kinzer, and then John Williams. Mrs. Craig received no pay as a committee member but earned two hundred dollars a month as a field representative. When Lorena Hickok, who served as a "confidential investigator" for Harry Hopkins, head of FERA, talked to Christianson in October 1933, she was told that the real problems were with the federal government, not with Governor Langer:

> Chief Justice [Adolph Marcus] Christianson told me that 'in most counties' no farm loans had been granted at all -- that he had heard of cases where applications made last May had still received no action. He blamed it on red tape and inad-

equate personnel. I am trying to find out just what a farmer has to go through to get a federal loan, but didn't get much help from him. He said most of the applications had to be made in writing and sent to St. Paul, which would of course slow things up. The whole machinery is so complicated! I heard of organizations today that I didn't know existed. . . .

In the county I visited this afternoon farmers had received federal loans, but the impression was that the loans were granted to pay back the Twin City bankers. . . . When I pointed out that, even though the money did go to the banks, it probably saved their farms for them, someone remarked, "Well, the farms aren't worth saving now."

They are not at all impressed with Mr. [Henry A.] Wallace's acreage reduction plan. This, they say is why: . . .Wheat was selling in North Dakota for 70 cents a bushel today. They say it costs 77 cents a bushel to raise it.[154]

In other words, from the point of view of North Dakota farmers, the fault for their plight was not in Bismarck but was instead in the weather conditions, the Twin Cities, and in Washington, D.C.

The first that Judge Christianson heard of solicitation of employees was that Mrs. Craig had been asked to purchase a subscription to the *Leader* and had refused. On June 15, Ewing told Judge Christianson that he had been told employees were solicited and, if so, any money should be returned. On August 15, Judge Christianson wrote a resolution which was passed, forbidding any political contributions. He said, "The Governor always told us we were running the business and he was going to allow us to do what was right about it. And we did the best we could. Ewing objected to Kinzer because of a letter he wrote to Hopkins criticizing action he took, and indications [were that] he was out of sympathy with the aims of the Relief Administration, so Kinzer resigned and I suggested John E. Williams to replace him."[155]

Minnie D. Craig

Mrs. Craig had been present when Harold McDonald solicited funds for the *Leader* from people he thought worked for the state of North Dakota. When McDonald solicited her, she refused to contribute. She testified that McDonald used no pressure on her and that she saw and heard nothing to indicate any pressure was used on anyone else in the office.

Minnie Craig's testimony that nothing untoward had occurred with McDonald's solicitations should have resonated with observers of the trial. As Speaker of the North Dakota House of Representatives, she was a sophisticated politician. She had secured that position, not only through the support of William Langer and her fellow Nonpartisan League legislators, but also through her ability to garner support from other factions in the legislature who were opposed to the League. The vote was unanimous, following League endorsement.[156] As the first woman so honored, her selection received attention in the national press. But as one fellow legislator commented, it was not her gender, but her probity and good judgment that recommended Minnie Craig to her House colleagues. He said, "We can trust her. We know her to be absolutely honest, broad in vision and tolerant of other people's rights, sympathetic to needed reform and untiring in effort to achieve it. We are mindful of the fact that through her legislative experience and her happy disposition, through her voice and seasoned judgement, she has the attributes that go to make a successful speaker. We have chosen quality."[157]

As a member of the State Relief Committee, as well as a field representative of the committee, Minnie Craig was also well aware of the privation suffered by North Dakotans in 1933. For this reason, among others, she chose not to seek reelection in 1934.[158]

Sherrard Ewing

Ewing testified as the field representative of the Federal Emergency Relief Administration. The State Relief Committee, headed by Judge Christianson, had been assembled before he arrived on the third Monday in January 1933, the month Langer was installed as governor.[159] Ewing thought it was a good committee.[160] He corroborated the process, noting that by federal law, the money for state relief had to be applied for by the governor. The committee filled out the forms and the governor had to sign them and send a letter asking for the money. Ewing testified that he never talked figures with Governor Langer. Langer simply signed and approved every request of the committee.[161]

Edith Scott

Scott was employed in the State Relief Office. She testified that when Harold McDonald solicited her, she told him she could not contribute. She then talked to Kinzer, who was head of the office at the time, and he told her that there would be no pressure on her if she did not contribute. The prosecution questioned her about the fact that her salary had been reduced, and she answered that she had gone from a monthly salary of ninety dollars down to eighty-five. On cross-examination, it was revealed that she had been absent from work one afternoon and for fifteen to twenty minutes of another day during the month before her pay was cut. (Other witnesses said she was absent for several days, and that she had not put in overtime as all the other secretaries did during a busy time.) Later, after Kinzer was no longer in charge, she received raises to ninety and ninety-five dollars, but her salary had remained at eighty-five dollars for several months after John E. Williams replaced him.

Harold McDonald

McDonald was the young man who solicited the infamous $179.50 from employees in the State Welfare Office. He had been instructed to solicit only state employees, but all state offices had been moved to downtown office buildings, after a fire had earlier destroyed the old state capitol. Since the new one had not yet been built, the hastily arranged relocation of state agencies interspersed them with offices administering newly created federal programs. Macdonald assumed that the offices he visited were staffed by state employees, and he asked them, just as he had asked others, to contribute to the *Leader*, and told them how they could get their money back by selling subscriptions if they chose to do it. He testified that he made no threats to anyone.

Frank Vogel

As the highway commissioner and a friend of Langer's, Vogel testified that he had been opposed to the idea of establishing the *Leader*. His experience was that the NPL was bound to be criticized for this move and that past political NPL newspapers had been unsuccessful. He contributed five percent, as he did when he had been employed under the (Roosevelt) Democratic administration when the figure was ten percent. (Judge Miller ordered this part of his testimony stricken from the record). Vogel allowed a solicitor to talk to highway department employees, provided no pressure was used. No employee was fired for failing to contribute, although Vogel testified that he had fired a few people for other reasons. Frank Vogel did not know who had contributed and who had not. He testified that if an employee were fired from the highway department, he would check to see if that person had pledged money and if he had, he would tell the *Leader* to cancel the obligation. He did write some letters to employees if he heard that they were not paying their bills, whether to grocery stores or anywhere else, but these transactions did not constitute pressure with regard to *Leader* subscriptions.

Several employees of the relief office and the highway department were called. They told of discussions in the offices and among employees about whether they should contribute. Some asked R. A. Kinzer or Frank Vogel about it and were told it was optional and that there would be no pressure on them. The *Bismarck Tribune*, however, had been running hysterical allegations of mass firings that never occurred.[162] In talking among themselves, these state employees decided after reading the *Tribune*, and other papers of like disposition, that they should contribute to the *Leader* fund after all. In other words, far from reporting on a heavy-handed recruiting scam by Langer and the NPL, the *Bismarck Tribune* caused more money to be contributed than would otherwise have been the case. Nowhere in the brief presented by P. W. Lanier and the U.S. government prosecution in 1934, and the later Senate investigation in 1941, was any evidence introduced to the effect that firings of any kind had occurred as a result of solicitations for *Leader* subscriptions.

The Charge to the Jury (Instructions)

Defendants Joseph Kinzer, Yeater, and Hample were acquitted by order of the Court.[163] Presumably, there was no testimony to implicate them in any alleged offense. The judge also told the jury that Oscar Erickson remained as a conspirator and defendant but was "not on trial at this time before this jury."[164] That left R. A. Kinzer, Harold McDonald, Frank Vogel, Oscar Chaput, and William Langer to face the charges.

Judge Miller was known for his unique way of instructing jurors, and in this case, he chose to comment on the facts of the case, something federal judges are allowed to do but a practice that was and is unusual in North Dakota. Since I started practicing in federal court in North Dakota about 1945, federal judges from Charles Vogel (no relation to the author) on have said that they do not comment on the evidence, and that it was for the jury to decide what the facts were. Judge Miller did not adhere to that practice in the Langer case, commenting at considerable length, close to an hour, according to the defense lawyers. Though not recorded by a court reporter, one attorney for the defense recorded about ten minutes of them.

One duty of any trial judge is to summarize the contentions of the parties. In this case, Judge Miller spent thirteen pages summarizing the government case [favorably] and less than one page on the defense contentions. All he said about the defense was that it claimed there was no intent and no joint action.[165] At one point Judge Miller illustrated his concept of the law by referring to robbing banks or a post office, using the following analogy:

> ... A person robs the Post Office in Bismarck. That is a crime against the United States; it is the crime itself. But the conspiracy statute provides that if two or more persons should conspire to rob the Post Office of the United States, that is a different offense. If a person was charged with robbing the Post Office of the United States at Bismarck, it would be necessary for the Government to prove that he actually robbed the Post Office, but if the indictment is under Section 37, and two or more persons should conspire to rob the Post Office at Bismarck, all the Government would have to prove would be, one, they did conspire and agree together that they would rob the Post Office and that some one or more of them did something towards carrying out the object and purpose of the conspiracy, that is to say, for instance, if one of them should go down and go into the Post Office and look it over and see where the doors were and where the safe was for the purpose of reporting back to the other conspirators; the crime then is committed.[166]

At another point, rather than let the jury make up its own mind, Judge Miller dismissed the defense argument that there was no proof offered by the government that "the drafts drawn against the *Leader* and credited again to William Langer's accounts were for the identical sums or included that portion of the deposit in the *Leader* account that came from the federal employes [*sic*]," by using a farming analogy:

> Gentlemen, that is a quibble. All the money in The Leader account was commingled in one account the same as a dozen loads of grain in an elevator are commingled and when you take out a bushel of it you take from all the commingled grain; so that when any draft was drawn on The Leader fund, which included the Federal five per cent assessment collected, it was a part of that fund, of course, which was drawn against.[167]

As for the actual money involved in the case, Judge Miller said that the evidence showed that the defendants collected from relief personnel only about one hundred eighty dollars, but the jury could conclude that this was because the federal government, not Langer himself or other state officials, heard about it and put a stop to it.[168]

Miller told the jury to look closely at the subscription-selling feature, and that it was not the intent of the United States that, in addition to giving employment to the unemployed, those people were to give five percent of their salary to somebody, or pay a debt of Langer's to somebody else. He said the employees had earned their salaries, and now they had to earn five percent again by selling subscriptions. In other words, he told the jury that the intent was proved, even though intent was one of the matters of fact to be determined by the jury. He suggested it was coercion for the boss to say, "I have subscribed, you better think it over."[169] There was no testimony in the trial itself that any boss said anything of the kind.

As for Frank Vogel, who had testified that he opposed the *Leader* scheme from the start but had contributed himself and allowed highway department employees to be solicited for contributions, Judge Miller compared him to a man contacted by someone planning to steal cattle, who asks to be allowed to use the first man's barn to hide the stolen cattle overnight. When the owner of the barn permits this to be done, even as he continues to object to it, he becomes guilty of conspiracy:

> ... So with reference to Vogel, if Vogel knew that the Langer scheme was unlawful and a fraud, and he cooperated with him in any way, such as the letters here that are in evidence of his demanding that employes [sic] recognize their obligation to *The Leader* and pay it and in permitting them to be induced to do it, it is for you to determine whether he did cooperate with him. If he did cooperate and aid and assist he does come into the conspiracy, and that is the only way he comes into this case.[170]

In other words, Judge Miller compared McDonald's solicitation to cattle rustling, and compared allowing the solicitation of contributions to concealing stolen goods and aiding and abetting a felony.

R. A. Kinzer and Oscar Chaput were lumped into this conspiracy as well, either as willing or unwilling accomplices in Governor Langer's scheme to hustle *Leader* subscriptions, which became in Miller's comments to the jury, a scheme to rustle federal dollars. Despite the fact that prior to the charge to the jury, the prosecutor had dropped every overt act charged to Vogel that related to the solicitations in the highway department, Judge Miller insinuated that Vogel had participated in a conspiracy to divert federal funds relating to McDonald's solicitation of workers in the State Welfare Office.

U.S. Congressman Usher Burdick described how Judge Miller spoke to juries in this case and others when he testified in front of the Senate Committee on Elections and Privileges in 1941.[171] Burdick's view of Judge Miller's prejudice toward many defendants was based upon his direct observation of the judge's demeanor in the courtroom in cases that preceded the Langer case. When Burdick was assistant U.S. attorney, he often did the trial work in most prosecutions, being lowest in rank.[172] Burdick said he proceeded to try any case the right way, and whether the outcome were an acquittal or a conviction, he did the best he could. Judge Miller, however, often made it very embarrassing for him and difficult to do his job. He said about Judge Miller: "When he wanted a man convicted, he practically handled that whole thing himself, and when he did not want a conviction, I could not get by him, and his method of charging the jury, while in print it was all right—if you would see him deliver the charge, you would say it was all wrong."[173] Burdick gave an example of Miller's jury instructional style, describing a typical statement that read like an impartial instruction on burden of proof, but ended with an admonition laced with body English: "'If, on the other hand, you are satisfied beyond a reasonable doubt of the guilt, it is your duty to convict him." According to Burdick, the words were accompanied by shouting and hitting the table with his hand, for emphasis.[174] Of course, the transcript would not show the judge's actions, only his words.

Burdick cited another example of Miller's siding with the prosecution in a comment directed to Francis Murphy, a North Dakota defense attorney, who was also present at the Senate committee hearings. He reminded Murphy, "Well, Francis, . . . that was pulled on you in a case where I was on one side and you were on the other." Burdick went on, "There is not a jury in America that would not come to the conclusion that the judge was on one side of the case, and that embarrassed me, because I did not want to defeat Francis here, by such means, but every time the judge rose and hit the desk, I got a conviction."[175] James Hanley was another witness to Judge Miller's bias against Langer.[176] He had been a "regular" (anti-Nonpartisan League) Republican candidate for governor in 1926 and speaker of the House of Representatives and was clearly not someone who could be accused of being sympathetic to William Langer for partisan political reasons. Nevertheless, he had concerns about Miller's prejudice.

Before the first Langer trial, Hanley went to see Judge Miller, along with the lead defense attorneys, Ed Sinkler and George Thorp, to ask about a procedural matter. At the time Hanley had been friendly with Miller and considered him a fine judge, but it was his experience in the Langer trial that changed his mind. Thereafter, he became convinced that Judge Miller was prejudiced. When Miller said that he thought that any lawyer who defended Langer in the case was getting "hot money," it was then that Hanley realized that the attitude of the court was different. Hanley resented such a prejudicial statement and told other legal counsel about it.[177]

Questions from the Jury

On June 16, during jury deliberations, the jury asked the judge several questions. One was whether other defendants were responsible for the actions of the two solicitors, Chaput and McDonald, who either intentionally or by mistake solicited federal government employees. Another question was whether defendants could be responsible for acts of hired agents when the agents do an act contrary to the orders of their superiors and the superiors are unaware that such acts have taken place. Judge Miller gave one answer to both questions, calling them "substantially the same":

> The Court now tells you what the law is: It is not necessary or essential to the existence of a conspiracy that each conspirator shall have knowledge of all the details of the conspiracy. Where a party of men combine with the intent to do an unlawful thing and in the performance of the unlawful intent one of the parties goes a step beyond the balance of the party and does an act which the balance do not themselves perform, all are responsible for what the one does. In other words, in the pursuit by various parties of an unlawful conspiracy each is responsible for the acts and doings of the others. If one procures or conspires with another to commit a crime he is guilty of everything done by his confederates which follows incidentally in the execution of the common design, even though it was not intended as part of the original plan.[178]

The defense claimed an exception (i.e., an objection, to preserve the issue on appeal) on this instruction from Judge Miller that "when parties agree on an intent to do an unlawful act and in the performance of that act one party goes beyond the others, all are responsible"—and properly so. Miller's assertion from the bench usurped a crucial jury decision—whether the defendants had, indeed, agreed to perform an unlawful act and what their intent was.[179] The power of Judge Miller's analogies in his comments was such that the jury asked the court to reread the part of the instructions on violations of state law, as it may relate to a continuation of a conspiracy, and "that part of your charge in which you illustrated by reference to the Post Office robbery conspiracy," during their deliberations.[180] Both were reread. In effect, Judge Miller had said that if a group of people agreed to rob the Bismarck Post Office, and one went there to check the location of the doors, they would all be guilty of conspiracy to rob a post office, whether or not they took part in the crime. This instruction was not only prejudicial but also erroneous, because it ignored the rule that a conspiracy that is abandoned is not a crime.

Verdict and Sentencing

The jury returned on Saturday evening the same day, June 16, with a guilty verdict. Judge Miller was delighted and made his pleasure public. Instead of the customary thanking of the jury for doing a civic duty, he told them that he was "delighted and pleased," and that the jury merited "the respect of the whole state and nation."[181] In view of the process of jury selection, Judge Miller's bias, his rulings on evidence, his slanted instructions to the jury, and his comments in the presence of the jury panel that the defendants were either innocent or cheap crooks, it is not surprising that the jury returned a verdict of guilty, or that the Court of Appeals, after Langer had already been deprived of the governorship and renomination in the June 1934 primary, reversed the conviction. Neither of them had much choice in the matter.

One juror who did have serious reservations about the verdict did not have the physical stamina to take on his peers. Otto Roder was taken ill during the trial and had asked for a cot. He was later reported to have told the mayor of Minneapolis, while in that city for medical care, that he thought the defendants innocent but had to vote against acquittal in order to get the medical help he needed. He died shortly after the trial.[182]

There were other outrageous irregularities in the conduct of the trial. Although the jurors were supposed to be in the custody of the marshal at all times and forbidden to read newspapers or listen to the radio, an affidavit of E. R. Sinkler, one of the defense attorneys, stated that he saw the jurors buying newspapers and reading them.[183] It was also reported that Deputy U.S. Marshal Howard Strack was seen frequently entering the jury room during deliberations, although it was his duty to enter only if the jury had a communication for the judge. This report would have an effect on the second trial.

The battleground then shifted from Judge Miller's court to venues that were more favorable to Langer and his codefendants—the election process and the United States Court of Appeals for the Eighth Circuit. The election process did not take long. The trial had begun on May 31, the jury verdict was received on June 16, the primary election was on June 27, with the sentencing set for June 29. Langer, of course, had to stay in Bismarck while the trial was going on, leaving him only eleven of the last thirty days to campaign. Despite his limited campaign opportunities and the fact that he was now a convicted felon, the voters of North Dakota gave Langer the biggest plurality ever received in a contested election of a North Dakota governor with 113,027 votes. It is obvious from these results that, among other reasons for their support, the majority of voters in North Dakota thought that their favorite candidate had been the victim of a politically motivated judicial mugging.

On June 29, two days after the overwhelming vote in the primary and before the sentencing hearing, Langer had gone to Warner Agency in Fargo and asked them for surety bonds for himself and the other defendants. They got bonds from one in-state company and one out-of-state company authorized to do business in the state. When they came before Judge Miller, later in the day, Judge Miller sentenced Langer to the maximum term of imprisonment for this conspiracy—eighteen months—and a fine of ten thousand dollars. He sentenced Frank Vogel, R. A. Kinzer, and Oscar Chaput to terms of thirteen months and fines of three thousand dollars each. Harold McDonald received a sentence of four months to be served in the Burleigh County jail. The judge refused to accept the bonds Langer had arranged for because he contended that they only guaranteed that the defendants would appear, and he would not accept their word on that. Miller demanded instead a personal bond, and one that was sufficient to allow the money to be used to pay the fines, and he wanted the personal bonds accompanied by cash or property amounting to nineteen or twenty thousand dollars. He said that if Langer and the other three did not come up with that amount by the time train left that afternoon, they would be taken to a federal penitentiary in Kansas.[184]

Judge Miller's vindictive reversal of common law bond procedures was suddenly cut short by an extraordinary act of generosity and trust. As Langer explained in the U.S. Senate hearings in 1941, Joe Runck, the son of one of his good friends from Casselton, about twenty miles from Fargo where the sentencing took place, drove in and put up personal property in the amount of twenty thousand dollars. Langer said that Runck "had heard about this [the first conspiracy trial] in Casselton and came in and asked about some of the other defendants he had never heard of, and said if they would not run away, he would go bond for all of them." Runck told the clerk that if his $20,000 of property did not satisfy the judge, "he had $80,000 more."[185] If it were not for this voluntary action of a near-stranger, the governor of the state of North Dakota, the highway commissioner, and the other defendants would have had to spend time in the custody of the marshal, and within hours would have been headed for Leavenworth Penitentiary in Kansas. This, in spite of the fact that the primary purpose of the bail bond procedure is not punitive but to assure the appearance of a defendant, and owners of substantial property are routinely allowed release on their own recognizance or personal bail. That Judge Miller demanded a cash or property bond of a man who had been a lifelong resident of North Dakota, owned property in Burleigh and Cass Counties and elsewhere in the state, and had been elected as the governor, and of the other defendants as well who were also lifelong residents or had lived in North Dakota for many years and had property in the state, demonstrates once again, his malice.

Skirmishes Between the Court Battles

On July 12, 1934—after the conviction and sentencing, and after the overwhelming majority in the election eleven days later, which gave the Nonpartisan League a big majority in the House of Representatives— Governor Langer called a special session of the legislature to convene on July 19. In the meantime, Langer's right to hold office after his conviction was appealed to the North Dakota Supreme Court, which ruled on July 17 to remove Langer from office immediately. Thus he was allowed to serve only about three-quarters of his two-year term. The decision could have gone either way. Four prestigious law review articles show the precedents were equally divided and equally persuasive.[186] Thus the law as interpreted in other courts would have permitted the North Dakota Supreme Court to allow Langer to remain in office pending appeal. In a companion case against Highway Commissioner Frank Vogel the result and the precedents were the same.[187] The legal questions were whether the conviction in federal court of what in federal law was a felony, but in state court was only a misdemeanor, required the removal of the defendant from office, and whether the removal was permissible only if the conviction occurred in a court of the state in which the officer served, or whether it could be in some other court, state or federal. With a split in the precedents, the court had a choice which to follow, and the judges chose to disqualify the defendants from office.[188] As a result of the court's ruling, Lieutenant Governor Ole Olson was declared governor, and he canceled Langer's call for a special session, just two days before the legislators were to convene. Historian Dan Rylance notes that while Olson had been Langer's running mate in 1932, he and Langer had "broken politically" over a variety of issues, and Langer had chosen Walter Welford to run with him in the primary in 1934, which Langer and Welford won. Nevertheless, as the sitting lieutenant governor, Olson served out the remainder of Langer's term in 1934.[189] Despite Olson's effort to forestall them, the NPL members of the House of Representatives assembled anyway, pursuant to Langer's call, intending to impeach the newly declared governor, but the majority of the senators, who were not Leaguers, prevented a quorum in the Senate.

The Nonpartisan League, no doubt concerned with history, as well as with the fate of their governor, and blocked by Judge Miller in a presentation of their facts made a record of its own, in the one venue that would listen, an unofficial meeting of the North Dakota House of Representatives. Speaker of the House Minnie Craig assigned fifteen members of the House to a fact-finding committee,[190] which began hearing testimony at an opening hearing presided over by Judge J. M. Hanley in Mandan, North Dakota, on August 8, 1934. Members of the committee included William Falconer, William Godwin (majority floor leader), and others. Here, the witnesses who were not allowed to testify in Judge Miller's federal court had the chance to speak out. Because the state legislature as a whole was not legally in session, the record of the proceedings of this committee were never a part of the official legislative record. Partial copies exist, and state newspapers carried reports of the committee's work.[191]

The first witnesses, Fred J. Argast and Roy Frazier, former members of the Nonpartisan League Executive Committee, testified as they would have in an admissible offer of proof, and said that Langer had really expended more than the nineteen thousand dollars promised by the NPL in return.[192] Lee Nichols, a member of the State Relief Committee, corroborated Langer's testimony as to the accidental solicitation of employees in the "State Relief Office." He also testified that the relief office for North Dakota started out with funds merely loaned to the state by the federal government, and that the members were, and considered themselves to be, state employees, dispensing state funds, at the time of McDonald's solicitation. It was only later, after the fact of the solicitation, that the loans to the state were changed to federal grant status, thus making the federal role more direct. In addition, Governor Langer never had anything directly to do with the operations of the state committee that dispensed the federal funds, either indirectly under state auspices as a loan, or directly under federal auspices as a grant. The failure of Prosecutor Lanier and Judge Miller to allow for this distinction on the part of Langer's defense is what gave McDonald's actions the appearance of criminality, when, in fact, no such criminality occurred.[193] Through the testimony of Congressman Usher L. Burdick, H. C. Schumacher, and others, the de facto committee took the opportunity to show how the jury was hand-picked, motivated by U.S. Marshal Gunvaldson's hatred of Langer

No witness testified that McDonald made any threats to those he solicited. The closest any witness came to saying anything of the sort was from a witness who said McDonald acted cocky. This witness, however, said that he, too, signed a pledge to support the *Leader*, because of false reports he had read in the papers that people were being fired for not agreeing to solicitations from McDonald and others.

In the first trial there was also considerable testimony of solicitations in the highway department, but all the overt acts alleged to have taken place there were dismissed, and the Court of Appeals later made it clear that there was no violation of federal law in soliciting funds from state employees.[194] One person who claimed to have been fired there for not contributing, George Hepner, was a division engineer at Minot. He was not, in fact, fired, but was offered a transfer, after Frank Vogel received a report that he was out of favor with the Ward County commissioners and could not get along with his employees. Vogel said he was a good engineer but a poor administrator. Hepner admitted there was talk of a transfer, and he was told to see Frank Vogel at Bismarck, but he did not do so and was not fired, but found another job elsewhere.[195] The whole of the government's case thus rested on two very flimsy counts: a mistaken set of solicitations involving relief employees more clearly identified with the state of North Dakota than the federal government office to the tune of $179.50, and a single five-dollar-a-month reduction in salary of an employee who admitted to missing work in the month her salary was reduced. From these two molehills came the mountain of a U.S. government case which overturned the verdict of the North Dakota electorate, not once, but twice. The key to this remarkable intrusion of federal power into state government was the animus of his political enemies, including Judge Andrew Miller,

U.S. Attorney Powless W. Lanier, and U.S. Marshal Ole Gunvaldson.

As for Langer's appeal to the Eighth Circuit Court of Appeals, that review took much longer than eleven days; indeed, an opinion was not rendered until almost nine months after the guilty verdict in the first trial. The appeal was expensive, anxiety-provoking, and involved an extensive and complicated legal procedure. Although the ruling would come too late to save William Langer's first term as governor and his legitimate nomination to a second term, all of the testimony relating to the solicitations in the remaining seven counts of the indictment were overturned by an appeals court and held insufficient to prove any federal [or state] crime.

Chapter 4
Reversal by the Eighth Circuit Court of Appeals
March–May 1935

"A conspiracy or plan to assess state employees was not an act violative of any federal statute, and hence, so far as the federal government was concerned, not criminal."
—U.S. Court of Appeals, *Langer v. U.S* [196]

No matter how much anyone appealing a judicial decision wants to speed up the procedure, appeals take time. Not only did the North Dakota Supreme Court remove Langer from office in July 1934, but the court ruled him ineligible to run in the November 1934 general election, despite the fact that he received the biggest plurality ever received in a contested election of a North Dakota governor.[197] Since his appeal to the Court of Appeals took longer than the remainder of his two-year term, his first opportunity to again run for office was postponed to 1936. As a convicted felon, Langer was also disqualified from the practice of his profession, law. While he was not formally disbarred, he made an agreement with the State Bar Board that he would not practice law unless and until the conviction was reversed.[198]

Ousted from office and no longer practicing law, Langer, who had paid the expenses of the defense of himself and some of the other minor defendants, suffered a severe financial reversal. He went from well-paid professional to ex-lawyer with no means of support except for some farmland. Yet the voters were with him, as the results of the primary had shown. While he might have become disillusioned with politics and public affairs or looked for some more dependable occupation, he did not withdraw but instead became more determined than ever to make a comeback and continue with his political career and his legal profession.

While his enemies rejoiced over what they considered their success in driving him from office and legal career, Langer, Frank Vogel, and other loyal associates, planned for a future after the Eighth Circuit Court of Appeals or the Supreme Court reversed their convictions. Unbiased and knowledgeable observers would have concluded that their chance of a successful appeal was dim—after all, most criminal convictions are affirmed on appeal. But Francis Murphy, a great lawyer, and Langer, who was also a great trial lawyer, knew that the record of the first trial was full of error, due to the rulings, instructions, and animosity of Judge Miller.

Among their other advantages were their enormous public support and the fact that neither Langer nor Frank Vogel had lost their formidable political skills. I have a memory from my early teens of being in some small town in southeastern North Dakota with my father, Frank Vogel, hundreds of miles from home, and of how consternated he was to walk down the main street for five or ten minutes before he met someone he knew. That experience rarely happened to him anywhere in North Dakota. There was, in fact, a friendly dispute between Langer and Vogel to who knew the most people in North Dakota.

In addition, Frank Vogel, unlike many politicians, did not reserve his concern over elections until a few months or a year before the next convention or election. Like all political pros of today, he was thinking about elections and delegates and candidates and League membership from the day after an election, won or lost, to the next election day. He kept in touch with the leaders in each county and very often in each precinct. A source of Vogel's strength was that he followed the policy of never making promises he couldn't keep and keeping every promise he made, even if it were difficult or inconvenient. Frank Vogel was the man most trusted by the League faithful, and this trust carried over to Bill Langer.

An illustration of Langer's attention to detail comes from the days when I was secretary of the McLean County Nonpartisan League, which reliably gave the NPL majorities every election in those days until after the switch to the Democratic column. Langer came to my law office in Garrison about some months before an election and said that in order to win, he would have to have a majority of 1,100 votes from McLean County. I replied that I thought we could do it. Later, when he was in Garrison again, we talked again and again he used the same number, 1,100, as the majority he need to win. Again, I said I thought he would get it. After the election was over, and he had won, I reminded him that he had said he needed 1,100 and that we had given him a 1,500-vote majority. He said with a perfectly straight face, "Bob, I told you we had to have 1,800."

So the political planning went on even during the dark days, in the face of criminal convictions and no income, while exultant opponents were boasting of their victory and the end of the Langer era, or as it was sometimes phrased, the "Langer-Vogel machine." More practical or less dedicated officials might have quit. But Langer and Vogel were not quitters: they were fighters, and they kept on fighting. They intended to be ready when the reversal of the verdict came.

Francis Murphy did not participate in the first trial, but he served as lead counsel in all three of the later trials. In those days, appellate courts did not review the transcript of the trial; instead, the lawyers had to agree on a narrative of what the evidence was. Francis Murphy prepared the record on appeal from the conviction in that case in the fall and winter of 1934. Much of the following material is summarized from the thousands of pages of actual records from that narrative of Langer's first trial. Murphy also wrote the brief and made the argument in the Court of Appeals on March 14, 1935, citing forty-four court errors.[199] The three judges on the appeal court—Judges A. K. Gardner, J. W. Woorough, and A. B. Walkenburg—rendered their decision on May 9, 1935, overturning the convictions.[200]

After many pages devoted to discussion of the contentions that the money distributed by the State Relief Office belonged to the state, that the indictment was insufficient, and other contentions, all of which were stricken or rejected by Judge Miller, came these words:

> It appears from the evidence that while appellant McDonald was acting as a solicitor for the Leader, he solicited contributions from certain clerks in the state emergency relief office. The total of pledges from relief employees was $469.50 while the total pledges from state employees was $58,282.22. There is evidence that there was a sign on the door where these relief clerks were employed, referring to "State Emergency Relief."
>
> McDonald's testimony is to the effect that he did not know that these employees were not employees of the State of North Dakota, nor that they had any connection with the federal government. The North Dakota Capitol Building had burned down, and the state offices were scattered throughout Bismarck . . . the overt acts are quite consistent with the contention of appellants that there was no plan to solicit federal employees, and that the act of McDonald in soliciting such employees, not being in furtherance of the plan or conspiracy, was not binding on the associates.

But it is contended by the government that the scheme or plan that was confessedly agreed upon and participated in by the appellants was itself unlawful because violative of certain North Dakota statutes. But if this were true, and we may say in passing that we think it was not, it would simply constitute a separate and distinct conspiracy and could not be substituted for the conspiracy charged in the indictment . . . a conspiracy or plan to assess state employees was not an act violative of any federal statute, and hence, so far as the federal government is concerned, not criminal.[201]

The Court of Appeals disposed of other defense contentions. Having found it necessary to reverse Judge Miller's verdict on one reversible error, it did not choose to discuss others which also might have required reversal.[202] It is customary for appellate courts, when reversal is necessary on one point, not to discuss other grounds for appeal, especially if they do not anticipate that the question will arise on a new trial. Since the new trial would presumably be held before a different judge, the Court of Appeals must have assumed that the other "alleged errors" would not be repeated.

In light of subsequent events and in the interest of the law and the subsequent historical record, it is regrettable that the other issues were not disposed of, since they later came back to haunt Langer in the court of public opinion. Nevertheless, any lawyer is capable of arriving at an opinion as to whether violating federal and state law in the jury selection process is reversible error; whether allowing evidence of solicitation of state employees is reversible error in a case alleging violation of a federal law; and whether refusal to allow evidence that money turned over to Langer by the *Leader* was paid pursuant to a contract with the Nonpartisan League executive committee to repay a loan from him was reversible error. There is little doubt as to what the decision would be: that these matters were also reversible error. The fact that the Court of Appeals did not discuss these serious issues does not mean that there was no merit to the other grounds. It seems strange that the Court of Appeals did not simply order the prosecution dismissed, which would have prevented a second trial because of the constitutional prohibition against double jeopardy. But when defendants ask the appellate court for a new trial, that is what they are likely to get if they are successful, and apparently that is what happened here.

Among those questions not discussed by the Court of Appeals, there are six, which by themselves would have required reversal, in the opinion of this writer. This syllabus of errors is adapted from a list compiled and alleged in defense briefs and motions in the records of the Court of Appeals.

1) Admission of evidence barred by the Court of Appeals

The Court of Appeals had said that no state law was violated. It also said the evidence of solicitation of state employees was not admissible as proof of a conspiracy against the federal government, and "could, therefore, have no bearing on the question of intent, nor on the vital question of conspiracy." In view of Judge Miller's admission of this evidence, and his instructions to the jury that the evidence as to the state collections tended to prove the federal case, which the Court of Appeals said was not true, this ground alone would also require reversal.

2) The federal jury selection system required selection of jurors who were qualified under state law (i.e., men and women)

Chapter 81 of the 1921 North Dakota Session Laws made women eligible for jury duty. That law, passed after adoption of the Nineteenth Amendment to the U.S. Constitution, provided that "all citizens . . . are competent to serve on grand and petit juries." Grand Forks County had had women on juries in 1922, as did other counties.[203] The defense established that no woman had ever been called for jury duty in North Dakota federal court. This should have been grounds for reversal, but Judge Miller denied a motion based on this and other objections to the jury selection process because, he ruled, this was the way it had always been done, and if he granted the motion the trial would be delayed, and some federal employees who had been subpoenaed might not be able to attend the trial. He added, incredibly, that the method being used would result in juries as fair as any other method. Years later, other criminal convictions were reversed because of systematic exclusion of women jurors. While the first Langer trial was going on, the North Dakota Supreme Court, in *State v. Norton*, ruled on June 9, 1934, that, "It is a matter of common knowledge that women have served as jurors in many, if not all, of the district courts of this state. This has been the judicial practice ever since the passage of Chapter 81 in 1921."[204] In view of this "common knowledge," the practice of the state courts since 1921, and the requirement of federal law that juries in federal courts be selected according to state practice, it is obvious that Judge Miller's refusal to include women on the jury panel violated a constitutional right of the defendants.[205] Defense attorneys repeatedly objected to the method of selecting the juries (both grand and petit), and the judge repeatedly overruled all objections and denied all motions on the subject. Years later, the United States Supreme Court held that systematic exclusion of women, so that only 15 percent of jurors were women, violated the Sixth Amendment.[206] In the Langer trial, all women were excluded.

3) Disproportion of jurors from urban areas

In another violation of the jury selection process by Judge Miller's court, the defense proved, by the testimony of the Clerk of Court and his deputy, that the federal jury selection system resulted in a vast preponderance of urban residents, while North Dakota as a whole was about 80 percent rural. This practice should have been grounds for a reversal, since it did not provide a random selection and it did not comply with state law, as the federal law required.

4) A double standard for admission of evidence on the matter of Langer's contributions to the *Leader*

Judge Miller allowed the government to bring out testimony that some of the money collected for the *Leader* newspaper was paid over by the League to Langer. Then, after allowing this testimony to go to the jury, the judge refused to allow the defense to call as witnesses the members of the executive committee of the League to testify that Langer had advanced to the League more money than he received, that the committee had agreed in advance to repay him, and that was why they had done so. Judge Miller ruled, even after offers of proof by the defense, that the evidence was "immaterial," but left the government evidence in the record, thereby leaving the inference for the jury that there was something illegal about the payment, without allowing the defense to introduce any evidence to contradict that inference.

5) A double standard concerning contributions made by NPLers on the one hand, and Democrats and Republicans on the other.

Judge Miller also refused to allow any evidence that the Roosevelt administration then in power (and prosecuting the case) was collecting political contributions from federal employees. That was also irrelevant, he ruled. When Frank Vogel, in response to a question as to whether he had paid in money for the *Leader*, said that he had and that he had also paid contributions to the Democratic Party when he was employed by the federal government, Judge Miller ordered the answer stricken. He thus deprived the defense of its right to contradict the testimony of the government, which should justify reversal in itself.

It should also be noted that all of the Langer trials were held prior to the adoption in 1939 and 1940 of the Hatch Act, which prohibits some political activities of federal employees.[207] Political patronage was not forbidden prior to that time, and neither was political activity by non-civil service employees. This point cannot be emphasized enough. Judging past actions by present standards is always a dangerous business, and particularly in politics. All parties in FDR's and Bill Langer's day routinely solicited campaign funds from federal and state employees, and all relied on their right to use patronage to reward its followers. The fact that there were reformers who were decrying these practices, and that their standards would later be applied does not change the realities of political and financial survival for Langer and the NPL at that time.

6) Highly slanted jury instructions that favored the prosecution

Though the judge in federal court is allowed to comment on the evidence, their comments should obviously be fair. Judge Miller's were not, as several examples will show:

- He stated that the reason only about one hundred eighty dollars was collected on pledges from the employees of the State Emergency Office might be that the federal government heard about what the defendants were doing and stopped them. This conclusion was not supported even by evidence from the prosecution.

- He commented that the employees had earned their salaries and now they had to earn 5 percent all over again.

- He compared Frank Vogel to a man contacted by another man planning to steal cattle, a comment in keeping with a newspaper editorial but hardly appropriate for a federal judge.

His instructions to the jury were questionable, particularly with the disproportion of thirteen pages relating to the government's theory of the case and only one page for the defense.

These four instances were all indications that a judge's duty to state fairly the contentions of both parties, the defense as well as the prosecution, was not met in the first Langer trial. While each example varies in merit, their cumulative effect was certainly grounds for reversal.

The reaction of the press to the Court of Appeals' decision was decidedly mixed. The *Leader* came out with a big banner headline, "Langer Cleared," a three-column head on the news story saying "Conviction Reversed by U.S. High Court," and a one-column headline, "Frame-Up Shown by Records."[208] On the other hand, the *Fargo Forum's* report of the reversal of the convictions by the Court of Appeals was a front-page headline, "Welford Ready to Fight Langer Move."[209] The reader had to go through several paragraphs of text before he learned that the Court of Appeals had reversed the conviction the *Forum* had emblazoned in big headlines months earlier.

Later, in the same issue, Langer was quoted as jubilant and saying that the government spent $125,000 (equivalent to about $1.7 million today) to prove he was an honest governor. He blamed Harry Hopkins, head of FERA, U.S. Postmaster General James Farley, and North Dakota Senator Gerald Nye. He might also have added the names of Andrew Miller, P. W. Lanier, Sr., William Lemke, and Ole Gunvaldson. Langer also said that under Democratic Governor John Burke, the Democrats collected 10 percent from employees, and under IVA Governor Shafer the IVAs collected 15 percent, and that he, Langer, had wiped this practice out and every contributor had an opportunity to get his money. He also said, "Not a single employee lost his job or was coerced for his failure to agree to the plan, and the United States Government in all its investigations could not find one."[210] In this statement, he was absolutely correct—the few counts involving claims of forced contributions were either not proved or dropped by Prosecutor Lanier.

The *Fargo Forum* spent as much space on whether Langer would demand his office back as it did on the decision of the Court of Appeals. Prime attention was given to the court's affirmation of federal jurisdiction and other preliminary rulings favoring the government, rather than the final decision that the evidence was insufficient. A *Forum* editorial two days later finally put as good a face on the result as possible, but made no apologies for its slanders through the years covering the first trial.

From the date the decision came out, Bill Langer, Frank Vogel, the other defendants, and thousands of faithful supporters, went to work to win the next election. Their enemies also went to work, angry at having lost in the courts, and determined to win somehow, somewhere, in their effort to destroy Langer and the NPL.

United States Attorney Lanier was not deterred by the dismissals and decision for a new trial. It is rare for a prosecutor to retry a case lost on such grounds as insufficiency of evidence. Such persistence should cause questions to be raised as to the motive of the prosecutor, as well as to the motives of the New Dealers who had appointed him. Thus Lanier, instead of accepting defeat and going on to other duties, searched the opinion of the Court of Appeals for something favorable and thought he found it in a statement by that court that it was possible to commit the crime of conspiracy to impede the operation of an act of Congress by using funds granted to the state for that purpose. He resolved to push ahead with a retrial.

In making that decision, Lanier chose to ignore the plain warning in the decision of the Court of Appeals that he would have to prove that the purpose of the conspiracy, as distinguished from an incidental and unintended result, was to impede the specific Act of Congress and would have to prove that the operation of such a law was actually impeded. When Judge A. Lee Wyman so instructed the jury in the final trial, Lanier complained publicly that the judge's instructions made it impossible to convict. On the evidence, it was already impossible, but Lanier continued to pursue his goal even in the face of that ruling. In the first trial he had had the aid of Judge Miller, hostile to the defendants to an astonishing degree, as well as hand-picked grand and petit juries, hostile to the defendants, especially Bill Langer. When the playing field was moved from a tilt against the defendants to level ground in all subsequent trials, Bill Langer, Frank Vogel, and their fellow defendants would win.

Chapter 5
The Affidavit of Prejudice and the Perjury Trial
December 3–6, 1935

> *"We can't prosecute men for their opinions. That is, we can't do that in America yet. There may be a time when we will, but up to date we can't."*
> — Judge A. Lee Wyman, just prior to directing a verdict of acquittal in the perjury case[211]

> *"I am the only person ever to be arrested in any English-speaking country for filing an affidavit of prejudice against a Judge."*
> — William Langer[212]

After the conviction in the first trial and the reversal of that conviction, and before the beginning of the second, Langer and his supporters loudly proclaimed the injustice of the trial, both for the intrinsic unfairness that they felt to be the case and for the obvious political ammunition that it provided for any subsequent campaigns for governor. While the reversal of the conviction for lack of evidence should have been the end of the whole affair, the defendants soon understood it would not be. They reconciled themselves to a second trial, but they were not prepared to undergo another trial before the same judge.

In view of the public criticism of the first Langer trial and of the judge, it was reasonable for the defense lawyer to expect Judge Miller to withdraw from the subsequent trial and ask to have another judge appointed. The judge, however, did not withdraw. So Langer's attorney, Francis Murphy, called on him and suggested he should.[213] Judge Miller had many times previously told lawyers, including Murphy, that he wanted to know if a client wished him to withdraw, as he would prefer to do so voluntarily rather than to face an affidavit of prejudice that clients were allowed to file to ask for a different judge. In spite of Murphy's suggestion, however, Judge Miller did not recuse himself from the next Langer trial.

After Judge Miller refused to withdraw, Francis Murphy predicted that an affidavit of prejudice would have to be filed. It was prepared and certified as made in good faith by one of the attorneys, J. K. Murray, who had been present during Langer's first trial whereas Murphy had not. Once Langer, Vogel, Erickson, and Kinzer signed the affidavit, Murray filed it with the court.

An affidavit of prejudice is a document which can be filed by either side, saying that there is reason to believe that the judge is, or may appear to be, biased. In North Dakota state courts these days it is called a request for change of judge, and each side is entitled to have it granted once as a matter of right. In the 1930s, the federal judge himself decided whether it should be granted—in other words, Judge Miller was to decide for himself whether he was prejudiced or not. He refused to disqualify himself, and instead engaged in some word games with the Court of Appeals, in which he claimed he was willing to be removed but did not file the necessary document to say so. The Court of Appeals suggested he follow the statute, but he did not.[214] Ultimately, the Court of Appeals ordered him removed from the case and on November 11, 1935, appointed Judge A. Lee Wyman of South Dakota to preside over the next Langer trial.[215] Substituting a judge from South Dakota may have been an unexpected development for the defendants, but the Court of Appeals can appoint any judge in the Eighth Circuit, consisting of many states, or even ask the Court of Appeals of a different circuit to send a judge. Examples abound: Judge Ronald N. Davies of North Dakota, rather than a judge from a neighboring state, was sent to Arkansas to handle the Little Rock school desegregation case in 1957, and a Missouri judge, Caskie Collette, was sent to North Dakota after Judge Charles Vogel was elevated to the Circuit Court of Appeals and no new district judge had been named to replace him in 1954.[216]

When Judge Miller announced that he was going to resign, the *Bismarck Tribune* praised him and pointed out he had presided over trials in thirteen western states, many of which were not in the Eighth Circuit.[217] Judge Miller, however, was not finished. He quibbled with Francis Murphy over the form of notarization of the affidavit of prejudice and told him the U.S. Attorney was not satisfied with the form, which Murphy had used many times before and which was identical with the form in a standard form book. To please Lanier and Miller, Francis Murphy had to change it to specify that the notary public had sworn in the witnesses, made them raise their right hands, and they had appeared before her. Experienced as he was in the ways of the law, Murphy said at the time that the only possible reason for this bizarre requirement was to prepare for a perjury charge and to prevent a defense claim that the witness was not properly sworn.[218]

When the affidavit of prejudice was filed, a grand jury was waiting. Murphy believed they had no other business scheduled at that time. Since a federal grand jury can only be called by a federal judge and the judge usually does so at the request of the United States attorney, there could only be one conclusion. Francis Murphy understood from the presence of the grand jury that the defendants would be indicted for perjury. He told the four defendants before they signed the affidavit of prejudice that they would to be indicted within twenty-four hours after the document was filed.[219] They were.[220]

William Langer was quoted in his official biography as a U.S. senator in the *Congressional Directory* as saying, "I am the only person ever to be arrested in any English-speaking country for filing an affidavit of prejudice against a judge."[221] P. W. Lanier's attempt to justify this unprecedented abuse of federal power against state officials was based on a dubious reading of *United States v. Berger*.[222] In fact, the United States Supreme Court's decision in that case suggests that a judge must accept the allegation in an affidavit of prejudice as true in making his determination of whether such an allegation indicates bias and allegations on information and belief are sufficient to raise the issue.

Judge Miller had to have known of the heavy criticism of his handling of the first trial, but he was not to be swayed. He told Senate investigators in 1941: "For, while I believed Langer and the other defendants convicted were all guilty, and so in effect stated to the jury when they brought in their verdict of guilty, and again repeated that belief at the time I sentenced the defendants, Langer and others, and still believed at the time I wrote the letter to [Circuit Judge] Stone that they were guilty, such a belief on my part did not meet the requirements of the statute."[223]

It was nonsense for Judge Miller to say that a belief in the guilt of defendants did not meet the requirements of the statute. The statute had no such requirement—a judge could recuse himself for any reason he chose to use in the exercise of his conscience, or for no other reason than that he might appear to some people to be prejudiced. Unlike others at the U.S. Senate hearings in 1941, including Judge Wyman of South Dakota, Judge Miller was not sworn in, and he was not asked the hard questions he could and should have been asked in the interest of justice. Instead, he was allowed to prepare the statement printed above and read it, with no follow-up questions. The exceptions made for him were not a courtesy afforded the office he held; if it were, Federal Judge Wyman would not have been sworn in either and questioned.[224]

The affidavit of prejudice filed by Langer and his codefendants contains a recital of events at the first trial which claim to show bias in statements made by Judge Miller in rulings he made, as well as in the instructions. It is several pages long and contains twelve paragraphs. Prosecutor Lanier alleged in the perjury indictment that only two of the twelve charges in the affidavit were perjurious. The first was when Langer and his codefendants asserted Judge Miller's speech to the jury was "intended to inflame them against the defendants; that he said the court had been attacked by unscrupulous groups which he described so as to appear to include the defendants, that he referred to communists and implied that the defendants were included, and gave the impression that the defendants were public enemies." The second perjurious item, according to Lanier, appeared in paragraph six, "which states on information and belief (meaning that the defendants have heard from others and believe to be true) that the judge had prepared and signed commitments to jail or the penitentiary for the defendants during the trial."[225]

It is interesting to read the parts of the affidavit that were not alleged to be perjured. They include allegations that the judge allowed the jury to read inflammatory news articles and hear inflammatory radio campaign speeches; acted contemptuously toward the defendants and showed approval of the prosecution; and stood above some witnesses giving evidence against the defendants, smiling and nodding to show approval. As Francis Murphy wrote to Langer, the failure to allege perjury as to the most serious charges mounted to a tacit admission that they were true.[226]

Held December 3-6, 1935, after the second trial for conspiracy and before the third, the perjury trial was a fiasco for the prosecution. It appears that Lanier thought he could prove perjury through testimony of people in the courtroom as to what they understood from the judge's remarks to the jury. Judge Wyman properly ruled that litigants have the right to assert their beliefs as to the partiality of judges and that any impressions that other people form from observing the same events are irrelevant to that right. In effect, he said no observer can testify as to what the judge intended to do. The clear inference was that Judge Miller, not the defendants, should have been the person testifying as to what he intended by his speech to the jury and what he did on the matter of the commitments to prison.

Although Judge Miller was present in Bismarck at the time of the trial, Lanier did not call him as a witness. Judge Miller's chambers and home were in Fargo, and the Court of Appeals had disqualified him from having any part in the trial. With only one set of judge's chambers in the federal building in Bismarck and only one courtroom, it is difficult to imagine what judicial business Miller could have been conducting in Bismarck while the trial was going on, but he was there, and he was not called as a witness. Lanier did call several other witnesses, however—an Associated Press reporter and other observers, who had heard the comments to the jury by Judge Miller—and Judge Wyman disallowed their testimony because it was only their understanding of what was said and did not constitute evidence of what was actually said.

Lanier then attempted to prove the falsity of the claim of preparation of the commitments for jail by calling Deputy Clerk Talcott to testify that no commitment had ever been filed in the clerk's office. Judge Wyman rejected the testimony, correctly pointing out that this was not proof that Judge Miller had not prepared commitments. Lanier then rested his case, having offered no admissible evidence. Francis Murphy then made a motion to direct a verdict of acquittal, which Judge Wyman granted, and the Common Law world's first—and probably last—prosecution for perjury for filing an affidavit of prejudice came to an ignominious end.

At Lanier's suggestion, the Federal Department of Justice ordered a transcript of the perjury trial and had an experienced Justice Department lawyer, Dan Jackson, review it. His report contained the following:

> ... for some reason, which I cannot conceive, Mr. Lanier did not propound unobjectionable questions to the witnesses..and from this record it appears that Presiding Judge Wyman repeatedly instructed counsel for the Government in what was material to the issue, what was statement of fact as alleged in the indictment, and that he would permit proof of the falsity thereof ... He properly sustained an objection to the newspaper story. ... I can see nothing in the record before me which would indicate any unfairness on the part of the trial judge [Wyman] and on the contrary if this is a true record of the proceedings the court went further than I have found Federal judges usually go to hold up the hands [in support of] of the prosecuting officers.[227]

In other words, Lanier had no case and never should have brought it.

Jackson also pointed out that the question as to the commitments was whether they were prepared or not, and only Judge Miller would know that, but he was not called as a witness. Yet, in spite of the fact that the whole prosecution was unprecedented and the result, given the lack of proof, inevitable, the very fact that the case of perjury was filed against Langer has been used as evidence of his legal improprieties, rather than on Judge Miller and P. W. Lanier, as one might expect.

The perjury trial cost the U.S. government a great deal of money. Prior to the indictment by a grand jury, twenty-three jurors from around the state were brought to Fargo and drew mileage and per diem pay at government expense, and at least fifty-one members of the jury panel at the first trial were interviewed and many of those brought to Fargo to testify to the grand jury, all at government expense. Their testimony, predictably, was that they were not prejudiced. All of the defense attorneys at the first trial, except J. K. Murray, who signed the certificate of good faith as to the filing of the affidavit of prejudice, were also subpoenaed. Apparently there was some thought given to indicting Murray, too. The expense of this episode was likely to have been in the tens of thousands of dollars.

In granting the directed verdict, Judge Wyman had a few comments that lovers of the Bill of Rights might want to remember. He noted, "The allegations in the affidavit of prejudice merely tend to state the conclusions of the men signing the affidavit, their allegations of their impressions, and if they are honest in those opinions it can never be made the basis of a perjury suit. We can't prosecute men for their opinions. That is, we can't do that in America, yet. There may be a time when we will, but up to date we can't."[228] No one except P. W. Lanier, Sr., so far as appellate records show, ever had the audacity, or the lack of knowledge of law and history, to charge a defendant with perjury for filing an affidavit of prejudice. Judge Andrew Miller must also share that blame, since Lanier claimed he presented the matter to the grand jury "under orders of Judge Miller."[229] Regardless of the truth of that claim, Lanier was not required to follow any orders of Judge Miller in that respect. It is the function of the government attorney to decide what is presented to a grand jury, not a trial judge.

The indictment for perjury was a surprise to the Department of Justice. Before Lanier obtained it, he had often asked for help on research on other matters and had made frequent and urgent requests for information and witnesses, often with very short time deadlines. But the department had no inkling he was even thinking about a perjury charge, as is shown by a rather plaintive letter from Assistant Attorney General Joseph Keenan, who wrote Lanier on October 19, 1935, that he had "read in the press" that such an indictment had been issued by the grand jury and asked for a summary of the evidence and a copy of the indictment.[230] Lanier sent them, and wrote that the allegations of prejudice were scurrilous and untrue. He said his indictment was based on *United States v. Berger* and that Judge Miller "ordered" him to check the affidavit of prejudice and bring a perjury charge if it were untrue.[231]

Thus, the Department of Justice cannot be faulted for the bringing of the bizarre and unprecedented charge of perjury for filing an affidavit of prejudice, since the department's knowledge of the charge came after the event. But the department can be criticized for its indifference to justice in not recognizing and stopping this brazen attempt to limit the basic right of a defendant to an impartial judge, an unprecedented attack. In fact, the only historical incident that can properly be compared to it is the punishment of juries for bringing in verdicts not approved by the judge. The last time that happened was in 1670, when an English judge jailed jurors who refused to convict William Penn, later the founder of Pennsylvania, on a charge of seditious libel. A higher court then firmly held that no jury can ever be punished for bringing in a verdict contrary to the instructions of the judge.[232] That is still the law, in England as in the United States.

Langer's enemies and the daily press sought an explanation for the directed verdict of acquittal in the perjury case. The obvious one—that the U.S. attorney for North Dakota, P. W. Lanier, had brought a charge that could not be proved—would not serve their purposes. They focused instead on the fact that one of Langer's allies had brought Judge Wyman's son to Bismarck in the middle of the perjury trial. Langer knew nothing of the incident until it had already happened, and as soon as he found out about it, he paid the young Wyman the money he said he was owed and sent him back to South Dakota. The facts about this difficult situation were part of the testimony offered in the U.S. Senate hearings in 1941, but the public was left to draw its own conclusions in 1935.

The sequence of events that led to Gale Wyman coming to Bismarck began after the first trial and conviction. Langer's ally and a former assistant U.S. attorney, Usher L. Burdick, suggested to Langer that he should hire some knowledgeable person to watch the actions of the clerk of court's office and the U.S. marshal and his deputies during the next trial. Langer allowed James Mulloy, secretary of the Industrial Commission, to hire someone, and he chose Chet Leedom, a former U.S. Marshal from South Dakota. Leedom did observe the next trial before the Court of Appeals and reported some misconduct by the deputy marshal, Howard Strack, to Judge Wyman. The judge then called Strack into his chambers where he admitted the charge; he was ordered to abide by his instructions thereafter.[233] As the perjury trial began, Mulloy went to Deadwood, South Dakota, to bring Chet Leedom back to watch again for misconduct by the marshal's office or the clerk's office.[234] He found that Leedom was in the hospital for alcohol abuse and in no condition to travel. Mulloy, well known to be a problem drinker himself, then became concerned about being blamed for Leedom's being drunk, and he asked a young man, Gale Wyman, to go to Bismarck with him to explain why Mulloy could not bring Leedom back. Mulloy called Langer and said that Leedom could not come but his "right hand man" could and he would bring this "other fellow." Mulloy admitted he did not use Wyman's name.[235] Langer concurred and said that he thought Mulloy was referring to another South Dakota deputy marshal named Hood.[236] What he did not know was that the man was in fact the son of the presiding judge at Langer's trial.

When Mulloy and Wyman arrived in Bismarck and Langer learned who the "other fellow" was, he immediately recognized the danger of having the judge's son in Bismarck and told him to go back to South Dakota. Mulloy had promised him payment, and the young man needed money to go back. Mulloy had previously hired Gale Wyman to go to Sioux Falls to tell his father that the defendants wanted the jury list and that the people in Bismarck were planning a big dinner to indoctrinate the new judge. Again, Mulloy admitted he had not told Langer of this, but now Wyman wanted the two hundred fifty dollars Mulloy had promised, plus expenses of twenty-five dollars. Langer gave Mulloy a check for that amount, and Mulloy, who could not cash it on the weekend, endorsed it over to Wyman.

For obvious reasons, Langer could not write checks to the son of the judge in his own trial, and, just as obviously, he had to get him out of town after Mulloy had created a major perception problem. Mulloy may well not have had ulterior motives and acted as he did in an excess of zeal for what he then considered a good cause. Later, however, Mulloy turned against Langer and used his own ill-considered acts as a basis for imputing corruption to Langer.

Gale Wyman had a short visit with his father in Bismarck, during which they both later testified that the Langer case was not mentioned.[237] Nowhere, in fact, in any of the documents is there any suggestion that Judge Wyman was actually influenced by Leedom or his son or anyone else. The only claim that has made its way to the public is that the defendants tried to influence him. On the contrary, Leedom was there to see that the jury was not influenced improperly by the prosecution, and Langer's only interest in Gale Wyman, once he learned who he was, was to get him out of Bismarck. When Langer was asked in the Senate hearing why he had paid Gale Wyman $275, Langer's answer was, "I paid it because here was Gale Wyman's father as Judge. I could not afford to antagonize his son. If Gale Wyman had asked $1,000 of me, I would have paid it. I was there on trial and Gale Wyman demanding $500, $525, and his father is going to try me. What else could I do but pay him?"[238]

Despite this added complication, the debacle of the perjury trial finally reached its only possible conclusion. The Department of Justice is fortunate that it ended there. If there had been a conviction, and an appeal, with the decision published in the law reports, the department would have received a barrage of critical and devastating condemnation by legal scholars and historians. After all, a fair and impartial judge is a basic element of any fair trial and any acceptable judicial system.

Chapter 6
The Second and Third Conspiracy Trials
October 29-November 16
and
December 10-19, 1935

"I am the only candidate who has been tested by the Federal Government and found pure."

— Bill Langer[239]

The Court of Appeals had said the evidence in the first trial of conspiracy against Langer and his codefendants was insufficient to prove their guilt and reversed the guilty verdict. Nevertheless, the prosecution had the option to try the case a second time, which they chose to do. It was a decision that flew in the face of logic. Unless there was more or different evidence, no reasonable prosecutor would try the case again, so, one must ask, why was there was a second trial—and even more incredibly, a third?

According to Langer's lawyer for the second and third trial, Francis Murphy, the prosecuting attorney P. W. Lanier's answer, once implied and another time stated flatly, was that he proceeded with the trials because he "had his orders." He did not specify from whom these orders came—if not from Judge Miller, who was not his boss, then presumably from they came from Washington, D.C., and Harry Hopkins. I found no evidence of the latter in the records of Lanier's office. On the contrary, I found evidence that the Department of Justice was not even kept advised of developments.[240] Nowhere is there evidence of orders to Lanier to proceed. In my own experience as United States attorney for seven years, I never received an order from the Department of Justice or from any judge to bring or not bring a prosecution or a civil case. Earlier, Lanier had said that he had been "ordered" by Judge Miller to investigate the truth of the allegations in the affidavit of prejudice, and, if the facts sustained it, to obtain an indictment for perjury. Perhaps that is the "order" he referred to in his answers to Murphy. It appears from the record that the push to proceed with the three subsequent trials did indeed come from either Judge Miller or U.S. Attorney Lanier, or perhaps both. It was they who arranged to have a grand jury sitting during the second trial, so they could bring the perjury charge, and it was they who had another lengthy grand jury term to investigate the so-called Langer Defense Fund, which raised less than five thousand dollars.[241] Perhaps they hoped to find some solicitation of federal employees and immediately have an indictment from the grand jury. Whatever their hopes were, nothing came of all their efforts.

The method of jury selection for the second and third conspiracy trials was largely the same as that of the first, except that a few women's names showed up on the jury panel and Judge Wyman gave the jury list to the lawyers a few days in advance. When the method used by the Clerk of Court's office to screen potential jurors in the first trial became known, many people were surprised and angered. Congressman Burdick introduced a bill in the U.S. Congress to change the method but could not get it out of committee. At around the same time, Senator Thomas D. Shall of Minnesota introduced in the United States Senate a resolution to investigate the jury selection methods in federal courts. It was not passed.

The 1935 North Dakota House of Representatives, with the Senate (which was not controlled by the Nonpartisan League) concurring, adopted a resolution calling on Congress to change the system under which clerks and jury commissioners had "too much opportunity to select jurors personally agreeable to them" and asking Congress to "provide an impartial, unbiased and uncontrolled method for selecting Federal Jurors."[242] Many years later, in 1948, in a broad revision of the Judicial Code (28 USC), Congress did finally change and improve this patently unfair system.

Usher L. Burdick had been appalled by what he saw as the miscarriage of justice of the first trial. He continued to defend William Langer against his political enemies, both at the time of the trials and years later when he testified on Langer's behalf to the Senate subcommittee in 1941.[243] In his 1941 testimony, Burdick said that he had given Langer some advice about choosing lawyers after the first trial. The lead defense attorneys for Langer and his codefendants had been George Thorp and Ed Sinkler, prominent lawyers from Fargo and Minot, respectively. Both lawyers had good reputations and much trial experience, but, nevertheless, they failed to object to some of the obviously reversible errors in rulings of Judge Miller in the first trial. Burdick said the two men were good lawyers, but he told Langer, "Those lawyers were afraid of Judge Miller, and that is why you lost."[244] For his subsequent trials, Burdick advised Langer to get a lawyer who was not afraid of Judge Miller or the Devil, which meant Langer should get Francis Murphy, since, with the possible exception of Bill Langer himself, Murphy was the preeminent defense attorney of the time in North Dakota.

Murphy had been successful in reversing the conviction with the Court of Appeals, and he became the lead attorney in the later two conspiracy trials and the perjury trial. Having heard him argue the Oscar E. Erickson impeachment defense, I remember his summation as probably the best I ever heard, and having read the transcript of the Senate Langer hearings, in which Murphy represented Langer and far outshone the lawyers prosecuting the proceeding there, I can say with assurance that he deserved his high reputation.

The Second Conspiracy Trial

The biggest contrasts between the first conspiracy trial, with Judge Miller presiding, and the second, with Judge Wyman presiding, came in the fairness of the rulings on evidence and in the instructions to the jury in the latter. The instructions from both trials are recorded in the transcripts. As earlier chapters have recorded, Miller's were quite slanted against the defendants, while Wyman's were standard and even-handed.

As for the trials themselves, Murphy appears to have been correct in stating that the evidence was much the same as at the first. The list of witnesses was similar,

Oscar E. Erickson, one of the codefendants in the Langer trials, was too ill to appear in the first trial but was present for the second and third trials.
State Historical Society of North Dakota A1809

but somewhat shorter for the second trial, held October 29–November 16, 1935. The three people who had been members of the State Emergency Relief Committee—E. H. Brant, R. A. Kinzer (one of the defendants) and John E. Williams—testified for the defense, as did H. C. Frahm, chief engineer of the Highway Department, who had the same position in prior administrations. He testified that solicitation of employees in the Highway Department had no effect on efficiency or morale. Neither Langer nor Vogel testified. Lanier had, by his questioning of one witness, George Lydecker, about an aspect of Langer's testimony, opened the door to a reading to the jury from a transcript of the prior testimony of Langer in the first trial, something that was bound to favor the defense.[245] Another difference was that Oscar E. Erickson, who had been hospitalized at the time of the first trial, testified as a defense witness in the second.

The prosecution came up with two former defendants, Chaput and McDonald, the two main solicitors for the *Leader*, who had somehow been persuaded to change lawyers after the reversal of their convictions by the Court of Appeals. In the first trial, they had taken Langer's long-time enemy, John Sullivan, Mandan, as their attorney and he had them plead guilty to charges that were later dismissed by the Court of Appeals. For some other reason, their change of attorneys was made without notice to their attorneys of record: at the very least, a breach of professional courtesy, if not a violation of ethical obligations. The charges against both of them were later dismissed by the government.[246] According to Murphy, McDonald's direct testimony was so favorable to the defense that Murphy violated a cardinal rule of cross-examination and had him repeat it. Chaput was not called by the government at all.[247]

The second trial resulted in a hung jury. Although the press reported the division as ten to two, some jurors recalled it began as seven to five for acquittal and some said it ended as eight to four for conviction. The two jurors who were reported by the press to vote for acquittal were Ernie Reich of Casselton and Herman Charboneau of Barnes County. Charboneau said in an interview that the jury started with seven jurors favoring acquittal, but the seven were worn down to Charboneau and a juror named Janke, who gave in, leaving Charboneau alone for acquittal. Charboneau also said that Deputy Marshal Strack entered the jury room when there was noise; that the jury foreman had told the jury that a man who held out for acquittal in the first trial had been murdered; and that he was offered a bribe of five hundred dollars by two other jurors who wanted him to vote for conviction.[248] This statement was in Charboneau's "affidavit" given to the Senate investigators, but he was not called to testify nor was his "affidavit" referred to in the Senate Hearing.[249] In his interview, Charboneau said that some investigators, either federal or state, came to his house and put him in one room and his wife in another, and searched the house looking for bribe money, but of course found nothing. One can speculate that the two were the Senate investigators, Hood and Smith, who did not believe they had to have warrants to search or to examine possible witnesses.

Again, Langer's critics kept searching for some evidence of foul play to justify the failure to obtain a conviction. They thought they had found it when they heard years later that Ernie Reich, who was reported as one of two jurors for acquittal, got a job in the capitol in the Insurance Department, headed by Oscar E. Erickson. Some histories of the Langer trials include statements or suggestions that Reich was bribed. What those historians fail to note is that the job he got in the Insurance Department, at wages of seventy-five dollars a month, came two years later; that Reich was handicapped (he had only one leg); and that the Langer administration had the tendency to give jobs to handicapped people—so much so that there were frequent comments made about the capitol being taken over by them. Langer testified in 1941 that he had no knowledge of Reich's employment in the Insurance Department, and Erickson said that hiring Reich was his decision alone. To add fuel to the rumors of a bribe, another damaging story is that Frank Vogel, then highway commissioner, was said to have delivered a check to Reich for some eight hundred dollars. Again, the facts are that this incident also happened two years after the trial and that the check was from a firm with a highway department contract that employed Reich, who was said to be an excellent mechanic, to assist their salesman in selling machinery.[250] Neither of these two stories offer any evidence that Reich was promised anything at any time during the trial.

Charboneau never got anything, never wanted anything, and said, to the disappointment of the Senate investigators, even after a thorough grilling by them that fills more than 160 pages of transcript, that he only did his duty and wanted no job even though C. R. Verry and another unidentified man had insisted to him in 1941 that he deserved to have a job and ought to ask Langer for one.[251] It was difficult for Langer's enemies to believe that there was no smoking gun to explain jury verdicts in his favor or that juries made decisions according to the evidence.

The other controversy that arose out of the second trial was the presence of Chet Leedom, former United States Marshal in South Dakota and a friend of Judge Wyman. The press and some historians have claimed that Leedom's presence represented an attempt to influence Judge Wyman. In fact, Leedom was at the trial because of Usher Burdick's suggestion to Langer that he hire someone familiar with the federal courts to watch the marshals, the bailiff, and the clerk of court's office for jury interference.

In his testimony before the Senate subcommittee in 1941, Burdick said that he had told Langer that Judge Miller was prejudiced and that the court attendants appointed by him would naturally be prejudiced the same way. Burdick went on to say it had been reported to him that the court attendants had been visiting the jury frequently during the first trial. As a protective measure, he suggested that the person Langer found to do the watching should be someone with experience who knew about courts and proper court procedure, but he did not suggest Langer get someone from South Dakota. A one-time friend of Langer's who later became an enemy when no state jobs were available to him, James Mulloy, chose Leedom, recommending him to Langer as a man familiar with the federal court system and the handling of juries. Langer agreed to hire him to come to Bismarck and watch the clerk's office and marshal's office during the perjury trial, to detect any misconduct of those offices, similar to that which had happened at the first trial, where Deputy Marshal Strack had been observed to spend hours in the jury room, and there were reports that the jurors were allowed to read newspapers and listen to radio in violation of the court's orders.[252]

As chapter five indicated, at the time of the perjury trial, Leedom had been drinking too much to make the trip so Mulloy had unwisely brought the judge's son, Gale Wyman, in his stead. Relatively sober this time, and with a hotel room near Marshal Strack's, Leedom did find misconduct. He observed that Strack was again spending time in the jury room, and he reported this to Langer, who told Francis Murphy, his attorney, who then took it up with Judge Wyman, without mentioning Leedom's name. Judge Wyman called Strack into the judge's chambers and asked if the report was true, and Strack admitted that it was. He was told to reread the oath he took to allow no one to communicate with the jury, and was reminded him that this applied to him, too, except when the jury had a message to send to the judge.[253]

Langer and Murphy were not the only ones upset by Strack's actions. After the trial was over, the juror Charboneau, who had served on juries in several courts, told J. K. Murray that on the first night of deliberations when the vote was seven to five to acquit, Strack had told the jury not to continue discussing the case. Strack had come into the jury room without being asked by the jurors to do so, had spent about two hours alone in a room with one juror who had a sore foot, and had otherwise intruded on the jury deliberations during the second trial.[254] Judge Wyman's son, Gale, told the Senate investigators that there were other attempts to interfere with the trial—attempts by Lanier and Judge Miller to influence Judge Wyman. Lanier reportedly made attempts to go into Judge Wyman's chambers to discuss the case in the absence of opposing counsel, and Judge Miller, who had been removed as judge by the Court of Appeals, also went in to make suggestions to Judge Wyman. It reached the point where Judge Wyman told Judge Miller that he could handle the trial by himself and he did not need any assistance. The judge also, very properly, refused to see Lanier except when the defense lawyers were also present.[255]

Judge Wyman told Hood and Smith that he saw Leedom briefly once in his chambers with his secretary present but did not discuss the case. He understood that Leedom was there as a reporter for the Farm Holiday Association newspaper. Leedom, a former newspaperman and a good writer, did have press credentials from that newspaper. Judge Wyman's integrity was never questioned, nor should it have been.[256]

Between the second and third conspiracy trials, the Department of Justice received some good advice from its political friends, including former Democratic State Committeeman R. B. Murphy, who called the trials a political disaster.[257] Usher L. Burdick and George Wallace, Minnesota Tax Commissioner, who had previously been tax commissioner in North Dakota, also sent letters; both said that the prosecutions had become persecutions.[258] With this new information under its belt, the Justice Department became concerned, and sent out Dan M. Jackson, special assistant to the attorney general, to talk to people in North Dakota and decide whether or not to recommend that the department order the filing of a *nolle prosse* (a voluntary dismissal with prejudice of a pending case). Jackson went to Bismarck and talked to Judge Miller, who praised the good faith and competence of Lanier and recommended continuing the case, and to some newspapermen, averse to Langer, including Happy Paulson, editor of the *Fargo Forum*, and some local Democratic politicians, most of them similarly disposed. Admitting that he personally was reluctant to do so, Jackson recommended that the trial proceed, partly on the basis that more damage would be done by the *nolle prosse* than by continuing. He did not specify whether he was referring to political damage or damage to the judicial or electoral process. He did note that many of the people of North Dakota considered the trials as persecution and political in nature, had lost faith in the entire judicial system of the state, with the exception of the State Supreme Court, and appellate jurisdiction in the federal system.[259]

The Third Conspiracy Trial

After the hung jury in the second trial, Lanier brought the case forward in a third trial, held December 10–19, 1935. It was much like the second, but shorter. Judge Wyman's instructions to the jury in the final trial were similar to his in the second trial except that this time, he more specifically stated that to prove the conspiracy the government must show that the defendants conspired to impede the operation of an act of Congress—not, as Lanier claimed, that their solicitations of contributions were criminal even if they were was an incidental and unplanned effect of a legal effort to raise money. Lanier was quoted as saying that the instructions made it impossible to get a conviction. It is safe to construe his statement as

Nonpartisan League dinner, January 1935.
State Historical Society of North Dakota C0427

an admission that he could not get a conviction without the kind of slanted instructions and unfair trial he could count on from Judge Miller. Judge Wyman directed a verdict as to some defendants and the jury brought in a verdict of acquittal of the others on December 19, more than a year and a half after the affair began.

The final denouement of the celebrated Langer trials brought forth a burst of celebrations among a majority of the voters of the state but not necessarily from the newspaper editors. Predictably, the *Fargo Forum* buried the news in a one-column story under a headline: "Langer Silent About Future."[260] The *Leader* newspaper used its biggest headlines in its December 26, 1935 issue to proclaim the victory, exulting in a torrent of colorful language:

Rumors Assist Langer to Claim Governorship

> The reign of terror is over . . . despotic and vicious abuse of authority . . . debauching of our most sacred institutions . . . ruthless gang of peewee politicians, masquerading as 'the government' besported themselves in a Roman holiday to make life miserable for their betters and send men innocent of crime to prison . . . plain political persecution of the rankest sort . . . nauseated and disgusted with P. W. Lanier's persistent efforts to obtain a conviction on such flimsy charges . . . Gerald P. Nye, P. W. Lanier, the bootlicking newspapers, a few high moguls of the Democratic party in Washington and some of their payroll patriots . . .[261]

P. W. Lanier, however, did not even stop his vendetta after the third conspiracy trial ended in acquittal. He continued to ask for copies of tax returns for Langer, Erickson, and the *Leader*, insisting that income of the newspaper was not being reported, even though the Internal Revenue Service had told him that it was included in Erickson's returns and that there was insufficient evidence to proceed on a tax case.[262] Judge Miller, too, was "furious," and wanted an indictment of J. K. Murray, who signed the certificate of good faith on the affidavit of prejudice.[263]

It is clear that a less adamant United States attorney and judge, as well as the Department of Justice and Department of the Interior, might have saved all the expense and anguish of three trials if they had only read carefully the following language from the opinion of the Court of Appeals when it reversed the conviction in the first trial:

> The gist of the offense, as has already been stated, is the alleged conspiracy to obstruct the administration of a

government function. It is not claimed that the overt acts charged in themselves constituted substantive offenses. Unless there was such a conspiracy, the conviction of appellants cannot be sustained. Whatever we may think of the ethics or propriety of the practice employed by appellants to secure funds for political purposes, it is not a matter of concern to the Federal government, unless some lawful governmental function was thereby obstructed. In other words, a conspiracy or plan to assess state employees was not an act violative of any Federal statute, and hence, so far as the Federal government is concerned, not criminal.[264]

This opinion makes it clear that mere proof that a few federal employees were solicited did not prove that it was the intention of the so-called "conspirators" to impede the operation of any act of Congress. The Court of Appeals plainly says that the "conspiracy" must be one which is intended to impede the operation of such laws. The theory of the government in each trial was that a plan which had the incidental effect of collecting money from a few federal employees was enough to make a conspiracy to impede congressional action. No proof of an intent to hinder any law was ever offered in any trial, and in fact, no credible proof of any adverse effect on the operation of any federal law was established, while the defense put on an abundance of proof from the people who ran the Relief Office that there

The governor's mansion in Bismarck was home to William and Lydia Langer and their four daughters from 1932 to 1935 and again from 1936 to 1938.
State Historical Society of North Dakota A4382

was no such effect. One may certainly conclude that the prosecutions were motivated by something other than a desire to uphold federal laws. Since Bill Langer was politician who aroused great passions, both pro and con, it is difficult to arrive at any other conclusion than this: what drove the prosecutions was not an interest in justice, but a political vendetta.

What was the cost of the attempts to destroy Bill Langer and those associated with him? To them, of course, on a personal level, it was huge. But at the same time, the financial burden to the state and federal government cannot be underestimated. The following offers some details and estimates of what this overzealous crusade cost the public taxpayer.

In the first investigation of Langer, made by the Interior Department, the department admitted in the Senate hearings that it had spent eleven thousand dollars (about $135,000 in 2002 dollars). The Interior Department turned over its investigation reports to the U.S. Attorney, P. W. Lanier, and he took over, perhaps with a push from Judge Miller. Lanier had more investigation done by the Interior investigators and also asked Internal Revenue to investigate Langer's tax returns and asked the postal inspectors to investigate a possible mail fraud case. No cost figures are available on those two investigations or the cost of the many grand jury sessions.

While no official cost figures are available for the four trials that resulted from the government's legal attack on Langer, it is obvious that salaries of judge and U.S. attorney and court personnel, per diem and travel expenses of jurors and witnesses, and other court expenses for months of trial would be

Hear Lydia Langer
LYDIA LANGER
at
Lidgerwood, N. D.
Tuesday, Oct. 23 at 2:30 P. M.

OTHER SPEAKERS
J. M. ANDERSON
Republican endorsed candidate for Superintendent of Public Instruction
J. M. GRONNA
Republican candidate for Secretary of State

MERCHANTS OF LIDGERWOOD ARE CO-OPERATING ON LYDIA LANGER DAY AND ARE OFFERING SPECIAL BARGAINS

Come Early! Band Concert at 1:30 P. M.
(Pol. Adv.)

Lydia Langer made an unsuccessful bid for the governor's seat on the Republican ticket in 1934 after the North Dakota Supreme Court ruled that her husband, Bill Langer, could not run because of his conviction in federal court in June 1934.

State Historical Society of North Dakota 1060

huge. Langer estimated the total at $125,000, more than $1.7 million today, which, he said, was spent to prove he was a good governor. No wonder he said in a later campaign that he was the only candidate who had been tested by the federal government and found pure.

After almost twenty months defending himself in the courtroom, William Langer, released from the constraints of the conviction and removal from office, was free to run for office again. At the earliest opportunity, in 1936, he did just that, running for governor. Between the time of his conviction in the first trial in 1934 and the 1936 election, North Dakota had had three governors. When Langer was removed in 1934, the League-elected lieutenant governor, Ole Olson, became acting governor and served out the remaining months of the term. The League endorsed Lydia Langer to replace her husband as the League candidate in the general election of 1934, and she ran well. Langer, exaggerating slightly, although proudly, later said she got more votes than he ever had. But she lost to Thomas Moodie, the Democratic candidate.[265] Moodie, however, had voted in Minnesota

Thomas Moodie, shown here shaking hands with the outgoing governor, Ole Olson, only served a few weeks in early 1935 before the North Dakota Supreme Court ruled he was ineligible to serve because he failed to meet the residency requirement. State Historical Society of North Dakota 823-06

On February 2, 1935, Lieutenant Governor Walter Welford became North Dakota's fourth governor in nine months after the winner of the 1934 election, Thomas Moodie, was removed from office.

State Historical Society of North Dakota A3007

less than five years earlier, making him ineligible as governor as one who had not resided in North Dakota for at least five years. When his election was challenged and his Minnesota residence proved, he was removed as governor, after about a month in office.[266] The lieutenant governor, Walter Welford, endorsed by the NPL to run with Mrs. Langer and elected, then took office as governor. He soon was dominated by interest of the "Rumpers"—the derisive term used by Leaguers to describe dissident ex-Leaguers who had lacked the votes to win in League conventions so they broke away to hold gatherings of their own. Thus ensued a split in the League between Welford and his Rumper supporters, on the one hand, and Langer and the majority Leaguers on the other.

In 1936, the regular League convention endorsed Langer for governor and William Crockett for lieutenant governor, while the Rumpers endorsed Welford and T. H. H. Thoresen. Langer lost the primary election by 795 votes out of more than 180,000 cast. He then ran as an Independent candidate in the general election, and won in the three-way race, with 99,750 votes to Welford's 95,697 and 80,726 for the Democratic candidate, John Moses.[267] Bill Langer was back, and more political history was about to be made by one of its most colorful politicians.

Chapter 7
The Senate Investigation
January – November 1941

"After watching him for several years there and trying to work deals from him, from along the line of the Federal Government, we decided it was hopeless, and therefore decided we were going to bring this investigation around to— well, to see what could be done about it. Anyhow, we're opposed to his acting as United States Senator."
—I. N. Amick, a member of Mulloy and Verry's committee working to unseat Langer, 1941[268]

William Langer returned to the governor's office and his family—wife Lydia and their four daughters—returned to the Governor's Mansion in Bismarck following the election of 1936. It was not long, however, until Langer decided to challenge incumbent Gerald Nye for his seat in the U.S. Senate in the 1938 election. As historian Edward Blackorby described it, in 1938 "the general election demonstrated that 'Langerism" truly was the central issue in North Dakota politics."[269] Langer was defeated by what Blackorby called an "arrangement [that] had all the hallmarks of a political bargain, and most observers agreed that an understanding, tacit or otherwise, existed between the Democrats and the Rumper, anti-Langer, Republican coalition . . . to defeat 'Langerism' by electing a Democratic governor [John Moses]; Burdick also won, while Langer, his political sponsor, went down to defeat."[270]

In 1940, however, Bill Langer won the race for a position in the United States Senate. In a three-cornered race in the primary election, he defeated the incumbent senator, Lynn J. Frazier, and Thomas J. Whelan.[271] In the general election he beat Charles J. Vogel (not related to either Frank Vogel or the author) by about 22,000 votes. All were formidable opponents. Frazier had been a three-term governor of North Dakota from 1916 until his recall in 1921 and had

Pictured in this photograph of leaders of the Nonpartisan League on January 5, 1937, are the newly elected governor, William Langer (bottom center). Also identified are John Gray (bottom right), and in the second row: Jim Mulloy (second from left), Oscar Butterdahl, Oscar Erickson, Frank Vogel and Bill Godwin.   From the Robert Vogel Collection

served in the Senate for eighteen years prior to the 1940 election. In later years, Charles Vogel served as a judge for a federal district court of appeals, while Tom Whelan was named an ambassador to Nicaragua. In spite of the substantial majorities or pluralities the voters gave Langer, his enemies made one last effort to destroy his political career and nearly succeeded. Agnes Geelan described the scene in her biography of Bill Langer:

> On January 3, 1941, Senator-elect William Langer stepped forward with Senators LaFollette, Maloney, and McFarland to take the oath of office in the nation's capitol. The ceremony was interrupted by Senator Alben Barkley, majority floor leader, who announced that a petition had been filed with the Secretary of the Senate by a group of North Dakota citizens protesting the seating of William Langer.
>
> After a brief discussion and at the recommendation of Barkley, Langer was seated "without prejudice," subject to a parliamentary ruling that only a majority vote of the Senate would be needed to pass on the question of Langer's right to the seat.[272]

While the Senate Committee on Privileges and Elections, chaired by Senator Tom Connally, received the petitions and handled the investigation, Langer had again to wait—this time for nearly fifteen months—for justice to prevail, and it eventually did. In the meantime, he actively participated in the work of the Senate. The full Senate voted to seat him on March 27, 1942, and Langer served as U.S. senator from North Dakota until he died in office some eighteen years later.

The two North Dakota citizens who challenged Langer's fitness to be seated were both familiar faces on North Dakota's political scene and both of questionable character: James Mulloy of Bismarck and C. R. Verry of Minot. The charges against Langer ranged from the vague—that he had been accused repeatedly of immoral conduct—to the specific—negative versions of his handling of legal cases, such as the Johnson case and others described in this chapter. Every one of the charges had been campaign issues repeatedly brought forward by Langer's political opponents and repeatedly rejected by the voters. Anti-Langer witnesses, such as Clyde Duffy, C. R. Verry, Mulloy, as well as other pro-Langer witnesses, including Langer himself and

Bill and Lydia Langer cast their ballots in the 1940 election in which he was elected to the U.S. Senate for the first of four terms.

State Historical Society of North Dakota 0276-38

Usher Burdick, agreed that the issues were well known. Yet the Senate investigators, who had interviewed all these people on the subject, said exactly the opposite in their report to the Senate. Their only basis for this perversion of testimony, as indicated by pencilled notes on the archive copy of their report, is a few scattered remarks of a few people, not active in politics, that they personally had not heard of one charge or another. As the evidence reveals, the Senate investigators falsified the public record and claimed the voters of North Dakota were unaware of these charges, and the majority of the Senate committee repeated the lie.

At one time, James Mulloy had been Secretary of the Industrial Commission and Secretary of the Securities Commission, appointed by Langer and other members of the commissions. He had worked hard, at his own expense, for Langer's election in 1932. As indicated in earlier chapters, he had also tried to assist Langer by bringing a gatekeeper from South Dakota to keep an eye on the court proceedings in the perjury trial and the second conspiracy trial; however, his choice of men, Gale Wyman and Chet Leedom, brought more trouble than help. Langer, who had the possible fault of sticking by his friends too long, did not forget Mulloy's efforts on his behalf,

*The Langers had four daughters, pictured here in 1932. L-R: daughter Lydia, Mrs. William (Lydia) Langer, holding Cornelia on her lap, Emma and Mary. This photograph appeared in the **Mandan Morning Pioneer**.*

however.[273] Mulloy, who was efficient when sober, was reappointed to the Industrial Commission in Langer's second term, starting in 1936.[274] In addition to Governor Langer, the other two members of the commission were John N. Hagan, secretary of agriculture and labor, and Alvin C. Strutz, attorney general. They told Mulloy that they had heard reports of his drinking on the job when he was employed by the State Mill during the administration of Governor Walter Welford and warned him that they would vote to fire him if there was any repetition of that activity.[275]

When Langer chose not to run again for the governorship in 1938, Mulloy held and lost a number of state jobs. He worked for Oscar Erickson in the Insurance Department and was fired.[276] He worked for C. J. (Red) Myers in the hail insurance office and was fired. He worked for the State Laboratories Department and was fired. Frank Vogel told the Senate investigators that he was proud to say Mulloy had never asked him for a job because Mulloy knew he would be turned down if he did ask. It became obvious that no state official, no matter how sympathetic to Mulloy's family, could risk hiring him.

Shortly before the end of Langer's term as governor in 1937, it was discovered that Mulloy had altered the records of the Industrial Commission so as to allow himself to continue to draw pay from the State Mill and Elevator in Grand Forks, although he was no longer employed there and had moved to Bismarck. As soon as Governor John Moses took office as governor in 1938, Attorney General Alvin Strutz made the motion to fire Mulloy from his position with the Industrial Commission, as well as the job he held at the State Laboratories. The motion carried. Besides Strutz, the other members of the board were Governor Moses and State Treasurer John R. Omland. Mulloy never forgave Strutz. It was later discovered that Mulloy had also altered an order of the Industrial Commission to investigate him, and had written up the order to substitute the name of former Secretary John Wishek for his own name. No investigation of Wishek was ever contemplated.[277]

Among other problems, Mulloy had a well-earned reputation for not paying bills.[278] Early in his career, he worked in South Dakota as auditor for a chain of lumberyards, a job from which he was discharged. He said it was due to a difference of opinion with one of the partners. In testimony taken by the Senate investigators, he was said to have skipped out on a board bill in Faith, South Dakota, and to have written bad checks there. The manager of the Alex Johnson Hotel in Rapid City, South Dakota, was holding a bad check from Mulloy in the amount of fifty dollars. Doctors Roan and Strauss,

Bismarck physicians, had reduced Mulloy's bill on his promise to pay but had still not been paid. Oscar Erickson held an unpaid note Mulloy had given another Bismarck doctor, and Frank Vogel held another note. Ed Patterson of the Patterson Hotel in Bismarck had an unpaid judgment of three hundred dollars against him.

When Mulloy was Secretary of the Securities Commission, he would notify out-of-state securities dealers that he would be coming to examine them. He would then bill them in advance for expenses, collect the money, and spend little of the billed time making inspections. When the commissioners discovered this, they ordered that no out-of-state examinations be made without their prior approval. This, too, Mulloy blamed on Attorney General Alvin Strutz.

Mulloy also had personal problems. At one point, his wife sued him for divorce, alleging he had beaten her. They were reconciled, but the publicity was harmful to him and also to Langer, since the publicity came during his governorship when Mulloy was associated with him. All witnesses who discussed the matter agreed that his wife was a fine woman and they had a wonderful daughter. One witness said she was a better wife than he deserved. This statement was probably true, given that witnesses testified to the Senate investigators about Mulloy's having a mistress in Chicago and entertaining one strange woman after another, who posed as his wife in South Dakota.[279] In truth, he was a bad check artist, a womanizer, and an alcoholic. Many people tried to help him. Their reward was that he ran against one, Oscar Erickson, for the office of insurance commissioner, accused another, Strutz, of taking bribes, and alleged that another, Langer, was unfit to hold office. He blamed Langer and Vogel, not himself, for his inability to keep and obtain lucrative positions with state government and told several people that he would get revenge.

He admitted, in order to make the charges against Langer, that his charges, if true, made Mulloy himself a criminal, guilty of multiple felonies.[280] He admitted to having been arrested several times for bad checks, for fights, and for fraud. He said he never served a jail sentence, but he did not say what the disposition of the arrests was, or whether he paid fines or received suspended sentences.

Before filing his affidavit, Mulloy consulted with a Fargo lawyer, Howard Fuller. After invoking lawyer-client privilege, under which lawyers are forbidden to disclose communications from a client, Mulloy asked about the statute of limitations, the length of time allowed between a crime and the filing of a criminal charge. When Fuller said it was three years, Mulloy then narrated events that he said had occurred more than three years earlier, including his version of the arrival of Gale Wyman in Bismarck and his claim that it was part of an attempt to influence Judge Wyman. He recanted that story later in the Senate hearings, admitting that Langer and the others did not know he was bringing young Wyman to Bismarck and that he had no authority to hire Wyman for anything.[281] Fuller, who was acquainted with Judge Wyman, told Mulloy that he was misinterpreting the facts, that Judge Wyman was honorable, and that Mulloy should do nothing about his story.[282] Nevertheless, on December 30, 1940, only two days after the members of the Industrial Commission voted to fire him, Mulloy dictated and filed his affidavit.

The other original protester, C. R. Verry of Minot, ran a bill collection business. As was a fairly common practice, although he was not a lawyer, he often had bills assigned to him and then sued in court and acted as his own lawyer as non-lawyers have a right to do. He was secretary of the state senate in 1925 and chief clerk of the North Dakota House of Representatives in the years when anti-Nonpartisan League Republicans controlled that body (1927–31, and 1941).[283]

Apparently, the anti-League forces were not troubled by his reputation. In the 1941 session, Verry was accused of altering bills between the time they were passed by the House and the time they were delivered to Governor Moses.[284] When asked by Senate investigators, Governor Moses said that an investigation "by a journalist" showed "negligence" in the handling of the bills, but he was not prepared to say that the negligence was Verry's.[285] Other witnesses said the alterations were made only on bills relating to departments run by Nonpartisan League-endorsed officials and resulted in reducing their appropriations.

Even more to the point, Verry was notorious for being careless with the truth. In four instances, the records of the North Dakota Supreme Court provide evidence that he was unworthy of belief.[286] First, in *Farmers Security Bank of Park River v. Verry*, the Supreme Court opinion tells a sordid story.[287] Verry had been cashier of the bank and owed money to the bank, which was being examined by the State Bank Examiners. He was ordered by them to provide security for the money he owed, and he agreed to give deeds to certain land for that purpose. He asked that the deeds not be recorded for a few days. During that short delay, he recorded a mortgage for nine thousand dollars ahead of the deeds, depriving the bank of the promised security. When he was sued to set aside the deeds, his story was so unbelievable that the Supreme Court said, "Furthermore, the court does not give credit to the testimony of Verry or his wife."[288] Verry was asked at the Senate removal hearing if he had been involved in that case, and he admitted that he was but offered no explanation.

In a second case fifty years later, *Verry v. Murphy*, the same court affirmed a finding of the lower court that Verry was liable for fraud, and for false statements knowingly made, noting that his testimony was "unworthy of belief."[289] Two years later, the court affirmed in *Hermann v. Ramadan*, a decision that found against Verry's claim that he had not received rentals from a defendant who was a tenant of Verry's principal. A letter written by Verry, which was inconsistent with his testimony at the trial, was produced to impeach him. The letter was believed, not the testimony.[290] It is one of the oddities of Langer's history that both of his major crises (the conspiracy cases and the attempt to unseat him from the Senate) were instigated by bill collectors: C. R. Verry, who was one of two sources for the Senate fiasco, and A. M. Anderson, who instigated the investigation that led to the impeachment trials. Perhaps the men were reacting in their own peculiar ways to having their occupations made more difficult by moratoriums on farm foreclosures. James Mulloy had his own motives, as we have seen.

The Senate Proceedings

The Senate Committee on Privileges and Elections, who received the petition, was mainly Democratic, although the makeup changed when the new senators were sworn in. The committee appointed an investigator named Burton, but C. R. Verry complained about the choice because Burton had done something in North Dakota earlier and Verry thought he may have been influenced by Langer. So the new committee delegated three of its members, Senators Scott Lucas, Harold Burton, and Orrice Murdoch, to select one or more new investigators. On May 8, 1941, they chose two, Sam H. Hood and Elbert L. Smith, who were sent to North Dakota to investigate. They spent a little more than two months at the task. Senator Lucas took an active part in the later hearings, even taking over the presentation of the prosecution from the retained lawyers at times.

Nothing appears in the record about the credentials of Hood and Smith, except that one was said to be a lawyer and the other an accountant, and one was from New York City and the other a graduate of Southern Methodist University. Neither knew much law and both of them systematically violated basic procedural and constitutional rights.

The Charges

The principal charge Hood and Smith investigated, incredibly, was "that for the past twenty years respondent's public and private life has been of such a character that he has been repeatedly suspected and accused of conduct involving moral turpitude." In those days, as well as today, a lot of politicians were "suspected" and "accused" of things. Negative and mudslinging campaigns are nothing new, but removing elected officials from office because of what they are suspected or accused of is. To anyone, and particularly to lawyers, who know that accusations are proof of nothing, it is abhorrent that someone could be in danger of losing a high office because he had been "repeatedly suspected and accused."

That amazing accusation was followed by a partially falsified recital of the four trials, statements that Langer had bribed two jurors in the second conspiracy trial, that he had procured the selection of Judge Wyman for that trial and had influenced him to direct the verdict in the perjury trial, and that he had paid Gale Wyman and Chet Leedom to influence the judge. Little or no proof was offered on such charges, but they were things of which Mulloy and Verry and others suspected or accused Langer.

Langer had no input into the selection of witnesses of the investigators, except that near the end he was asked to, and did, submit a list of names of people who could be interviewed as to his integrity. They were interviewed and some of those conversations were included in the investigators' report, although in a selective and slanted way. The investigators disregarded the testimony of dozens of honorable people who served on boards with Langer or had been supporters of his, as well all members of boards to which he had appointed members, choosing to assume without evidence that Langer had control over all such persons, whether connected with him or not.

Earlier, Langer had declined to give names to the committee because he was not allowed to have a representative present when the "affidavits" were taken or to examine the same witnesses or to read the statements of previous witnesses, now found in the Witness Books. He and Francis Murphy recognized that naming their witnesses and submitting them to the ex parte procedure of the investigators would merely give the latter a chance to grill the witnesses and attempt to destroy their credibility, or at least forewarn the investigators of what they had to say. Langer and Murphy chose the risks of not participating rather then the predictable certainty that their witnesses would be abused by the investigators or "sandpapered," as lawyers sometimes describe the procedure.

The Investigation

The two investigators interviewed more than 160 witnesses, and their report, nearly four thousand pages long, including the transcripts of those witnesses they chose to include.[291] They also interviewed an unknown number of other people whose responses were not reported except to drop an occasional reference to their "statements" taken by the investigators. These unreported interviews included several important witnesses. The two investigators started out with the assumption (which, as Senator Connally suspected, they were instructed to accept as fact) that the charges of Mulloy and Verry and their followers were true. They then looked for support for those charges. They mostly interviewed people suggested by Congressman William Lemke, an avowed political enemy of Langer's, and by Mulloy and Verry, who submitted a list of more than sixty names. At first they also asked about the reputation of Mulloy and Verry but soon gave up that line of inquiry when they kept getting answers that the two would not be believed under oath. In apparent desperation to get some kind of favorable answers, they turned to asking this question: "If Mulloy's charges were corroborated by credible evidence, would you consider them serious?" That question sometimes got an affirmative answer, but many witnesses added that they would want to know who was doing the corroborating.

William Lemke was a leader in the Nonpartisan League in North Dakota and served in the U.S. House of Representatives from 1932 to 1940 and again from 1942 until his death in 1950.

State Historical Society
of North Dakota C3635

Smith and Hood told lawyers they had to testify about confidential communications with their clients, thus requiring lawyers to violate their ethical duties as lawyers. Shamefully, all ten or so lawyers interviewed did violate their oath as lawyers—sometimes under threat of being cited for contempt of Congress—and testified about the confidential communications.[292]

When witnesses reasonably questioned how their responses to the interviewers' queries might provide material evidence about Langer's fitness for office, they were told that this was for the investigators to decide and the witnesses must answer. So they did. When the occasional witness asked for a witness fee, as Red Myers did, he was questioned about his reasons for asking, the intimation being that he was uncooperative and in contempt of Congress.

This investigation obviously occurred before the Supreme Court put some limits on the power of congressional committees after abuse of that power by Senator Joseph McCarthy of Wisconsin and others in the 1950s. At the time of the "investigation," the general understanding was that the executive branch had no control over the legislative branch. The Supreme Court finally decided that the Constitution applied to both and the judiciary had to enforce it.

When witnesses were concerned about their testimony might become public, Smith and Hood promised them confidentiality, saying it would only go to the Senate committee.[293] They then promptly let Mulloy know what was said and a within a few days often asked him to testify in response. And, of course, the testimony was not confidential to the committee—it also was made available to the full Senate and ultimately the public.

Bill Langer boasted during campaigns that he had been sued many times but had never paid to settle a case and had never lost one. From the records available, his claim appears to be true.[294] He blamed many of the lawsuits on his political enemies, something that is true of at least some of the more sensational cases. During the Senate's search of Langer's entire life and career for examples of his "moral turpitude," many of the old lawsuits, disputes, and negative publicity resurfaced. Hood and Smith sought out and interviewed many of Langer's former clients in an effort to find those who had complaints against him, whether founded or unfounded. The most well-known and misused example is the Johnson case, discussed in chapter two, but other widely publicized cases were also used against him.

The Phelps Case

One of the more well known of the cases involved a divorce case from early in Langer's career. A woman named Mrs. Phelps hired Langer to represent her in a divorce, and after the case was over, she sued him, claiming that he had stolen money from her. The trial came during Langer's campaign for attorney general in 1916, and the newspapers spread the word about the lawyer who stole twelve thousand dollars from a divorcee. Langer won his case against Mrs. Phelps after accounting for every penny. In fact, the judge directed a verdict, meaning that he determined there was no basis for any claim and therefore nothing for the jury to rule on. The judge scolded her attorneys for bringing the action, but the news coverage of the result of the trial was not nearly as flamboyant as the original lawsuit. Langer was left to explain the rest of the story to the Senate hearing in 1941: that the matter was referred to the grievance committee of the State Bar Association, which held a hearing and reported to the Supreme Court that the charges were not sustained and recommended a dismissal and the Supreme Court adopted the recommendation and on March 30, 1917, dismissed the complaint.[295]

Ten years later, Mrs. Phelps also filed a claim with the Supreme Court, asking that Langer be disciplined for stealing money from her. A disciplinary committee investigated the charge and reported that she had no case and the Supreme Court agreed. Still, in 1941 the Senate investigators dredged up this old discredited tale and, without reporting the directed verdict and the actions of the committee and the Supreme Court, reported to the Senate that "the records of the Bar Board show that a former client made formal protest to the effect that after paying the Senator a fee in a divorce case, her interests were abandoned and he conspired with the defense in the matter of a property settlement." Since their own records show that the investigators had checked with J. H. Newton, clerk of the Supreme Court, on the outcome of the case and of the complaint to the Bar Board, the investigators must have known that the Phelps claim was groundless.[296] Their failure to tell the Senate about the vindication of Langer by the Supreme Court is inexcusable and shows the bias inherent in the investigation.

In his Senate testimony, Langer recalled another episode in this story from 1932. "The day I was elected governor," Langer said, "that same woman [Mrs. Phelps] filed proceedings in the Supreme Court claiming I had stolen $14,000 from her." He further explained that "the Supreme Court appointed a committee, consisting of Clyde Young, John Carmody [who had been on the Supreme Court], and

Emerson Smith of Fargo. B. C. Shaw, who had warned me about her, was my attorney. We went in and set out the facts, and asked the committee if we should withdraw. They said they would not insult us by asking us to leave while they deliberated, and said they wanted us to know they were dismissing the proceedings immediately."[297] Despite having checked with the clerk of the Supreme Court, the investigators did not report this outcome to the Senate.

The Hoover Case

Another case that came to the investigators' attention was one in which Langer sued a Minneapolis bank on behalf of a client, Charlie Hoover, after he had been turned down by other lawyers. Langer won a judgment for eleven thousand dollars in Hoover's favor. After a trial and an appeal to the Supreme Court and other proceedings, Langer collected for his client, and received a check from Hoover for fifty-five hundred dollars, a fee that covered both the trial and the appeal. When Hoover deposited the eleven-thousand-dollar settlement check in his local bank, however, the banker, who was an officer of the State Bankers Association, convinced him that Langer's fee was too high. He offered to finance a lawsuit against Langer to get it back, and Hoover agreed. In the suit that followed, Langer proved he had a written contract for the fee and won the case, but not without a lot of adverse publicity.[298]

The Deis Case

Langer was also subjected to rumors that he was a "womanizer." Of all public men I have known, Langer is the least likely to have such a charge leveled against him. Happily married to Lydia Cady, a woman he courted for seven years before they were wed, and the father of four daughters, Bill Langer had a loving and close family. Beverly Smith, the reporter for the 1954 article about Langer in the *Saturday Evening Post* noted, "Even Langer's enemies admit that his personal and family life is irreproachable, that he is a devoted husband and father."[299] The sole basis in any record for the slander about Langer and inappropriate relationships springs from the Deis case. In 1938, when Langer was running against the incumbent Senator Nye for the United States Senate, he was alleged to have committed adultery with a Mrs. Deis, with whom one of his former clients, Emma Oster Slovarp, had been living. When the case was finally heard in court, the jury deliberated less than a half hour before finding Langer innocent of all charges, but the publicity preceding the trial was hurtful and damaging, even though Langer was guilty of nothing.[300]

A lengthy lawyer-client relationship between Langer and the Oster family preceded the action. Jacob Oster had shot and killed a neighbor, Mr. Peterson, and was charged with first-degree murder. The Oster family retained Langer to defend Jacob against the charge of first-degree murder. Given the circumstances of the case, Langer intended to prove that Oster was only guilty of the lesser charge of second-degree murder. After spending the night in one of Peterson's outbuildings, Oster had observed the couple together, and in the morning, when the neighbor came out of the house, Oster, armed with a shotgun, ordered him to stop. Peterson ran, and Oster shot and killed him. Naturally, Langer wanted to talk to Mrs. Oster, but the state's attorney had taken her into to his own home and would not let Langer talk to her. Langer took this as a challenge. He hired a friend of hers to persuade her to talk to him, which she ultimately did. He wanted to tell her that the law provided that a wife need not testify against her husband and that she could not be compelled to do so.

The state's attorney, however, already aware of that fact, had persuaded her to allow him to get a divorce for her (presumably without charging any fee). Langer defended Oster in the divorce case on the theory that Emma Oster could not get a divorce because of the defense of recrimination (since repealed), which provided that if both parties were guilty of crimes or other conduct constituting grounds for divorce, no divorce could be granted to either one. The judge gave her a divorce anyway. Langer took this as another challenge and arranged to have a friend talk to Mrs. Oster about remarrying Jacob Oster.

The friend persuaded Mrs. Oster to talk to Langer, who told her that he didn't think she could testify against her husband in any case, but he didn't like the way the case was being handled, and he thought she ought to marry Jake again. She was willing, if Langer would agree that he would get her a divorce, without charge later if she wanted it. He agreed. Langer then got himself appointed deputy sheriff by the Burleigh County sheriff, got Oster out of the county jail, picked up Emma, and took the two to South Dakota, where they were remarried. He then returned his prisoner to the jail. Though this procedure was somewhat irregular, it was not the first time the Burleigh County sheriff or other sheriffs had allowed lawyers to take prisoners out of the jail temporarily, whether or not the lawyer was appointed a deputy sheriff.

When the murder case came up for trial, the prosecution called Emma Oster as a witness. Langer objected on the ground that a wife could not testify against her husband. The judge who had issued them their divorce testified to the divorce. Langer offered in evidence the new marriage certificate. The trial judge, no doubt somewhat astonished at all this, then ruled that Emma Oster could not testify.

Jacob Oster testified to the circumstances of the shooting and the presumed adultery of the neighbor, which Langer thought would justify a verdict of second-degree murder, or perhaps manslaughter. The prosecution, in rebuttal, produced some love letters Oster had written to another woman shortly after the murder, so the jury decided that maybe he was not as aggrieved by the presumed adultery as he claimed. They did, however, find him guilty of second-degree murder. He was sentenced to twenty-five years, less than the life term he would have received if he had pleaded guilty to first degree murder.

Some observers have been shocked that a lawyer, even if he were a temporary deputy sheriff, would participate in the remarriage of a woman in order to keep her from testifying to a murder. Such critics ignore the fact that Emma Oster could not have testified if another lawyer had not pressured her to get the divorce in the first place to make it possible for her to testify. That other lawyer was not running for office and was not an enemy of the daily papers, and those circumstances seem to have made a difference. In addition, courts had previously held that a divorce court order prohibiting marriage within a certain time after a divorce was not effective beyond the borders of the state in which the order was issued. Well-informed lawyers, including this author, were aware of this holding and sometimes so advised clients who were anxious, for whatever reason, such as a pregnancy, to remarry before the prohibition ended.

Later, Langer's enemies also made much of the fact that Mrs. Oster married again, to a man named Slovarp, without being properly divorced. They accepted her claim that Langer refused to get her a divorce, as he had promised to do. Langer, however, produced documentary evidence at the Senate hearing to show that he had prepared, served, and filed the divorce papers for her, and had notified her of the date of the divorce trial before Judge Fred Jansonius. He testified that he and the judge had waited for her to appear on that date and that she did not appear. Langer denied ever telling her she was divorced and pointed out that under North Dakota law a divorced woman could not get a marriage license without producing a certified copy of a divorce decree. Either Emma Oster did not tell the clerk who issued the marriage license that she had ever been married or else she lied to the clerk.

As Langer pointed out, Emma Oster had demonstrated that she didn't need a marriage license to live with a man—she was married to Oster when she moved in with Peterson, the man who was killed, and she had lived with Slovarp without a legal divorce, although Langer had done what he could to help her acquire one. Nevertheless, her claim that Langer promised her a divorce and did not get it for her continued to circulate.

After Oster was sent to the penitentiary and before she married Slovarp, Emma had moved in with a couple with the last name of Deis, who lived in Mandan. In 1938, Langer received a letter from P. H. Miller, a former non-lawyer county judge and a former state employee who had been appointed to office under the Langer administration. Miller had quit his state employment after Langer had not supported his grander ambitions and his supervisors questioned some of his actions. Miller's letter asserted that in conversations with Mrs. Deis, she had told him that Langer had been her boyfriend for seven or eight years and had made her "some promises." Miller also wrote that he might be going on a speaking tour soon, inferring that Langer should pay her off or get bad publicity. Langer, however, did not comply.

The letter was hand-delivered (perhaps because of some concern over using the mails to defraud) on October 11, just four weeks before election day, when Langer lost the Senate race to Gerald P. Nye. After the election and much advance publicity about the case, the scandalous complaint was finally served and filed. Langer's enemies flocked to the courthouse to read the lurid allegations. Friends of Mrs. Deis then offered to settle for declining amounts, eventually for as little as two hundred dollars, but Langer refused, asked for a prompt trial and got one a few weeks later.

Mrs. Deis testified that she had committed adultery with Langer in the governor's office on February 26 between two and three o'clock in the afternoon. Langer's attorney, Francis Murphy, asked her several times to repeat the date and time, and she did, each time very positive as to the day and the hour. What she and her three attorneys did not know was that during his first term Langer had a dispute over whether someone was present in his office at a certain time, so during his second term he had his secretaries keep a running log of who was in his office every day, with times of arrival and departure.

In court, Langer produced his records for February 26, which showed that at the time Mrs. Deis specified, he was meeting with the Industrial Commission (consisting of Attorney General Alvin C. Strutz, Commissioner of Agriculture and Labor John Hagan, and

Secretary James Mulloy) and with Archie Scott, manager of the state mill; John Gray, state treasurer; Berta Baker, state auditor; and O. T. Owen, tax commissioner, and that he had seen about sixty other people in the office that same day.

The attorneys for Mrs. Deis responded that perhaps the date might have been incorrect, but Francis Murphy, Langer's lawyer, had a cart wheeled in to the courtroom carrying the daily logs Langer had kept for the entire term of office and defied the lawyers for Mrs. Deis to pick any date they chose during the entire two-year term. Murphy promised he would disprove their claim on any date they picked.

When the case went to the jury, they were out for only fifteen minutes before they asked to return, but by then a jury was being selected in the next case, so it took a total of twenty-seven minutes before the jury verdict was received. Of course, the jury found in favor of Langer. Despite his innocence, some people refer to this lawsuit as proof of Langer's low standards of morality. The Deis case was highly publicized, except for the outcome. In 1941, when the Senate investigators talked to a couple of hundred North Dakotans, they further publicized it by asking almost all of them if they had heard of the charge that Langer had committed adultery, without ever mentioning his defense or the outcome of the trial.

Consider the effect on the reputation of a political figure of today if a representative of the United States Senate were to ask 168 prominent people in a state these questions, which were asked of many people, including C. C. Swain, president of Minot Teachers College: "Did you ever know of any suit that was filed . . . that reached the question of his moral character?" Or, questioned a senator's reputation, "from a moral standpoint, I am speaking now strictly moral, in the matter of his sexual life and things of that character"?[301]

The Fort Yates Jail Break-in

A charge to which Langer admitted was that he had broken into a jail. He had taken the action on behalf of two clients who were housed in the jail at Fort Yates, on the Standing Rock Indian Reservation south of Bismarck. They had been charged with first-degree murder for holding someone with whom they were fighting under water until he drowned. There was a hearing scheduled for the next day, and Langer needed to talk to his clients ahead of time. The winter weather was bad, but Langer drove to Mandan, and took the train as far as Cannonball, and then hired a car and driver. They found the road blocked with snow, so he hired a horse-drawn sleigh and driver to take him to Fort Yates. By the time he reached Fort Yates it was the middle of the night, and a deputy sheriff at the jail refused to let him see the clients, saying he did not have a key. The sheriff was not available, so Langer broke into the sheriff's office and desk and found a key. Langer said it came down to who could lick whom, the deputy or himself, but he got in and talked to his clients. He later tried the case and his clients were found guilty of a lesser degree of murder than which they were charged.[302]

The Lawsuit by the "Crippled Boy"

In early February 1934, about ten days before the biennial NPL precinct meetings preceding the county and state conventions at which League candidates would be selected, the *Bismarck Tribune* struck again.[303] It sensationalized for two days a lawsuit by a "crippled boy" named Buckley against Langer, as well as against an insurance company and the boy's guardian. The lawsuit against Langer claimed that the boy's case was settled for five thousand, but the boy got only nineteen hundred dollars, and now he wanted the rest. The inference, of course, was that Langer got the remaining thirty-one hundred dollars.

Nonpartisan League delegation to Washington, D.C., December 1933. Standing third from the left is Senator Gerald P. Nye, then A.C. Townley, Senator Lynn Frazier, Governor William Langer and Congressman James Sinclair.

State Historical Society of North Dakota E0904-1

It turned out that Langer was not the attorney for the boy but for the insurance company. Buckley's attorney, McCurdy, brought the lawsuit against Langer, the insurance company, and the boy's guardian and admitted that he didn't know who got the money so he had sued everybody connected with the case. District Judge Buttz threw out the case before any testimony was taken, saying that Langer was responsible only to his client, the insurance company, that the plaintiff ratified the settlement, and that the guardian was responsible only in the court that appointed him and could be required to account for the money there, before Judge Fred Jansonius. But of course the fact that Langer was being sued by a crippled boy was highly publicized.

Langer was sued or accused in other cases, which were all decided in Langer's favor or dismissed with nothing given in settlement. The four described in this chapter have been most often mentioned in the Senate investigation and in political campaigns, but the pattern is clear. The accusations were damaging to Langer's reputation and political aspirations, even though the evidence could not support the charges.

Taxes on the Great Northern Railroad and Langer's Land Sale

Two charges against Langer that were thoroughly publicized by his enemies involved financial issues: matters involving taxes on the Great Northern Railroad, supposedly connected with a sale of land by Langer to Thomas V. Sullivan, and Langer's sale of stock in a Mexican land venture to Gregory Brunk, a partner of V. W. Brewer, who was a broker of municipal bonds active in North Dakota in the 1930s.

Something Langer's enemies did not discuss but is important to know is that both Gregory Brunk and Thomas V. Sullivan were long-time friends, admirers, and supporters of Bill Langer. Their friendship and financial support of his campaigns long preceded the transactions in question. The friendships also long preceded Brunk's connection with any bond broker and Sullivan's connection with the Great Northern Railroad.[304] At the time of the Senate hearing in 1941, Gregory Brunk was an attorney in Iowa, Brewer was a bond broker in Minneapolis, and Sullivan an attorney in Chicago. All of them were questioned by the Senate investigators.[305]

Bill Langer and Gregory Brunk first met in 1928 or 1930. Both were admirers of Milo Reno, head of the Farmers Holiday Association, an organization of farmers advocating help for farmers in keeping their land during the great agricultural depression of the late 1920s and the great business depression that followed in 1929. Both had spoken at meetings of the Holiday Association. They became friends and regular correspondents, and Langer described Brunk as one of his two closest friends and advisers outside North Dakota.

Brunk attended League conventions and contributed to Langer's campaigns through the years. He even came to North Dakota and gave a talk at a League state convention, during which he promised to help the League program in any way he could. During one of the Langer trials he came to Bismarck and helped Langer check on potential jurors. Among his reasons for supporting Langer was that in Iowa he had seen a political prosecution of an upright state official on charges similar to those against Langer, and he worked without pay as an attorney for that official and helped get him acquitted of an unjust charge. He considered Langer's case to be a similar and equally politically inspired persecution, and he wanted Langer to be acquitted, too.

When Langer was removed as governor in 1934, Brunk came to Bismarck where he learned that the conviction in the first trial had prevented Langer from practicing law or running for office and that his financial situation had become precarious, so much so that a grocer, Roy Logan, was carrying his grocery bills; a tailor, Ed Klein, was selling him clothes on credit; and the gas and telephone companies had threatened to cut off heat and telephone service to his home. Furthermore, Langer needed to raise a thousand dollars within the next few days to pay the bill for printing the record on the appeal to the Eighth Circuit Court of Appeals. Langer was trying to raise money from his assets after the conviction in the first trial, and, in 1935, he asked Brunk to represent him and Marcella Wicks, a client for whom he had obtained a judgment for a 460-acre tract of land, in obtaining a payment from the Bureau of Indian Affairs of Langer's fee of some sixteen hundred dollars. Brunk succeeded in getting payment of the fee.

Bill Langer had been, and would later again be, probably the highest paid trial lawyer in North Dakota, but the expense of the first trial (during which he paid for separate attorneys for some of the other defendants), as well as constant campaigning, had drained away his assets. In 1937, when he became governor for the second time, he had practiced law from the time of the reversal of the conviction in May 1935 to his inauguration in January 1937, and managed to somewhat improve his finances, but they were still meager. Brunk, in the meantime, had studied North Dakota county and municipal finances, as had his partner, V. W. Brewer. Brewer, who had been a municipal bond broker for many years, specializing in North

Dakota bonds, had devised a plan to save money for counties and school districts and cities ("municipalities") by refinancing their outstanding debt.

During the Great Depression, when one-fourth to one-third of the residents of the state were on welfare, few people could pay real estate taxes, which were the chief source of funding for local governments and schools. Tax collections were insufficient to pay even the minimum costs of operating schools and local governments, so those organizations then had to resort to issuing bonds, and later, certificates of indebtedness, secured only by a pledge of repayment from tax money if and when collected. Of course, such debt carried a high interest rate, typically 7 percent for certificates, compared with the interest rate of about 4 percent on bonds.

When the limits on certificates of indebtedness were reached, many local governments started paying employees and suppliers with registered warrants, payable only from collections from future taxes not yet assessed. Some banks and creditors would accept these paper promises, if at all, only at a high discount, 10 percent or more. From 1935 on, real estate tax collections ran from 32 to 64 percent of taxes assessed. It was not until 1937 and later that tax collections became more normal.

The Brewer plan was to buy up, at his own risk and that of other brokers he could persuade to join him, all the bonds, certificates, and warrants they could locate, and then refinance all the debt with long-term bonds at a lower interest rate, perhaps 4 to 5 percent, thereby reducing the interest being paid out and restoring the credit of the municipalities by removing them from the category of delinquent debtors, and making all their debt current. He could do this only with local governments that had agreed to let him handle their refinancing in this way.

Many of the rural and western counties, who were the worst off, made such agreements with him. At considerable risk to himself and associated brokerage houses, Brewer bought up large amounts of outstanding debt of those counties, and then he succeeded in restoring their credit. In the process, he also helped to restore the high credit rating of the state, because a state that contains many delinquent subdivisions is given a low credit rating even if it is not itself delinquent.

Brewer spent more than two years on this plan, and his firm ended up with net income of about one hundred thousand dollars for all his risk and time. Brunk, who acted as attorney for the business, got about thirty thousand of it. There were expenses paid to local representatives who assisted Brewer, including some of Langer's lifelong enemies, like John Sullivan of Mandan and C. L. Lewis, whom Langer had fired and was now the editor of the *Ward County Independent*. Only one local representative, Hugh McCulloch of Washburn, was ever considered friendly to Langer.

During all this time, Brunk had studied North Dakota agriculture and government, and grown to admire the way the people of the state had conquered a difficult environment. At one point, he got Langer to come to Washington and speak to a meeting of big bond brokers, including New York bankers, Lehmann Brothers, and other big brokers. As a result, Moody's rating service raised the bond rating of North Dakota and its subdivisions a week later to a good investment grade, which made their bonds eligible for investment by banks and trust funds as well as for lower interest rates on its bonds.

During 1937, Brunk, now thoroughly convinced of the value of North Dakota land, even though its value was temporarily depressed, mentioned to Langer that he was thinking of investing in North Dakota land. Langer said, "For God's sake, if you want to buy land, buy it from me," and Brunk said he would do it. Langer had several thousand acres in Kidder, Burleigh, and Morton Counties, most of it purchased, some of it taken in lieu of attorney's fees. Langer had paid sixty thousand dollars for the land over many years. Brunk said he didn't want to pay fire sale prices, nor did he want to pay what Langer had paid for the land, so they agreed on a price of fifty-six thousand dollars; Brunk paid one thousand dollars down and the balance in irregular installments over several years. During the Senate hearings, Brunk testified, "I have seen big corporations and chain banks become perfectly holy, but when some fellow sets out to help people born on the wrong side of the tracks, then he is in trouble . . . I bought more than land, in my own mind. I thought I was buying an opportunity for this man [William Langer] to make a fair presentation of himself to this nation, and I believe I did."[306]

At the Senate hearing, the prosecution presented the testimony of three out-of-state appraisers: Ellis B. Southworth, Ersel Walley, and True D. Morse, from Minnesota, Indiana, and Missouri, respectively, and their testimony is in the transcript of the Senate hearing. These three men had looked at the land in 1941 and testified that they appraised its value, as of 1935, at $5,718. But their testimony was based on its value for cash, and two of them admitted that in 1935 there were no cash sales being made and very few on credit, and that it was a buyer's market. In other words, there were no purchasers who were ready, willing and able to buy for cash—and one of the requirements of a court valuation is the existence of such purchasers. In 1935, there were none.

A competent and experienced North Dakota expert appraiser, G. Leonard Dalstad, investigated the land involved in the Brunk transaction to determine what the land would be worth in 1991, and his estimate was its value would be $860,000. Even allowing for a generous ten-to-one inflation rate from 1935 to 1991, it would appear that $56,000 was a good deal for Brunk.

In 1938, however, when John Moses was running for governor, he was vocally critical of the Brunk purchase, which appeared to him corrupt, and he pledged that when he was elected, he would have the matter investigated and have any violators of the law put in jail. He was elected, and he got from the legislature an increased appropriation to the governor's office to fund the investigation. He put Clyde Duffy, a highly reputable anti-Langer lawyer who later ran against Langer for the Senate, in charge. He also hired James Mulloy, who appears unfavorably elsewhere in this narrative, as an investigator. Both Duffy and Mulloy testified at the later Senate hearings, as did a third Moses investigator, A. J. Klaudt. All three apparently were being paid by the governor's office, using state funds, when they testified. In spite of the money that was spent, nobody was prosecuted on bond deals or went to jail.

When Duffy testified to the Senate committee, he conceded that no evidence existed that Langer had intervened with any of the local governments that dealt with Brewer, and no evidence existed that Langer profited from any of Brewer's transactions. He also testified that the local counties, school districts, and cities benefitted a great deal financially by the Brewer-managed refinancing and from the lower interest rates on their debt, bonded and otherwise, that resulted from it. Those debts were charged with interest at about 7 percent, and, through Brewer, were refinanced at about 4 percent, a significant saving. He said that all of the county officials said that they had not discussed the refunding with Langer.

Duffy testified that he was not a financial expert and that he paid no attention to whether bonds were callable or not (it should be obvious, as Brunk pointed out, that no one would pay a premium for a bond that could be called in at face value at any time). He also admitted that he assumed that the bonds kept the same price at which they were bought, which any investor will recognize as highly improbable (after all, interest rates fluctuate, and prices react in the opposite direction, and other factors affect bond prices, too.) He did not check market values when they were resold. Of course, bond prices fluctuate over time. Mulloy, who had a different agenda from that of Duffy, admitted he knew nothing about the Brunk matter or the bond transactions.

In his testimony before the Senate Committee on Privileges and Elections in 1941, Brunk spoke of his great admiration for Langer because Langer, alone, of all the politicians he had known, kept his promises and cut appropriations (and expenditures) of the state by 52 percent, a record unmatched anywhere in the United States. He said, "I said more than once that a man who has the simple courage to cut the general appropriations 51 percent in one session of the legislature, and kick out 3 employees out of 5 would be needed in Washington. Nobody has told me why it would be in Brewer's advantage or mine to have him out of the governor's chair and in Washington."

In all the testimony in the trials, the Senate investigation and hearing, there was not one word of testimony that there was any connection between the Brunk land purchase and the Brewer-Brunk refinancing. Innuendo abounded, but no proof. The truth is that every one of the bond issues in question was offered for sale to the general public or any bond broker, and every offering was widely advertised in official newspapers for competitive bids according to law, subject to public bidding by anyone, and the highest bidder got the bond.

In other words, the evidence shows a long-term and very successful refinancing effort, not very profitable to the sponsors in view of all the risks they took, which saved North Dakotans a lot of money, on the one hand, and a private land transaction between Langer, in financial trouble, and his old friend Brunk, on the other hand. There was no proof that one was connected with the other.

Mexican Land and Railroad Taxes [307]

Bill Langer was also accused of lowering the taxes on the Great Northern railroad in 1938 because a lobbyist for the railroad, Thomas V. Sullivan, had bought worthless stock in a Mexican land venture from him for twenty-five thousand dollars in May 1937. This story, too, is full of holes. Sullivan was another long-time friend and associate of Bill Langer. Both were liberal lawyers in the years of the founding of the Nonpartisan League—the latter part of the 1910-20 decade. Sullivan was a law partner of James Manahan, a Minnesota lawyer who represented the early Nonpartisan League in North Dakota and Minnesota and also represented labor unions throughout the country. Sullivan later said they probably represented more labor unions that any law firm in the United States. In his autobiography, *Trials of a Lawyer*, Manahan describes Sullivan as "a brilliant young attorney very popular in labor circles."[308]

During some of the years, 1916–20, when Langer was campaigning for and winning the post of attorney general of North Dakota, Sullivan ran for attorney general in Minnesota three times, as the candidate of the Nonpartisan League or the Farmer-Labor party. He lost each time but came within a few hundred votes of winning on one occasion, the June 1918 primary when he ran against the incumbent, Clifford L. Hilton. Sullivan carried Jackson County, where he was one of the League lawyers defending A. C. Townley and Joseph Gilbert, chief League organizer, in the most bitterly contested political prosecution of many in Minnesota, tried only a few months earlier. Hilton's trial assistant had led the prosecution, and Hilton's campaign literature charged Sullivan with being "one of the Nonpartisan attorneys . . . . who has been prominent in defending the leaders charged with disloyalty" and said that there was no hint of disloyalty in Hilton. Langer spoke in Minnesota for Sullivan and Sullivan campaigned for Langer in North Dakota.[309] Both of them made many speeches for the League in North Dakota during the League's early organizational years, 1915 to 1920. Sullivan was one of the defense attorneys in at least five of the criminal prosecutions of A. C. Townley and other League organizers in Minnesota during and after World War I. The prosecutions were brought under a Minnesota statute passed in the war hysteria of 1917, under which a state agency, the Commission of Public Safety, was set up with no restrictions on it, funded with a million dollars, and given unlimited powers to spy on and to prosecute anyone who said or did anything the commission thought might interfere with enlistments. Townley and the chief League organizer, Gilbert, were prosecuted in Jackson County, Minnesota, for conspiracy to violate the act by making speeches which included such treasonous suggestions as that if boys were to be drafted, wealth should also be drafted. Townley had never been in the county where he was prosecuted.

In spite of a brilliant and prophetic dissent by United State Supreme Court Justice Cardozo, the law was upheld for constitutionality in another case involving Gilbert,[310] to the everlasting shame of the Minnesota judiciary and the Supreme Court of the United States, but years later a very similar law was declared unconstitutional by the United States Supreme Court in *Pennsylvania v. Nelson*, 350 US 497 (1956). Townley and Gilbert were convicted and each served the maximum sentence, ninety days in jail, and Gilbert served another year on a similar conviction in another county on a conviction in a similar case.

Sullivan was not only one of their attorneys, but also a witness, in the Jackson County case, the most famous (or infamous) of the Red Scare trials in Minnesota. There were dozens of them, and Sullivan was one of the attorneys in several of them. The lawyers in those cases, including Sullivan, were willing to face hostile judges and public opinion in one of the worst periods in United States history for attacks on constitutional rights until the recent events of the twenty-first century.

The Langer-Lemke feud and the Sullivan-Lemke connection[311]

William Lemke, later a longtime congressman from North Dakota, had a long-running feud with Langer, arising from their participation in a purchase of a huge tract of land in Mexico, about 1907. Lemke and Langer formed the Land Finance Company and Langer was one of many investors in the stock of the company. After a successful Mexican revolution, however, much of the land was expropriated, without compensation, by the new Mexican government.

Meanwhile, during the revolution, Langer and Lemke were in Mexico and were caught up in a situation where rebels were approaching the ranch, and Langer urged Lemke to head for the border with him. Lemke refused. After some delay, Langer left and caught a ride with two soldiers, who, as it turned out, were deserters being sought by the rebels. All three men were captured and sentenced to death by firing squad the next day. Langer managed to get in touch with United States authorities, who intervened just hours before the firing squad was to do its work, so he managed to get back to the border.

Langer always blamed Lemke for his brush with death, and Lemke criticized Langer for leaving him on the ranch, which was fired on, but Lemke was not harmed. After the revolution, claims were filed for compensation, and the land continued to be used by the owners but at little or no profit.

The people involved in the land incident had complicated ties: Tom Sullivan's wife had been secretary for William Lemke when he was attorney general of North Dakota (1921) and head attorney for the League, and Sullivan told the Senate investigators she always believed that the claims would be paid and the land venture would be highly profitable. So did he. She urged him to buy stock in the venture, even after the expropriation. The friendship between Langer and Sullivan continued in later years, as did Sullivan's even stronger friendship with Lemke. After Sullivan became attorney for the Chicago school system, he consulted with Langer about school problems, including attempts to censor school libraries. Both of them knew that there had been an uproar in North Dakota in the early League years over claims that the League advocated "free love," when someone found a book in the state library that mentioned those two words. The book had never been circulated to a school or student, but that made no difference to the critics.

Sullivan, with his experience of representing labor, was later hired by the Great Northern railroad to attempt to improve the railroad's deplorable labor relations with its unions. His retainer, out of which he paid all his expenses, was twenty thousand dollars per year, for part-time help on labor matters. While his friendship with Langer continued and he made contributions to the campaigns of Langer, Lemke, Nye, and Frazier (he did not contribute to Langer when he ran against Frazier in 1940), he took no other part in railroad affairs in North Dakota politics, except once. When Langer was governor, Sullivan was asked by the railroad management to talk to Langer about the railroad's claim that its profits on iron ore freight in Minnesota should not be considered in North Dakota assessments for taxes. Sullivan said he got nowhere with Langer, and the system of taxation was not changed during the Langer administration.

When Langer was indicted for conspiracy in 1934, Sullivan offered to come to North Dakota to help defend him (as Brunk had also done), but Langer chose to be defended by North Dakota lawyers. Because of their friendship, Sullivan knew that Langer was hard-pressed financially after the conviction in 1935 and his inability to earn money by practicing law until after the reversal of the conviction by the Court of Appeals. During a visit in 1936, Langer and Sullivan argued over Lemke, who was making his futile run for the presidency on the Union Party ticket, with Sullivan defending Lemke against Langer's criticism. Lemke and Langer were not speaking to each other at the time. During the course of the argument, Sullivan said he believed in the Mexican project and offered to buy Langer's stock. He did buy it, for twenty-five thousand dollars.

At the Senate hearing, Sullivan was not called as a witness against Langer. There was ample reason for the prosecutors not to call him. His lengthy statement had been taken by the Senate investigators, and it showed that he had always thought, and still did when he was interviewed in 1941, that the stock was a good investment. He said that Congress and the State Department were then putting pressure on the Mexican government to compensate owners of expropriated property, and they expected success, which would result in a very high return on his investment. He said his investment was the only one he had ever made that his wife approved of. He added that with the exception of the one conversation with Langer, his connection with the Great Northern had nothing to do with taxes, but only with labor relations.

In the Senate hearings, there was no dispute over the background of Sullivan or the relationship with Langer or Lemke, for that matter. The prosecutors only attempted to prove that the Mexican land stock was worthless, with Frazier and Lemke so testifying. However, Langer showed that Lemke had recently signed a claim for compensation from Mexico that showed a much higher value—in fact, three times as much as Sullivan paid for it—for the stock, and Langer's father's estate had valued the property at a higher figure, also. Sullivan testified that he (and his wife) thought the stock purchase was a good investment when made, and they still thought so at the time of the testimony, shortly before the Senate hearing. None of this appeared in the summary of testimony prepared by the Senate investigators.

What about the claim that Great Northern taxes were reduced? A little background will be helpful. As stated above, the sale of land stock to Sullivan was in May 1937, and when the state Board of Equalization met in August 1937, it raised the Great Northern assessed valuation seven hundred thousand dollars more than what Judge Miller had fixed as the valuation in 1936. A year later, in August 1938, the Great Northern assessment was lowered—but so were the assessments on the other railroads in the state—Northern Pacific, Soo Line, and Chicago, Milwaukee. That lowering was compelled by a series of court decisions in the Supreme Court of the United States; and similar or greater reductions were also made that same year in all the other states in which the same railroads did business.

During the early 1930s, the North Dakota railroads, led by the Great Northern, had adopted the cynical policy of paying only about a third to a half of their North Dakota taxes on time and suing to have the balance canceled on some claim or another that the assessment was improper. The lawsuits were usually heard by Judge Andrew Miller, the same Judge Miller who presided at the first Langer trials and who had been an enemy of Langer for two decades. He usually decided them in favor of the railroads.

One of the cases, *Great Northern v. Weeks* (Weeks was the North Dakota Tax Commissioner), was appealed to the United States Supreme Court.[312] The opinion was written by Justice Pierce Butler, who had been attorney for the Great Northern and other railroads before he was appointed to the high court. Three more of the justices had also been railroad lawyers. Langer described the opinion as giving no reason for ordering about a 10 percent reduction in the tax, and he was basically right. What it came down to was that the railroads were not making money, so they claimed their taxes had to come down. At the same time, of course, a time when about one-fourth to one-half of North Dakota people were on relief, no such rationale was applied to the real estate taxes on farmers or anyone else. Nevertheless, the states had to conform to the law as declared by the Supreme Court.

One effect of the railroads' refusal to pay nearly half of the taxes was that many local subdivisions, as well as the state, had to borrow money to keep going while the railroad tax cases worked their way through the court system. The railroads no doubt knew about the teachers who were not being paid, except with warrants or scrip of doubtful value, and the other problems existing in North Dakota.

Another factor in the Board of Equalization's decision to make a reduction in all railroad taxes in 1938 was that the preceding Welford administration had made a settlement with the railroads which purported to commit the state to the reduction—an unenforceable promise under the North Dakota constitution, since one legislature cannot bind the next one.

Bill Langer could not act by himself on railroad tax assessments. The Board of Equalization which made the decisions on assessments and valuations consisted of the governor, Langer; the attorney general, P. O. Sathre; and later Alvin C. Strutz; State Treasurer Berta Baker; Commissioner of Agriculture and Labor John Hagan; and Tax Commissioner Owen T. Owen, and later John Gray. Of these, Sathre at that time opposed Langer as did Gray. While the others had been on the same ticket as Langer, he certainly could not dominate them. Anyone who knew the steel-willed Berta Baker and Al Strutz, as well as Owen and Hagan, would consider ludicrous the assumption of the Senate investigators that Langer controlled the actions of the Board of Equalization.

The reduction the Great Northern received in 1938 was about fifty-eight thousand dollars in taxes paid. The railroad also agreed not to litigate that tax and drop proceedings contesting the tax of the prior year. The other railroads received similar reductions, averaging about 3 percent, slightly more than the Great Northern received. It should have been obvious to even the most bitter of Langer's enemies that the reductions were compelled by adverse prior court decisions. A private real estate deal between Governor Langer and a long-time friend, more than a year earlier, had nothing to do with the decision.

Chapter 8
The Senate Hearings and Decision
November 3, 1941–March 27, 1942

"As a matter of fact, this record, taken by these investigators, it seems to me from the start that the investigators went out there with the idea, 'Now we have got to get something on this fellow.'"
—Senator Tom Connally, Senate committee member, 1941 [313]

The Senate Committee Hearings and Debate

The Senate committee hearing, including summations by attorneys for both sides, November 3–18, 1941, and was different from the previous one-sided proceedings. The senators on the committee (including Senator Gerald P. Nye of North Dakota, an avowed enemy of Langer) heard the actual witnesses who had been brought to Washington, D.C., by both sides to testify. They heard Mulloy admit he had confessed to being a criminal and Verry admit his involvement in the suit that the Park River State Bank brought against him that ended up in the North Dakota Supreme Court. Most of all, they had the chance to see how a good lawyer, Francis Murphy, could destroy the contentions of the prosecution by his grasp of the facts and the mastery of the record made by the investigators, biased as it was. They heard the witnesses brought by Langer and Murphy tell what Mulloy was really like and what his motives were and how he had twisted the facts. The senators saw for themselves how effectively Francis Murphy and Langer and his records were able to trip up the prosecution's inferior lawyers. In addition to having the better lawyer and the facts on his side, Langer had one weapon that his detractors did not know about: he had every record of all thirty-seven years of his law practice. During those years, interrupted as they were by years of public service, he had built up more than ten thousand files and had preserved every one of them. So every time a witness referred to some client or lawsuit, even if it were a minor case tried thirty-five years earlier, Langer had his record to refute the accusations.

Any impartial reader would agree that the defense had much the better of the hearing. But the hearing was not attended full-time by all the committee members, some of whom came and went, including Senator Nye. Nor do we know what Senator Nye said to other members when they talked to each other outside of the committee hearing.

Witnesses called by those who wanted Langer unseated and those called by the committee itself were Usher L. Burdick, James Mulloy, C. R. Verry, Gale Wyman, Clyde Duffy, V. W. Brewer, Fred B. Ingstad, Andrew R. Feist, A. J. Klaudt, and the three appraisers referred to in chapter seven: Ellis B. Southworth, Erool Walley, and True D. Morse. Francis Murphy cross-examined them all, usually to the considerable advantage of the defense, which made many of its points through them as preceding chapters have shown. The prosecution also included a written statement of Judge A. Lee Wyman.

The defense called R. M. Stangler, J. M. Hanley, Francis Murphy, Usher L. Burdick, and Langer himself, who testified at considerable length, telling about his entire professional and political career (in the opinion of this author, probably the best oral history of North Dakota politics and law in the literature of the state). The defense also presented a statement by Alvin C. Strutz and an affidavit of Ed Sinkler, one of the attorneys for the defense in the first conspiracy case. A statement of Senator John Gurney of South Dakota was also read, praising Judge Wyman.[314]

One unusual aspect of the hearing was that both sides agreed that the testimony ("affidavits"), cited herein as Witness Books, taken by the investigators could be used as evidence and could be considered by the committee without being offered in evidence. Witnesses who testified for the "proponents," Verry and his committee and Mulloy, were often ineffectual, reluctant, and ironically helpful to Langer under cross-examination by Murphy. Robert Stangler, the nonpolitical and highly respected former manager of the Bank of North Dakota, and then manager of the State Mill, refuted the charges relating to Langer and the Bank of North Dakota. He pointed out that the bank had to keep funds on hand to run the state government, that its deposits varied during the year, and that the bank had purchased more local bonds and warrants than good banking practice would allow but it still could not buy all that was offered. In plain terms, he totally disproved any charges that the Bank of North Dakota assisted Brewer in his refinancing effort, and showed that the

Bank of North Dakota had done all it could, and probably more than it should have, to assist local governments but still could not buy all their instruments of debt. He showed that it only exchanged older bonds for newer ones offered by Brewer, without paying any commission and flatly stated that every purchase and exchange met with his approval and was not politically motivated. His testimony clearly showed that the critics of the bank did not understand municipal finance or the benefits and necessity of the refinancing, given the times. Usher Burdick testified about the biases and methods of Judge Miller, and many other witnesses, whose testimony has previously been outlined, also supported Langer's defense.

The Committee on Privileges and Elections, chaired now by Senator Theodore Green, who had succeeded Thomas Connally, submitted a majority report to the Senate on January 29. Signed by thirteen senators and presented by Senator Scott Lucas, the report stated, "Your committee finds that the charges of moral turpitude have been proven beyond all reasonable doubt and recommends that the integrity of the United States senate be upheld by denying William Langer the right to be a United States senator."[315] A minority report, filed by two members of the committee—Senators Orrice Murdock and Ellison D. Smith—followed on March 5. In opposing the majority's recommendation to unseat Langer, the two senators in the minority stated: "The petitioners have evidently adopted the view that if you say enough things about an individual and extend the period of time sufficiently long and use sufficiently abusive phraseology, those who will try the case will give up in exhaustion. To find Senator Langer guilty on the charges referred against him requires that we indulge in presumptive imagination, which we do not feel we are justified in and therefore refuse to do. We therefore recommend that the proceedings against Senator Langer be dismissed."[316] The full Senate reviewed the reports and debated Langer's fate from March 9 through March 27, 1942. Author Agnes Geelan reported details of the debate in her admirable book, *The Dakota Maverick*, and those will not be repeated here.[317] She mentioned one incident that was part of the Senate debate, however, that was not included in the committee testimony at all—the discovery of money and stock in a dresser drawer in the governor's mansion—but she does not complete the story. The discovery was made by two state penitentiary trusties. It consisted of three hundred thousand dollars worth of corporate stock and about two thousand dollars in cash. The trusties took some of the money, and one of them hired a taxi to take him to Fargo (about two hundred miles), an act which caused some comment and resulted in the arrest of the two men. The press and the enemies of Langer proclaimed that the stock and the money must be the proceeds of kickbacks or other nefarious activity on his part.

The charge about the money and stock was one of the early charges in the affidavits to the Senate, but the committee early on decided to withdraw it for lack of proof of misconduct. Nevertheless, the investigators blithely reported on it anyway, and it was discussed on the Senate floor in defiance of orderly procedure. What was not mentioned was that the stock, and presumably the money, belonged to Mrs. Langer. She had inherited it from her mother, the widow of a successful and famous architect in New York City who had designed the Metropolitan Opera building and many buildings at Columbia University. The stock was for shares of Pond's Extracts, Inc., and the inheritance could easily have been checked with probate records in New York, or corporate records or stockholder records, if it were not more convenient to let imagination run rampant, so as to imply wrongdoing.

Considering the kind of reports they were given to read, perhaps the committee members can be excused for believing the conclusions recommended by the investigators. This was wartime—war having been declared after the attack on Pearl Harbor the previous December—and senators had other things on their minds. Perhaps they should not have been expected to read and scrutinize nearly 4,000 pages of "affidavits" (in Witness Books) or the 850 pages of testimony taken by the committee itself, or even a highly slanted 71-page summary prepared by (or for) the committee. So the senators who were not on the committee may have even more excuse for not following the testimony in the case and relying only on the slanted reports. The debates, however, were revealing.

Following the debate, the Senate declared on March 27, 1942, by a vote of fifty-seven to thirty-two, to seat Bill Langer permanently, overturning the recommendation by thirteen members of the committee who read and heard direct testimony. Langer was a member of the United States Senate until his death, nearly two decades later, to the infinite distress of the enemies he had acquired in nearly forty years of public life and service. They made a kind of martyr of him, and he got some of the respect of a martyr while he was still alive.

In his thesis, Robert Horne compiled the cost of the Senate investigation, gleaned from the *Congressional Record*, to be $18,586, plus some contingent expenses not listed (about $227,000 in 2002).[318] *Time Magazine*, summarizing the Senate fiasco, estimated that the number of hours spent on the Langer investigation and hearings amounted to more than six thousand hours, including the time of the senators, who then, as now, were paid more than the average citizen. The total, in today's dollars, would surely run into the millions.

The Secret Roles of Senator Nye and Congressman Lemke

Senator Gerald P. Nye was a member of the Senate Committee on Privileges and Elections, and although the record says he took no part in its activities, the fact is that he sat as a member of the committee during the first five of the twelve days of hearings. He also steadfastly maintained, in speeches and the public press, that he had nothing to do with the Senate investigation of Langer or the hearings that were held. However, testimony by "affidavit" of Howard Fuller shows otherwise.[319]

Fuller handled the case in the North Dakota Supreme Court that unseated Langer as governor, and he was the lawyer first consulted by James Mulloy, the one who told Mulloy that the statute of limitations had run on his part in his story. His "affidavit" in the Senate records disclosed Senator Nye's participation in the Mulloy complaint to the Senate.

Before Mulloy came to see him, Fuller received a phone call from Senator Nye saying that someone would be contacting him about filing charges to unseat Langer and that Nye did not want to appear to have any connection with it, officially or otherwise. Nye said Fuller should make sure that there was some merit to the charges before anything was done about them and that he should let Nye know what developed and what he thought about it. So Nye was in on Mulloy's activities before any charges were filed or even put in writing.

Fuller further said that Mulloy was always accompanied by Charlie Joyce (who was a Lemke henchman), and that although neither Mulloy nor Joyce asked for money that day, the next day Joyce came back and asked for help to pay their hotel bill. Fuller reported that he gave him fifty dollars for that purpose, which he included as an expense item in his bill to Nye and Nye repaid him for it. He was not asked, and did not specify, whether he was paid for the time he spent with Mulloy, and if so, by whom. His meeting with Mulloy extended over at least part of two or more days. It is also worth noting that when Nye told Fuller that someone would consult him, he also authorized Fuller to reimburse the people and bill Nye the cost of their return trip to their homes.

Fuller also made clear that he had lived and practiced law in South Dakota and knew Judge Wyman and Leedom, and was positive that nobody could influence Judge Wyman, although he thought

Langer might believe it could be done. Fuller also thought that Mulloy's story put the worst interpretation on facts that were not necessarily incriminating and that he would be creating a scandal on the federal court system that was not deserved. He said he recommended as strongly as he could that Mulloy forget the whole thing and thought he would never hear any more of it.

A hotel keeper in Fargo, C. P. Stone, who was Mulloy's former brother-in-law and still on friendly terms with him, said that Mulloy had told him in December 1940 that he (Mulloy) had been promised five thousand dollars from Senator Nye for giving his affidavit to the Senate. Mulloy filed the affidavit at the end of the month, but there is no indication that he ever received any such sum.

It is also of interest that Congressman Lemke, another Langer foe who had for years campaigned on the theme that Langer received "kickbacks," not only admitted to the investigators in 1940 that he had no proof of such kickbacks but also admitted that he had contributed some "small amount" to the expenses of "getting the affidavits." The amount was fifty dollars. He later retracted this statement and said the fifty dollars was paid for something Mulloy did in South Dakota. If true, it was probably expense money for the trip Mulloy made there to talk with people who were later interviewed by the Senate investigators at his suggestion.

In 1941, after Lemke had been telling voters for several campaigns that there were kickbacks, Lemke was asked if he knew of "any kickbacks, so called, that Mr. Langer personally received?" He responded, "I do not, not of my own knowledge."[320] This statement provides a remarkable contrast to a report in the *Bismarck Tribune* of December 31, 1938, which quotes Lemke as demanding that action be taken to "restore money lost to the state through the kick-backs, kick-ins, and questionable transactions in securities" of the outgoing administration. Other of his accusations of kickbacks through the years abound, all contradicted by his sworn Senate testimony quoted above.[321]

The Role of the of "The Coalition" and Governor Moses

The attack in the United States Senate was not financed privately. In large part, it was financed first by the North Dakota taxpayers and finally by the United States taxpayers. John Moses was governor of North Dakota for three terms, elected in 1938, 1940, and 1942, on a "Coalition" ticket, filing in the Democratic column. He had previously been a Republican and had earlier supported Langer. The convention that endorsed him in 1940 was described by the *Leader* as "a small clique, headed by the *Fargo Forum*, which is and always has been overly opposed to the Nonpartisan League."[322] Whatever else they may have been, they were united in a determination to "get Langer" and have the taxpayers pay for it. They did not get Langer, but the taxpayers paid including the salaries of some of those who gave testimony at the Senate hearings, like James Mulloy, who was on the payroll of the governor's office when he testified in Washington, D.C.[323]

In 1939, the Nonpartisan League and its opponents each controlled one house of the legislature. Governor John Moses, in his first inaugural speech, asked for audits of the State Mill and Elevator, the Bank of North Dakota, the Hail Insurance Department, Highway Department, Workmen's Compensation Bureau, Land Department, a bonding fund, and "possibly others, especially the State Hospital," and said that if the charges "are false, the individuals charged are entitled to vindication. If the charges are true, the people of North Dakota are entitled to have that fact established and the offenders prosecuted." According to news reports, Moses requested fifty thousand dollars for the investigation ($647,000 in 2002 dollars).[324] The House voted to meet his request, but the Senate reduced the amount to twenty-five hundred dollars, which the anti-Langer people voted down entirely rather than accept the smaller amount. However, Moses got his office appropriation raised, so that he had eight thousand dollars, instead of the two thousand dollars Langer had been allocated for the governor's contingency fund. According to the *Leader*, additional amounts were added to the Bank Examiner's office and other offices so that Moses had a total of fifteen thousand dollars to spend. He hired Clyde Duffy, a prominent Devils Lake attorney, to be the special examining commissioner, at a salary of fifty dollars per day (more than six hundred dollars a day in 2002); A. J. Klaudt, an accountant (salary unknown); and James Mulloy, to be an investigator, at a salary of one hundred fifty dollars a month. Mulloy later furnished Senate investigators Hood and Smith with much of their information, suggested people they should interview, and accompanied them to many of their interviews. During the Senate committee hearings, Mulloy even sat with the "attorneys for the petitioners," until Senator Connally complained that he had no business sitting there. All three were apparently being paid by the state when they testified as witnesses in the Senate hearings in 1941.

When the 1941 campaign came along and Governor Moses won again (though the League again controlled most other offices), he wanted more investigations and asked for more money—thirty-five thousand dollars to appoint a special examining commissioner to investigate any public official the governor named. Senate Bill 166, passed by the 1941 legislature, gave him fifteen thousand dollars under a new law that authorized the governor unlimited power to spend it investigating any department (but only Nonpartisan League–controlled departments were separately named) and to order lawsuits and other legal proceedings and to give witnesses immunity from prosecution. The governor could authorize expenditures, without any restrictions, and could grant immunity to any witness who claimed the privilege against self-incrimination. The *Leader* reported that Moses had squandered thousands in his last term and got no convictions, and now wanted to conduct another "fishing expedition," and ended by saying "we don't need a dictator." It added that not even the legislature can grant immunity.[325] The authority was certainly a violation of the basic doctrine of separation of powers between administration, legislature, and the courts. Indeed, District Court Judge Fred Jansonius later ruled that one of Moses' proceedings violated the state law specifying that only the attorney general and state's attorneys could represent the state government in court. His ruling did not, however, specifically decide that the whole witch hunt was unconstitutional.[326]

All in all, the fifty thousand dollars or more of state money (equivalent to $612,000 in 2002) produced misdemeanor prosecutions of James McGurren, highway commissioner, and an assistant of his, both of whom were acquitted, and a verdict in favor of the Reverend Clarence Van Horne, registrar of the Motor Vehicle Department, who was sued in a civil case claiming misuse of money. It also produced removal (but no criminal charges) by Governor Moses of two members of the State Board of Administration, which governed the state colleges and institutions.

There was no prosecution of Langer or any other elected official, which was, of course, the real purpose of all the time and money spent. The results of all the investigations were turned over to Hood and Smith, however, and they put what is now called their own "spin" on the investigations and delivered them to their bosses in the United States Senate, where other huge amounts of scarce money were spent in the attempt, again unsuccessful, to "get Langer." If persistence is a virtue, the "Coalition" certainly had it. And the taxpayers, state and national, paid the price. Though no successful prosecutions resulted and no convictions, Governor Moses did not keep his promise to acknowledge "vindication" for those wrongfully accused.

Conclusion

The foregoing chapters answer many of the questions that were raised about Bill Langer and his record during his lifetime. But a few questions have persisted, even after his death. Who started the prosecution, or persecution, depending on one's point of view? Why, after the only guilty verdict, which came in the tainted first trial, was reversed for insufficiency of the evidence, did the United States Attorney persist in trying the case again? And what motivated both the tenacious persecution and the even greater resistance to the legal tyranny?

After the reversal of the first trial's guilty verdict, most prosecutors would have said the decision had been made and would have gone on to other duties. But here, not only was the case tried a second time but a third time as well. I have been a prosecutor, state and federal, and defended many criminal trials, and such grim tenacity is unknown in my experience. Why did the Senate committee vote to unseat Langer and why did a substantial minority of the Senate do the same, in the face of the overwhelming evidence in the files to disprove the allegations against him?

Lawyers and a few historians who know something about law and law enforcement have wondered if the impetus came from the Roosevelt administration. Others have speculated that the push came from Harry Hopkins. The answer, I have found, lies closer to home. The persistence was due to the animosity of Judge Andrew Miller, U.S. Marshal Gunvaldson, and the prosecutorial zeal (and perhaps political ambition) of U.S. Attorney P. W. Lanier, Sr.

There are passing references in the record to a complaint by an A. M. Anderson of Valley City and to the president of an organization of civil engineers, but nothing further is written about them. As previously shown, the Anderson letter was indeed the beginning, but that letter, in itself, does not hint at the full prosecution, which came mostly because of the efforts of some prominent Democrats to get patronage from the nonpolitical State Relief Committee.

The suggestion has also been made that a friend of Eleanor Roosevelt, Lorena Hickok, who made a fact-finding trip through the country looking at "relief" (now called welfare) problems, suggested fraud in North Dakota. But while she describes the desperate situation in North Dakota in the book written from her notes, *One Third of a Nation*, there is no suggestion of fraud in the state, where she spent about a week. Nor is there any such suggestion in her letters to Harry Hopkins, her superior in the Interior Department.[327]

The U.S. attorney's records show that the Department of the Interior, headed by Harold Ickes, received complaints of lack of patronage from North Dakota Democratic party officials. When Harry Hopkins, in charge of relief efforts, heard of the solicitation of *Leader* subscriptions in the State Relief Office, he ordered Langer removed from the relief program and then ordered an investigation made by Interior staff members, not the FBI, as was often assumed. No indication exists that they offered Langer any opportunity to reply to the charges before they removed him from his nominal position as a conduit for funding requests and for transmittal of checks for relief funds. It is safe to say that Hopkins and Ickes started the ball rolling, and once the Interior's investigation was completed, they turned the results over to the district U.S. Attorney to decide on prosecution or further investigation. That procedure is standard and mandated. Thus, it was he, P. W. Lanier, Sr., who picked up the ball and ran with it.[328] He decided to prosecute the first, second and third conspiracy cases, and he decided, with a push from Judge Miller, to instigate and prosecute the perjury case. Judge Miller may have nudged him on the other prosecutions also. Lanier had run for Congress as a Democrat in 1932 and was appointed United States Attorney when the new Roosevelt administration was inaugurated in 1933. He later ran for the United States Senate, and may, therefore, be suspected of some political motive. In any case, he chose to prosecute and prosecute repeatedly.

Lanier immediately criticized the incompleteness of the Interior investigation. There are letters in the file from the investigators, apologizing for being unable to get witnesses to say that they had been pressured to contribute to the *Leader*. There are also letters from Lanier to the Department of Justice complaining that the Interior Department investigators were incompetent, along with a request to have the Federal Bureau of Investigation take over the case. The

Bureau, which had a policy not to handle cases worked on by other agencies, declined.

The perjury case and its prosecution was a particular surprise to the Justice Department. On October 19, 1935, Assistant Attorney General Keenan wrote to Lanier that they had read in the press that Langer and other defendants had been indicted for perjury and asked him to send a copy of the indictment and advise them of the facts on which it was based. In his reply to the Justice Department, four days later, Lanier revealed the complicity of Judge Miller in this unprecedented violation of freedom of speech. He wrote, "Judge Miller instructed me to investigate this matter before the Grand Jury, and if under the law and the facts in my opinion an indictment for perjury would lie, to present the case to the Grand Jury."[329]

Of course, Judge Miller made it easy by calling the grand jury into session. In the meantime, Lanier had all sixty members of the jury panel for the first trial interviewed and a statement taken from every member of the trial jury, except one who was out of the state and another who had died, and all of them and all the defense attorneys except J. K. Murray, who drafted the affidavit of prejudice, were called before the grand jury at Fargo.[330] Normally, a district judge would only call grand juries at specified intervals (it was annual intervals then in North Dakota) or when the government lawyers ask for them. It is the U.S. attorney who decides what cases to present to the grand jury. When it came to Langer, both District Judge Miller and United States Attorney Lanier apparently cooperated in having grand juries available often in order to bring in indictments on any suspicion of perjury, or to prosecute for any new claim of misuse of government funds.

Lanier also conveyed his own feelings to the Department of Justice when he reported after the second conspiracy trial, in which there was a hung jury, that he considered the result "a victory for the Government." Since the only results had been to keep Langer out of public office for the last six months of the 1933–34 term of office as governor, prevent him from running for governor or any other office in 1934 or from making a living practicing law for a substantial period of time, we can assume that these were the results the government (as represented by Lanier) was seeking.

Lanier's motivation and the lack of pressure from the Justice Department may also be indicated in a letter he wrote to the Justice Department on October 19, 1934, suggesting a prosecution against Langer for income tax violation be commenced before the general election the next month, in which Mrs. Langer was the League candidate for governor. He said he wanted this action taken because Leaguers were saying that the trials were unfair and the prosecution was a persecution. The Justice Department mildly replied that a prosecution before an election would only add fuel to the persecution argument.[331] If the motivation were not political, what reason could there be for hurrying to obtain a new indictment before the election? There never was a prosecution for income tax violation, even after the Internal Revenue Service investigation that Lanier requested. Langer said the only result was that he got a refund of part of the tax he had paid.

There never was any reason for Langer to pay income tax on his income as governor. He was governor during 1933–34 and 1937 to early January 1939, and it was generally understood in those years that the federal government could not tax state salaries, and the state could not tax federal salaries. It was only decided later by the United States Supreme Court on March 27, 1939, that each had jurisdiction to tax wages paid by the other.[332] It is no wonder that the Internal Revenue Department and the Justice Department had to remind Lanier that he had to get permission from Internal Revenue to file criminal income tax cases, and no such permission to sue for a tax violation by Langer was ever granted, in spite of Lanier's many urgent demands that he be allowed to do so.

After the conviction in the first trial and while the appeal was pending, the press carried a report that someone had suggested executive clemency (presumably a pardon by the president, which is handled through the Justice Department). Lanier's reaction was to write a letter to the attorney general saying that any executive clemency "would bring a reign of terror to North Dakota."[333]

Trial dates were May 22–June 16, 1934; November 1–15, 1935; December 3–6, 1935 (perjury trial); and December 10–25, 1935, and grand juries were in session in Fargo on April 10–13, 1934, in September 1935, October 10–16, 1935 (perjury charge), and apparently at other times also. The expense must have been huge. The decision to spend it was made in North Dakota, not Washington. Even if the Department of Justice had wanted the prosecutions to proceed, it surely would have deferred to the opinion of the local prosecutor if he had decided that the case would be lost and should not proceed or that there was no new evidence to present. My experience as a United States attorney (1954–61) is evidence of that deference. I ran the show in North Dakota my seven years in that position, and no one in Washington ever told me what to do. Though the Department of Justice probably has the power to revoke decisions of U.S. attorneys, they did not during my tenure; in fact, they rarely even made suggestions, unless they were asked. I do not attribute this to any virtues of mine—I simply doubt that the department, under the two administrations I served under, or any other, attempts to dictate to any local prosecutors, who know the situation in their home states better than anyone in a Washington department could know it. As we have seen, they once considered ordering a dismissal of Lanier's final Langer trial before it started, but decided not to make such an order. I am convinced there was no direction from Washington of the Langer prosecutions. Lanier admitted to Francis Murphy that there was no new evidence for the second and third conspiracy trials. All in all, the evidence is overwhelming that it was he who pushed for the multiple trials, and never gave up.

Reading the transcript of the Senate Hearing many years ago, I concluded, as any fair reader must, that Langer had much the better of the argument as to the propriety of the actions for which he was criticized. In other words, he answered and disproved the charges against him. This raises the question: Why did the Senate Committee, in the face of that testimony, vote to recommend that he be unseated, by a vote of thirteen to two? Could it be that there was other evidence, not in the transcript, that was conclusive against Langer? It is true that the parties agreed that the "affidavits" could be considered as evidence by the committee and the Senate. Was there something in those "affidavits" devastating enough to overcome the strong case made by Langer's defense?

I did not have the time to solve those questions then, nor did I have access to the records of the Senate. But later I had the time and have located the records of the Senate (copies in the Chester Fritz Library in Grand Forks, North Dakota), records of the Clerk of United States District Court and the records of the United States attorney (in the National Archives–Central Plains Region, Kansas City, Missouri), records of the Interior Department (in the Roosevelt Library in Hyde Park, New York), and records of the Department of Justice (in the National Archives, Washington, D.C.). Langer's own voluminous records in the Chester Fritz Library of the University of North Dakota contain material of value, including transcripts of three of the four trials. I made summaries of the testimony in the Senate hearing, the records of the clerk and United States Attorney Lanier, the transcript, and the Witness Books taken by the Senate investigators, and have consulted some of Langer's records and old newspaper files (principally, the *Leader*, *Fargo Forum* and *Bismarck Tribune*). This research has provided answers that satisfy me and will, I believe, satisfy readers as well. One answer is that my original impression is correct. Langer did answer and disprove the charges against him. The Witness Books are even more strongly in his favor than the testimony before the Senate committee, in spite of shameful efforts to slant the investigation against him.

Why, then, did so many in the Senate vote against him? The answer is that Sam Hood and Elbert Smith not only slanted their investigation, they also shamefully misrepresented the results in their report, omitted much evidence favorable to Langer, and falsified much of the record they, themselves, had made. Fortunately, Langer had the facts in his favor, a superior attorney, and he prevailed in the end.

When the Senate voted against unseating Langer, the majority of the voters of North Dakota were exultant. The daily press, predictably, took a sour attitude, repeating the falsehood that the voters had not known about the issues until the Senate aired them and asserting that the Senate had failed in its duty. Bill Langer himself was as unrepentant and combative as usual. After waiting until all the Senate's bills for the abortive proceeding had been paid and the entire matter closed, on October 19, 1942, he put out in a news release and in the *Congressional Record* of that date, a challenge to Governor Moses to debate him. The entire challenge is printed in the *Leader*, on the first page, and an editorial said Moses should "put up or shut up" if he is any man at all.[334]

Langer's challenge sets out that Governor Moses had accused him of illegal actions in connection with bond sales by several counties and had used legislative appropriations to investigate him, but he had now been cleared by the Senate. He then challenged Governor Moses to debate him in the county seats of any three counties in which bonds had been sold, with Governor Moses to choose the counties. I found no record of any response to the challenge. But others understood the significance of what had happened and what the future would have in store.

Frank Vogel, for example, wrote Langer a congratulatory letter as soon as news of the seating reached North Dakota. He wrote:

> Well, old top, ten years is a long time, particularly long when each year brought a new fight in a new way. This is the culminating point toward which your efforts have been laid and you are to be congratulated for never admitting defeat, no matter how gloomy the picture looked . . . I hope that this is the end at least for four and one half years. I hope you will be left alone to

use your talents for the good of thousands of your true friends who stayed with you thru [sic] it all. My God, what loyalty. Many called on me during all the publicity. It did not worry them at all. They had shut their minds completely and did not believe a damn word of it. You owe them much, Bill, and you can now repay in services to them and I know you will.

We are not as young, Bill, as we were when we started this Putsch. But as I look back, I would not have missed it for all the honor, glory and money in the world. God, it has been a splendid fight.

You can do much, Bill. Cultivate even the rascals that fought you in the Senate. You may need their votes on legislation for North Dakota and I know you well enough to know you can have them eating out of your hand.[335]

As usual, Frank Vogel had it right. Bill Langer did repay his supporters and the people of North Dakota for their support. He got the votes of his enemies in the Senate on issues important to North Dakota, and he had them eating out of his hand. And it was a splendid—and ultimately, an unequal—fight between Bill Langer and his enemies.

To add to the tragedy and irony of the whole affair, years later, the Supreme Court of the United States ruled that the Senate had no right at all to punish any elected member of Congress for alleged misconduct which occurred prior to being seated in Congress. In *Powell v. McCormack*, it ruled that there were two possible ways for a House of Congress to exclude an elected member of that House.[336] One was by "exclusion," but this method could not be used to refuse seating to an elected member who met the constitutional requirements of age, citizenship, and residence and was challenged for conduct which occurred prior to the beginning of the term to which he was elected. The other, which required a two-thirds majority vote, was to "expel" a member for conduct after he was seated.[337] Powell was attacked for conduct prior to his election, and the court held that he could not be deprived of his seat, since he admittedly met all the constitutional requirements of age, residence and citizenship.

Langer, of course, met those same requirements, and all of the attacks on him were for conduct or alleged conduct which preceded his election. In fact, the Senate specifically ruled that the case did not involve any allegations of misdeeds after his election. For the same reasons, there was no basis whatever for unseating him. Again, just as in the criminal charges against him in 1934 and 1935, the whole effort was a waste of time and money, and an abuse of his constitutional rights. And yet, some historians and some politicians would have people believe that Langer was the malefactor and his detractors were the righteous custodians of the public welfare.

The larger question, perhaps, is why Langer's detractors hated him so passionately, and why, in contrast, his friends and supporters were so fiercely loyal.

Bill Langer was big, handsome, and intelligent, and he could be charming. The same could be said of many politicians, including many who go nowhere. But what other qualities did Langer have that made him an almost larger-than-life political figure? He had courage. He was afraid of no one. He did a great many things that were unpopular with a majority of the voters, and he endured a lot of ridicule for many of them. But he believed they were important and necessary for the public welfare, and he acted in accordance with his beliefs, popular or not. Some people remembered and were loyal to him through all his troubled career. A few examples may illustrate this.

Langer deserves a place in the history of the Women's Rights movement. He was active in keeping the Equal Rights Amendment alive during the eighteen years he was in the Senate (1941–59). One example comes from early in Langer's career in 1919 when he was serving as attorney general. In his first break with A. C. Townley and the League Executive Committee, he defended Minnie J. Nielson when an attempt was made to prevent her from serving as superintendent of public instruction. As governor he appointed many women to state offices. Early in his Senate years, he asked President Roosevelt to let representatives of the National Women's Party call on him to ask him to make a radio speech and issue a proclamation commemorating the twenty-third anniversary of the proposal of the Equal Rights Amendment (ERA).[338] In many sessions, up to and including the year he died, he introduced the ERA in the Senate, sometimes as the sole sponsor, sometimes with a few others.[339] Every year it was voted down and he was ridiculed for his quixotic actions. He was never afraid of tilting at what others thought of as windmills, but he considered real barriers to equality or justice.

He considered himself a Nonpartisan Leaguer first, a Republican sometimes. In one campaign he was criticized by Republicans for voting with the Republicans only 60 percent of the time. His response was to claim that the charge was a dirty, lowdown, damnable lie—he had voted Republican only 40 percent of the time and he could prove it.[340]

While governor, he filled the state capitol with qualified handicapped employees, and the standing comment of the cruel was that the building was a home for the crippled. He ignored such comments. As senator, he annually produced a list of all the things that could be paid for if the appropriations for the military were reduced. Dozens or hundreds of hospitals could be built, all children could be vaccinated against dreaded diseases (anticipating President Clinton's request), the whole population could be given urinalyses (imagine the ridicule that received from the mindless precursors of talk show pundits of today). He ignored the ridicule and seldom responded to it, or to any other attacks. He seemed to welcome them all.

He often turned attacks into pluses for himself. For example, the *Journal of the American Bar Association* (not a liberal publication, then or now) once had a story about how Langer—whose eyesight was failing due to diabetes, although he was very clever at concealing that fact—had a friend read aloud a British newspaper article that was very critical of Langer. Embarrassed, the friend suggested that he stop reading and throw away the article. Langer objected and had him continue, interrupting often to say, "My, doesn't he write well!" In addition, Langer called in a secretary and instructed her to send a copy of the article to every newspaper in North Dakota, with a note saying, "This is what the British think of Bill Langer."[341] It did no political harm at all. Bill Langer, in fact, did not think much of the British. When Winston Churchill was about to arrive in Boston aboard a British warship, Langer sent a telegram to the Rector of Old North Church, saying "Hang up two lanterns! The British are coming!"[342]

He was persistent in his crusades. Correctly, he thought that corporate, "white collar" crime was seldom adequately punished. Corporations cannot be sent to jail, so they only pay fines when caught and convicted, and many consider this just another cost of doing business. But officers of corporations who order or tolerate the commission of crimes can be, but seldom are, sent to prison.

So, every year, in his capacity as member or chairman of the powerful Judiciary Committee of the Senate, or even when he was a member of the Post Office Committee, any witness who had supervision over federal law enforcement agencies such as the Federal Trade Commission, the Securities and Exchange Commission, Postal Inspectors, or the Fraud Section of the Criminal Division of the Department of Justice, had to go through a dreaded litany of questions. I heard Langer go through the litany once, and did not envy the bureaucrat. It went something like this:

Langer: How many corporate officers has your agency sent to jail this year?

Witness: Senator, we have collected $300,000 in fines from corporations and obtained 15 convictions.

Langer: But how many officers have been sentenced to imprisonment?

Witness: I can check on that and let you know, Senator.

Langer: Don't bother. I have already checked and the answer is "None." Why don't you come right out and admit it instead of beating around the bush?

Witness: Well, I wasn't sure about it.

Langer: I suggest you go back and tell your bosses that they had better do something about this deplorable lack of guts, and see to it that white collar criminals who steal or defraud people of millions of dollars are treated just like burglars or holdup men who do the same. And tell them that I expect to be on this committee next year when your authorization comes up again, and I will ask these same questions of them. If the answers are not more satisfactory than yours are now, somebody might wish they were."[343]

One year he took note of the fact that the Rural Electrification Administration(REA) had made loans in greater volume and amount in other states than they had in North Dakota, and he decided to do something about it. What he did was not what is usually done by legislators—make speeches to an empty chamber or send out a press release. He insisted that the administrator of the REA or his deputy accompany him to meetings in many, if not all, the fifty two counties in North Dakota to discuss rural electrification. The administrator astutely sent his deputy, who had little choice in the matter. I attended two or three of the meetings, which typically began with Langer introducing his guest to the crowd, mostly made up of farmers and their wives who had no electricity on the farms:

Langer: This is Richard Dell, who is the Deputy Administrator of the Rural Electrification Administration, which has been ordered by Congress to electrify rural America. I brought him here to explain to you why it is that Vermont, which is a rural state like North Dakota, is 85% electrified, and North Dakotas has only 15% of its farms electrified.

B The main reason is that North Dakota has a sparse population and Vermont is more concentrated, so it is cheaper there.

Langer: Now, Dick, Congress didn't say anything about putting electricity only on little, tiny farms that only produce a little maple syrup, or enough milk to sell in the next little town. What I want you to do is to tell Mary Schmidt, down here in the second row, who helps her husband farm 500 acres, why it is that people in Vermont have electric lights and milking machines, and she has to go out and milk the cows by hand in the light of a kerosene lantern.

Dell: Well, North Dakota has just one farm to the mile and Vermont has four.

Langer: Dick, that does not help Mary one bit. She still has to crank the cream separator by hand. And over there is Ole Anderson, my old friend and sixteen dollar sucker,[344] who lost half his calf crop last year because he couldn't get an electric pump to replace the windmill that broke down, and his wife, Sigrid, who is still doing her washing with a John Deere portable gasoline engine for power, and cranking the clothes of her six kids through rollers by hand, and hanging them on a line because she can't get any electricity. You tell them why you treat them worse than those little hobby farmers in Vermont!

This kind of discussion continued on for a hour or more, in all or most of the fifty-two counties of North Dakota. Dick Dell promised to go back to Washington and do what he could for North Dakota farmers. From that point on, North Dakota electrification speeded up a lot.

In another campaign Langer was accused by his opponent of being nothing but an errand boy in Washington. His response was that he certainly was the errand boy for the voters of North Dakota, the best they ever had, and he would be proud to keep on running their errands in Washington. He added, "I have never been the errand boy of the big banks, railroads and the oil interests. I let the ROC [Republican Organizing Committee] do the dirty work."[345] As a matter of fact, he and his staff were by far the best at constituent service that North Dakotans ever saw—no other senator or congressman in this writer's lifetime has even come close, not even when they hired some of his former secretaries.

Bill Langer also had a different attitude toward the press than most politicians. Instead of trying to manipulate them, he defied and ridiculed them, and the media reciprocated. The feud began early in his career. For example, while he was still attorney general (1917–21), he was criticized in the press for his strong enforcement of the prohibition laws. His response was that he would continue to do his duty "in spite of the criticism of corruptionists and criminals, including their accessories of the Kept Press."[346]

He decided early that instead of trying to manipulate or cater to the press, as many politicians do, he either ignored them ("just spell my name right"), or ridiculed them. One year he might be making speeches saying he was running a contest to see which newspaper in North Dakota was the biggest liar. If he was in the southeast part of the state, he would say that the *Fargo Forum* had a big lead, and if he was in the northwest, the *Minot Daily News* was ahead, followed closely by the *Bismarck Tribune*. Or he might say that he was running a competition to find the ugliest man in North Dakota, and that Alden McLachlan (of the Associated Press), who was covering all his meetings, was the winner.

He once was invited to speak to the North Dakota Press Association, which included both the daily papers (almost always opposed to him) and the smaller town papers, which were somewhat divided. So he made a speech, saying it was his duty as governor to help out all of the people of North Dakota and that he was willing to help the press too. He said that in order to help the public he had originated a plan to keep them better informed by creating a newspaper, the *Leader*, and having it financed by voluntary contributions of state employees, which was quite successful. Now he was willing to be helpful to the members of the other newspapers, too, so he suggested that they set up a similar plan of financing an increase in their circulation figures.

During one of his campaigns for governor, he pointed out that the private utilities were overcharging the state for electricity. For example, the charge to the state for electricity to the capitol, the penitentiary and the Training (now the State Industrial) School was seven cents a kilowatt. He pledged that he would get it reduced when he was elected. He was elected, and he invited the utility (Montana-Dakota or its predecessor) to contract to sell electricity to the state for one cent per kilowatt. The utility refused. So Langer persuaded the Nonpartisan League-controlled legislature to appropriate money to make a study of the cost of a new plant to generate electricity for the state. The utility still resisted, so Langer saw to it that a study was made. It showed that the state could save a huge amount of money and make electricity for three-fourths of one cent per kilowatt. The bill for the study was paid and bids for construction were about to be prepared. At this point, the utility saw the error of its ways, and agreed to a new ten-year contract, at one cent per kilowatt. The savings, of course, were huge.[347]

Similarly, in another campaign, Langer said it was a shame that North Dakota still had two toll bridges, privately owned, and he would see to it that the tolls were eliminated.[348] One, across the Cannonball River, was easily taken care of, but the other was owned by the Great Northern Railway, across the Yellowstone River, near Williston, and was used by trains as well as cars and trucks. The Great Northern was adamant that it would continue to charge for vehicular traffic.

Langer met with railroad officials, but without result. In fact, the railroad claimed that the bridge was actually on the Montana side of the state boundary and that North Dakota had no jurisdiction over it. This sort of opposition just inspired Bill Langer to further effort. He had engineers from the state highway department make a survey of the site of the bridge, and found that it was in fact (but just barely) on the North Dakota side of the border. Langer arranged for protest meetings in Williston, with farmers testifying about how expensive it was for them to bring their products to market in Williston because of the toll, and the Williston merchants gladly joined the protest movement. The railroad caved in, and the Williston Chamber of Commerce had an appreciation dinner for the Great Northern vice-president Dorety (who was also the attorney who had argued the Great Northern tax cases in the federal courts), who made the ultimate agreement to waive tolls if North Dakota did some of the maintenance on the bridge. All was sweetness and light, at least on the surface, and the farmers paid no more tolls on the bridge.

The greatest of all the actions of Bill Langer that endeared him to many North Dakotans, and antagonized many others, were his moratoriums on farm foreclosures.[349] Coupled with the moratorium was the policy of the Bank of North Dakota in preserving the rights of farmers to repurchase land if they had lost it or turned it over to the bank. That policy was to continue to hold the farm for the former owner or any member of the family, and if someone else offered to buy it, to give the debtor or his family the first chance to buy. It is now more than sixty years since Langer left the governorship, yet there are still people in North Dakota who will say that Bill Langer or Frank Vogel (as manager of the Bank of North Dakota), or both, saved the farm they live on, or made it possible for their grandparents to live and die on the home place.

Frank Vogel, in many speeches, contrasted the experience of the two largest farm real estate lenders (and mortgage holders) in North Dakota during the depression years. One was the Federal Land Bank and the other the Bank of North Dakota. He said that the Federal Land Bank foreclosed and sold the property at the depressed prices of the time, while the Bank of North Dakota did not foreclose unless the farmer abandoned the effort and turned over the property to the Bank, and occasionally foreclosed if the situation was hopeless, but in either case the Bank would continue to hold the land in its own assets, for years if necessary, for resale to the debtor or any member of his family, and if there was an offer from another buyer, the farmer and his family would be given an opportunity to meet the bid. The result of the two differing policies was, he said, that the Federal Land

*A political cartoon by W. H. Shields that appeared in the **Leader** on April 17, 1933, after Governor Langer declared a moratorium on farm foreclosures.*

Bank lost huge amounts of money by their sales at depressed prices, and the Bank of North Dakota lost very little and kept a great many farms for borrowers and their families. Sometimes forbearance pays off.

In other states, when there was unrest over farm foreclosures, there were a few deaths from violence, milk trucks were overturned, judges threatened, and the National Guard called out to protect the bankers and sheriffs in holding foreclosure sales. Langer took office as governor in January 1933, at the height of the wave of anti-foreclosure actions which led to penny auctions at foreclosures in fifteen other states. Farmers joined together to dissuade potential bidders and bought farms at foreclosure sales for a few dollars, all for the benefit of the debtor. There was violence in other states, and seventy-nine penny auctions in fifteen states, but none in North Dakota.[350]

In North Dakota, Governor Langer and, later, the Legislature, forbade foreclosures or allowed them only under very limited circumstances, and Langer called out the National Guard only to **prevent** foreclosures. He was the only governor in the country to do so.[351] Although the Guard was called out by Langer fewer than sixty times, and some of those calls were issued at the request of local sheriffs who were in sympathy with the moratorium (or feared disorder if the foreclosure proceeded), the public pressure behind them probably kept creditors from proceeding with hundreds more foreclosures from occurring at all.[352] And, in spite of the dubious constitutionality of the original action, not one district court judge ever ruled it unconstitutional.[353] Perhaps some local judges also read the election returns.

In 1937 and 1938, North Dakota had a drought and, as a result, the grain crop was low in quality, with shrunken kernels. The Industrial Commission learned from the North Dakota Agricultural College (now North Dakota State University) that the grain made flour of quality equal to that of normal-sized grain. The Industrial Commission, headed by Langer, had the State Mill pay double the Minneapolis price for wheat in 1937 and 50 percent above it in 1938. Minneapolis millers, of necessity, met the price. The cost to the mill was insignificant in comparison to the gain to the farmers. As Bill Langer told the Senate hearing, the North Dakota State Mill paid for itself in one day when it raised the price of wheat. The manager of the mill estimated the saving at $12 million, an enormous sum for 1937, equivalent of $150 million in 2002 dollars.[354] Twenty years earlier, the state sold two million dollars of bonds to finance both the mill and the bank.

Langer really believed that it was part of his job to help his constituents, whether they had been friends or enemies, so much so that his supporters sometimes complained that he did more for his enemies than his friends. Actually, there was probably little or no difference in his willingness to use his powerful position to help any constituent, regardless of prior support, or lack of it.

He was also the most effective campaigner of that, or any other, era of North Dakota history. He was a master of the platform, who might even invite his opponent on the platform and make him highly uncomfortable with fulsome praise, invite him to speak, and then occasionally interrupt with more praise or a joking aside. He would schedule six or seven speeches a day. Each would take longer than he had planned for, and he would arrive later and later as the day wore on. Nonetheless, the crowds would wait for him and he drew packed houses wherever he went. His voice got hoarser as the campaign wore on, and he often ended up with a wheezy whisper and a session in the hospital when the election was over, but he talked to more people per campaign than anyone else ever did, at least until television and radio attempted (but failed) to give the impression of a live appearance. He wore out drivers, while making more live speeches to more people than anyone else in North Dakota ever did. These are only a few of the stories told about Langer, stories which created a legend and made him invulnerable to attack in his later years.

He paid a price, however, for the defiance of railroads, utilities, press and banks and other large corporations. His opponents were always better financed, and the daily newspapers were always ready to vilify Langer and his friends, especially after he pointed out how much public money the dailies got for publishing official printing. One of the dailies even financed the most publicized lawsuit against him: the Johnson case described in chapter two.

He could also be magnanimous with opponents and even long-time enemies, as a few examples will show. After he was opposed by Thomas Whelan and Charles J. Vogel in a hotly contested race for election to the United States Senate, he supported the former for appointment as ambassador to Nicaragua, and the latter as United States district judge and, later, as judge of the Eighth Circuit Court of Appeals. Some of his paranoid enemies saw his support as proof of a deal that they would let him win, but any such accusations can easily be proved false by reading news reports and speeches of the campaign, Charles Vogel's letter to the Democratic campaign managers in Washington and concession letter to Langer. Such support of his opponents may have been good politics, but it requires a lot more grace and tolerance than most politicians are likely to display. The prime example, however, of magnanimity is Langer's approval of Lanier's reappointment as United States attorney after Lanier had persecuted him in four separate criminal prosecutions in 1934 and 1935. Lanier came up for reappointment in 1937, when Langer began his second term as governor, and again in 1941, when Langer was in the U.S. Senate. A U.S. senator, by long custom, can prevent any civil appointment in his state merely by saying to the Senate or a Senate Committee that the nominee is "personally obnoxious" to him. Langer certainly had ample reason to utter those words in 1942, and as a member of the Judiciary Committee, which passes on appointments, a fine opportunity to do so. Langer never said the words, or any words like them. Instead, as a member of the Judiciary Committee, he personally reported to the full Senate, on February 27, 1942, the "favorable report of the Committee" on the appointment of "Powless W. Lanier, to be United States attorney for the district of North Dakota."[355] The Senate confirmed him the next day.[356]

It could be argued that Langer's action had a political motivation, because the Senate had not yet voted on the proposed unseating of Langer by the Senate. However, Langer's use of a traditional, and jealously guarded, right of a sitting senator would not likely be penalized by senators who wanted to maintain a right that they treasured—to reject appointments in their own state. I doubt it would have made any difference in the final vote. I know of no other North Dakota politician who was as generous to his defeated opponents. His failure to object to later reappointments proves the generosity.

He was an unusual politician, for his times or any other times. He struggled more than most against his opponents, but he also served with integrity and vision, determination and courage, in the face of opposition that would have made a lesser person turn from public life forever. In the long run, it was an unequal contest between him and his enemies.

Appendix A:
Langer and the Historians

William Langer faced many battles to uphold and protect his reputation during his lifetime. The struggle to present the full story of his political career since his death is no less challenging. From a grade school history book, first published in North Dakota in 1942, to articles in history journals and chapters in books about North Dakota's political history written in the 1980s and 1990s, authors have related Langer's story in a way that has far too often failed to tell "the truth, the whole truth, and nothing but the truth." In recapping Langer's involvement with the Nonpartisan League and the infamous and politically motivated trials that have unfairly tainted his reputation and that of some of his closest colleagues, historians have left readers with false and misleading impressions of one of North Dakota's longest-serving and most faithful public servants.

Conrad Leifur's *Our State, North Dakota*

North Dakota schoolchildren in the 1930s and 1940s were required to take a course in civics in the upper grades. The standard text in the North Dakota portion of the course was *Our State, North Dakota* by Conrad W. Leifur, who was a teacher in the Bismarck school system.[357] Editions of his book were published in 1942, 1945, 1953, and 1958, the early years of Bill Langer's senatorial career. Historian Larry Remele described the Leifur text as "the standard textbook for secondary schools for more than three decades and the history that influenced more North Dakotans than any other until the late 1960s."[358] The following excerpt from Leifur's 1942 textbook helps explain what the impressionable young people of North Dakota were being taught about Bill Langer and the Nonpartisan League only ten years after the events that were being described. In later editions, however, Leifur deleted or corrected some of the more egregious statements quoted below, and by 1958, Langer's name is only mentioned three times and with little emphasis. Leifur wrote:

Upon becoming governor [in 1932] Langer soon took complete control of the affairs of the Nonpartisan League, and set about to build up a strong political machine. One of the first objectives in this direction was a large campaign fund. Much of this fund was presumably to go to the support of the *Leader*, the Langer-controlled League newspaper. It was reported that to raise this fund every state employee, whether employed in the capitol at Bismarck or in any of the many state institutions or departments located elsewhere, was required to pay 2 per cent of his salary to this fund. Anyone who refused to pay risked the loss of his job. Many lost their jobs anyway because of not belonging to the right political party. One of Mr. Langer's campaign promises was to 'clean out' the 'gang' at Bismarck and give the jobs to friends of the league. It appeared that so many friends of the league were promised jobs that there were not nearly enough to go around. Even the creation of many new jobs did not begin to take care of all who had been "promised." The "cleaning out" business was probably carried too far when it was extended to the Agricultural College. Several of the most valuable professors, from the point of view of the agricultural development of the state, were discharged and the Agricultural College lost its standing among colleges in the North Central Association.

To prevent . . . foreclosures from taking place, Langer issued various moratoria. At one time he declared an embargo on agricultural products, forbidding their shipment from the state. When the hope that farm prices would rise as a result of this embargo failed to materialize, the plan was abandoned.

Governor Langer was removed from office on July 18, 1934, having been disqualified by the North Dakota Supreme Court. The basis for this disqualification was the fact that he had been convicted in Federal court on a charge of conspiracy, growing out of the practice of requiring state and even Federal employees to pay a part of their salaries to support his political machine. Upon this disqualification Ole Olson, lieutenant governor, became acting governor and served the rest of the term. Mr. Langer had already been re-nominated by the Republicans, the Nonpartisans having the control of that party, for a second term as governor, when the conviction took place. Mrs. Langer was then nominated to take his place as a candidate for governor, but she was defeated by Thomas H. Moodie. The Federal court of appeals reversed the conviction, allowing the Langer case to be tried again. A second trial brought no verdict, as the

jury disagreed. At the third trial Mr. Langer was acquitted . . .
In 1940, again in a three-way race, Langer defeated Lynn J. Frazier and Thomas Whelan for the Republican nomination for United States Senator, and went on to defeat the Democratic candidate in the fall. Due to the many questionable situations which accompanied his conduct of the governorship, a committee of North Dakota citizens petitioned the United States Senate not to seat Langer. However, on March 27, 1942, the Senate voted fifty-two to thirty in favor of seating him.[359]

An analysis of the content and presentation of Leifur's "history" may offer a corrective to what were given as the facts about Bill Langer and his place in history.

First, the only time the pejorative word "machine" is used in discussion of state politics is in connection with Langer. Second, the implication about Langer's fund-raising is that he and the Nonpartisan League were exclusively engaged in such a campaign and only they ever asked state employees to contribute to campaign funds. In fact, every administration before and many since have done the same thing. Langer and the League were always outspent by their opposition by a large margin, and every party solicited state and federal employees for campaign funds. The *Leader* over the years printed photographs of canceled checks from state employees to political parties, both federal and state, as well as copies of requests to state employees to contribute to the gubernatorial campaigns of George Shafer, Walter Welford, John Moses and others. The Hatch Act regulating how funds were raised was not passed until 1939.[360]

Leifur's statement that state employees were "required" to contribute or risk "the loss of his job" are pure propaganda, as was his reference to "even federal employees" being "required" to contribute.[361] The Court of Appeals accepted as fact that the solicitation of a few employees of the "State Emergency Relief" office happened unintentionally when the solicitor McDonald mistook those employees to be state workers, partly as a result of the confusion of relocated offices after the state capitol building had burned down in 1933. Why does the author say otherwise? Those issues were thrashed out in many a campaign, and every accusation answered. They are manifestly absurd, in the first place, because there were thousands of employees, and even 2 percent of their salaries would have been a much larger sum than the campaign funds or the *Leader* ever got. The number of people whose "firings" were attributed to failure to contribute was very few, and those few were explained, at the trials and in the Senate hearings, by reasons that had nothing to do with failure to contribute to either Langer or the *Leader*.

Attributing the loss of a state job in Langer's tenure "because of belonging to the wrong political party" implies that this had never happened before or since. The fact is that every administration regularly "cleaned out" state employees when administrations changed.[362] The Langer administration was not unique in that respect. Furthermore, the firings at the beginning of the administration could not have had anything to do with the *Leader* plan, because the administration took over in January of 1933, the "cleaning out" took place then, while the plan for the *Leader* was not devised until long after the change of administration took place. The first *Leader* was published July 17, 1934.

Leifur's statements about creating new jobs for political supporters because there were not enough to go around, flies in the face of the fact that the Langer administration cut appropriations by more than 50 percent and thereby made certain that there were far fewer jobs in the state administration than there had been previously.

The references to the North Dakota Agricultural College and embargo matters require more discussion than this book affords, but it must be said that the embargo, declared October 16, 1933, did not "fail." It was effective while it lasted. Wheat prices (especially durum) rose dramatically and quickly. What caused the withdrawal of the embargo order was a successful constitutional challenge resulting in a court-ordered end to it on January 15, 1934.

Nor did Langer's moratoria "fail." Thousands of farmers, who stayed on the farm because of the moratoria, gave credit to Langer for their survival, and more thousands gave credit to Frank Vogel, manager of the Bank of North Dakota, for renting the land back to them, and refusing to sell to others until the prior owners or their families got back on their feet and could buy it back for what the bank had in it. For decades after the Depression and the Langer administration's efforts to help farmers, even at the end of the twentieth century, people approached this author to describe how Bill Langer or Frank Vogel, or both, saved their farms. Those North Dakotans must have been surprised to read in their children's civics books that the moratoria was a failure.

While Leifur praised the administrations of many other governors elsewhere in his book, he has nothing good to say about the Langer administration, ignoring the 50 percent cuts in state appropriations (which was partly responsible for the Agricultural College contretemps), the purchases of shriveled wheat by the state mill that raised wheat prices, the purchases by the Bank of North Dakota of warrants from financially strapped local governments that enabled them to keep operating, the keeping of schools open in many districts, and many other memorable accomplishments.

Leifur gave no reasons for the reversal of the conviction in the first Langer trial. By not explaining that it was for lack of evidence, or that the judge who presided was not allowed to preside at subsequent trials, or that the Court of Appeals said that no federal law was broken, and they doubted that any state law was, the impact of the reversal is diminished. In addition, the Republican primary nomination of Langer did not take place before the jury verdict in the first trial; it came eleven days later. In spite of the conviction, and in spite of the fact that the trial prevented him from campaigning, he got the biggest primary majority in history.

Elwyn B. Robinson's *History of North Dakota*

Elwyn B. Robinson, long-time historian at the University of North Dakota, wrote what has been accepted as the state's "standard history": *History of North Dakota*, published by the University of Nebraska in 1964, and reprinted with a new foreword and afterword by the North Dakota Institute for Regional Studies in 1995. Although this writer makes no claim of being a historian, I have written elsewhere about my disagreement with Robinson's account of the North Dakota Constitutional Convention of 1889.[363] And, reluctantly, I also must dissent from some of his account of the Langer era.[364] The following are a few of the points Robinson makes from which a reader can judge whether or not the documentary record supports his view.

Robinson says that Langer's main appeal was to the German-Russians, "many of whom could not read English and distrusted well-groomed candidates." Langer spoke German, but the writer, who heard many speeches, some in counties with many German-speaking voters, never heard him give an entire speech in German.[365] And as a prosperous lawyer and graduate of two universities, one in New York City and one in North Dakota, and as a busy lawyer who spent a lot of time in the courtroom, he certainly was a "well-groomed candidate," much more so than William Lemke or Usher Burdick, for example. And many of North Dakotans who supported the Nonpartisan League could and did read well and widely, in the *Leader*, and elsewhere.

Robinson gives Langer credit for a "bold operation to meet the crisis in Bismarck" and details some of his efforts. His attack, however, follows fairly quickly, as Robinson describes Langer having "cleaned out the executive departments and appointed persons loyal to himself," as if that had not been done every time there was a change of party in power since the Dakota Territory days.[366] In Robinson's description of the genesis of the Nonpartisan paper, the *Leader*, he notes that Langer "openly solicited his appointees to buy subscriptions equal to 5 per cent of their annual salaries, a political tithe for the faithful. Langer defended this as an honest campaign-fund solicitation: the jobholders could recoup by reselling the subscriptions, and those who refused to subscribe were not fired." He goes on to describe Harold McDonald's inadvertent solicitation of the State Relief Office, "where the clerks were paid from federal funds. State employees pledged $58,202 and relief employees only $469." As authority for this paragraph (and much later material) Robinson cites the much later report of the Senate Committee on Privileges and Elections. But here, as later, he cites the charges made in the Senate hearing, but not the answers to those charges, contained in the same report, as well as the minority report, and, more specifically in the so-called Witness Books that contain the actual testimony of the witnesses interviewed by the Senate investigators. He fails to point out that for an accidental gathering of $179.50, the state was kept in a turmoil for a generation.

Robinson does concede that the Roosevelt Administration, "cheered on by the conservatives in the state, set out with considerable hypocrisy (it was then said to be levying assessments on postmasters in North Dakota) to destroy Langer." He need not have used the qualifier "it was then said." In fact, it was often proved, and seldom denied, and at the first trial Frank Vogel testified that he had 10 percent when he was a federal employee (not a postmaster), but Judge Miller struck out the testimony.

Robinson says nothing about the trial, at which the charges were answered in detail, except that it was long and was presided over by Judge Miller, and that the judge was "an old enemy," who announced that he was "delighted and pleased" with the verdict and sentenced Langer to eighteen months in prison and a fine of $10,000. This is all true, but such an important event in North Dakota history, which it shaped for a generation and still affects, deserves more from a historian. As for the appeal, in which the Court of Appeals reversed the judgment, Robinson said only that "Langer was eventually cleared after a long legal battle."[367] He mentioned the second conspiracy trial, and the disagreement of the jury, and went on to say, "After a perjury trial, December 3–6, Langer was found not guilty." It would have been more factual and fairer to say that Langer (and others) were charged with perjury for filing an affidavit of prejudice against Judge Miller, turning the rights of defendants on its head. Even more importantly, Robinson's "standard history" ought to have explained that the acquittal on the perjury charge came on a directed verdict by an outside judge, before the defense offered any testimony, with the judge remarking that the time had not yet come in this country when people could be prosecuted for what they think. As for Langer's second term as governor (1937–39), Robinson has little that is good or even-handed to say about Langer or the League. He says that Langer "coerced" the legislature to pass an income tax law, and on the next page that the 1939 legislature "backed by Moses, refused to appropriate money for larger pensions."[368] In Robinson's view, if something happened in the Langer administration, it was due to the governor's coercion; if it happens during the Moses administration, it is done by the legislature with the backing of the governor.

Similarly, he refers to Langer's winning of the "hostility of many" and Moses compiling a "notable record." In view of their subsequent records, this statement is puzzling, to say the least. The "hostility of many" is presumably a reference to the so-called "bond deals," accusations of which were the mainstay of many an election thereafter. Again, Robinson refers to the accusations made before the Senate Committee on Privileges and Elections and set out in the report of the committee, but not to the answers to those charges, contained in the same committee hearings.[369] Robinson again states a charge made at the Senate hearings without any reference to the refutation of it—that during the second trial, Langer paid Judge Wyman's son $525.[370] He omits the pertinent facts that Gale Wyman was in Bismarck without Langer's knowledge, and that in order to get him out of town he had to give him money Mulloy had promised, without Langer's authority. In view of all the evidence, it is misleading and unfair to say, as Robinson does, that "Langer himself admitted paying some $525 to Gale B. Wyman, son of the federal judge who presided at his second and third trials in 1935," with no further explanation.[371]

Robert and Wynona Wilkins's *North Dakota: A Centennial History*

University of North Dakota professors Robert P. Wilkins and Wynona H. Wilkins, in their book *North Dakota: A Centennial History* treat Langer and the League more fairly than the above sources, but still have a few disputable comments.[372] They correct many errors and omissions in the previous histories: recognizing Langer's accomplishment in cutting appropriations by 50 percent during the desperate legislative session of 1933 and the effectiveness, temporarily at least, of the embargo and moratoria during Langer's two administrations.[373] As I have written above, they also recognize that Judge Miller was "an old enemy" of Langer's. Nevertheless, they repeat some of the old errors and misconceptions of Robinson (whom they greatly admire) and add a few new ones.

The indictment against Langer and others is described, inadequately, as "for collecting funds for political purposes from federal employees." After mentioning the verdict of not guilty in the third trial, they go on to say, "Langer subsequently testified that he had paid a sum of money to the son of the judge presiding at the trial which ended his misadventures with the law. Its role in the outcome of what proved to be the final trial, however, has never been determined."[374] This latter innuendo is unjustified. As has been shown, Langer's explanation seems to have been enough to satisfy the United States Senate.

The authors' chronology is also awry. The payment of money to young Wyman to get him out of town occurred earlier, not during "the trial that ended his misadventures with the law," and there were two more trials after he left town, so it could hardly have had any role in the outcome of the final trial resulting in an acquittal. According to Mulloy's testimony, neither Gale Wyman nor Leedom was present at the last two trials.[375]

The Wilkinses also follow Robinson in attributing League successes only to the mistakes of the opposition, never to its own programs, asserting that the history of the League was nothing but "a sideshow" and "that the great socialist experiment was a failure," all of which would be disputed by knowledgeable observers of both parties in North Dakota. The Bank of North Dakota, the State Mill and Elevator, and many other state programs and statutes that still exist, are proof to the contrary.[376]

The Wilkinses are unduly kind to William Lemke, as are most published historians, including Robinson. They observe that he "stretched the guidelines of the Home Building Association [HBA] to build for himself a $20,000 house and two car garage at Fargo."[377] In fact, Lemke borrowed money from the State Fund, which was limited to loans for houses costing no more than five thousand dollars, and spent more than four times that on his home at 1222 Ninth Street South in Fargo.[378] He had drafted the authorizing legislation for the fund, and his violation of the rules caused the other candidates and the Nonpartisan League much embarrassment. His political opposition capitalized on Lemke's abuse of that fund by providing tours of

Fargo during campaigns, so that voters could see the "Lemke mansion." Bill Langer, in a letter to the author said that the 1921 recall of League officials—Governor Lynn Frazier, Attorney General William Lemke, and Commissioner of Agriculture and Labor John Hagan, was caused by the scandal about that house, and that the difference between the five thousand dollars Lemke said he spent on the house (and was all he could borrow) and the twenty-two thousand dollars actually spent on the house was made up by contributions, of which Frank Vogel raised two thousand dollars in McLean County alone.[379]

Despite this fiasco, during the early years of the League, Lemke was a tireless legal adviser for the organization and one of its triumvirate of leaders, along with A. C. Townley and F. B. Wood, who, as the executive committee, rather dictatorially ran the organization until, in 1922, it was reorganized with a much more democratic organization. He made mistakes, such as tolerating or even encouraging the passage of laws such as the so-called "Anti-Liars law" (never enforced) which would have punished "false" criticism of state officials and a law setting up a state sheriff—not much different from the justifiably abhorred Sedition Act of the national administration of President John Adams. But he deserves much credit for the early successes of the League.

The Treatment of Langer in *The North Dakota Political Tradition*

The North Dakota Political Tradition, a collection of articles by several North Dakota historians published in 1981, edited by Thomas Howard, varies in accuracy and quality.[380] Historian Robert P. Wilkins provided a chapter on the state's early political history, quite accurately covering the era preceding the Nonpartisan League, especially the McKenzie era. It is misleading, however, to say that the techniques used by NPL organizer A. C. Townley were not that different from those used so effectively by the McKenzie machine for years.[381] There may have been some similarities before 1922, when Townley left the main organization, but in that year the Nonpartisan League in North Dakota adopted new procedures that were more democratic than any of the other parties. After that time, the League used simultaneous or near-simultaneous meetings in more than 2,200 North Dakota precincts, followed by similar simultaneous meetings at the county level, with secret ballot voting on delegates to the state convention, which used secret balloting, a procedure that made central control impossible.

McKenzie operated behind the scenes, through cronies and out-of-state money. Townley did not. He certainly, along with Lemke and F. B. Wood, dominated the League until 1922. Neither Alex McKenzie nor A. C. Townley nor anyone else could control the kind of a democratic setup the League had after 1922. This writer attended scores of its meetings and can make this statement confidently based on his firsthand knowledge of the facts. Wilkins also states that Langer "usurped" the Nonpartisan League, ignoring the fact that he was endorsed from 1932 through 1956 by the same kind of democratically elected conventions as the League had held from 1922 onward, as well as the same kind of democratic convention that moved the League to the Democratic Party column in 1956.[382] That is not usurpation, it is democracy.

The admirable chapter in *The North Dakota Political Tradition* by Larry Remele, "Power to the People: the Nonpartisan League," is the best recent history of the Nonpartisan League. Among other things, it documents some of the mistakes made by the early League, as well as the willingness of the League's Republican opponents to support Democratic or other candidates, provided only that they oppose the League, and the effect on the Nonpartisan League of the "Red Scare" and Palmer Raids after World War I.

A few quibbles might be offered. Lemke may have been "an honest and sincere person" in the early years, as Townley was, but they both degenerated later, as evidenced by Lemke's repeated charges of "kickbacks" to Langer, which he later admitted was supported by nothing specific that he knew of. And Lemke did more than "err" by taking out a home loan with the State Homebuilders fund—he violated the rules by taking a loan in a much larger amount than was authorized for anyone, and the repercussions were long-lasting. All in all, though, the Remele chapter is to be recommended.

The same cannot be said of Glenn Smith's chapter in *North Dakota Political Tradition*: "William Langer and the Art of Personal Politics." To begin with, Smith evaluates Langer as having a "mediocre academic record."[383] Agnes Geelan, in her well-researched biography, *The Dakota Maverick*, says his early record was ordinary, but when he was graduated from Columbia University, he was "valedictorian and president of the senior class and up to 1960 stood #1 or #2 in the list of all Columbia Law School graduates," and won the Rolker Award as the senior "deemed by his classmates to be the most worthy of special distinction . . . for scholarship, participation in student activities, or pre-eminence in athletic sports, or a combination of all of them."[384] Smith says that Langer throughout his life never held party loyalty to be a virtue.[385] If the NPL was a party (and it was by any reasonable definition), that is not true. If Smith is referring only to the Democratic or Republican Parties, then he may be correct. Langer's primary loyalty was to the Nonpartisan League.

Referring to Langer's endorsement by the anti-League Republicans in 1920, Smith acknowledges that Langer did not agree with their program and disliked many of its leaders. He then gratuitously adds that Langer "was willing to accept IVA support under almost any circumstances." Would Smith have had him refuse it? Langer said in the Senate hearing he told the IVA convention he agreed with the League program, and still got the IVA endorsement, and contemporary evidence confirms this. So it would seem that the Independent Voters Association, the regular Republicans, would support anyone opposing the Nonpartisan League under almost any circumstances.

Smith tells of Langer's agreement to reorganize the League, and says he "created" a precinct-based organization. Actually, the League had always had one, since 1922. Smith says it was used to create "loyal Langer supporters" and that "it was not incompatible to support both Langer and the League—in that order."[386] If the organization was so designed, how did it happen that Langer got the League endorsement for the governorship in the 1932 convention by only one vote, after Frank Vogel talked to delegates all night? And how did it happen that Langer often had a lot of trouble later in League conventions on candidacies and platform? And how did it happen that the League, in a democratically run convention, took itself into the Democratic column in 1956?

Smith makes an amazing claim that Langer in 1932 "had no real program of legislation, unlike the early Townley League that had very concrete, specific programs. He talked of reducing real estate taxes and state expenses, which, in the depression, was popular rhetoric."[387] Though he later mentions (and criticizes) tax cuts in the legislature, and the adoption of a sales tax, Smith ignores the unprecedented cut (more than 50 percent) in state expenditures that Langer had promised in his campaign and delivered on. Labeling Langer's efforts as "popular rhetoric" is unjustified. It probably was "rhetoric" for Roosevelt, elected the same time as Langer, who raised expenditures when he was in office, after promising reduced appropriations, but not for Langer and the League, who kept their promises. The platform also promised moratoria, and that promise was kept. So were many others.

With regard to the Langer moratorium on mortgage foreclosures, Smith mentions that Langer called out the National Guard thirty-one times, but fails to mention that calling out the guard to prevent foreclosure sales was just the opposite of the action of other governors, or that the existence of the moratorium prevented the commencements of many foreclosures.[388] He minimizes the effect of Langer's grain embargo by saying the price rise was mostly due to a purchase by the federal government. The farmers of North Dakota, who gave Langer the credit, must have been surprised if they read this.[389] Actually the federal purchase came after the embargo, and the federal government was buying wheat abroad at the same time, which would tend to lower prices.

Regarding the Federal Emergency Relief Administration, Smith says that Langer, in practical operation, was much more than nominally in charge as governor and says he took an active interest in, and set policy concerning, the release and distribution of much of these relief funds, that applicants were asked who they voted for governor and forms had to be signed by local NPL precinct committeemen.[390] These statements are flatly contradicted by the testimony of Judge Christianson and other members of the state committee. Yet Smith claims that there is "much evidence" to support contentions that Langer used the funds for political purposes and that Judge Christianson did not know much about the operation.[391] This, too, in the testimony is denied by all the members of the state committee, both friendly and unfriendly to Langer. The author cites no evidence to support any of these statements. Anyone who knew Judge Christianson would scoff at the notion that he would not know about the operation of a program he headed. He was a man with a high sense of duty and he had high standards, and would never head an organization without being in charge of it. He testified that he worked twenty-hour days and wore out his tires heading the organization.

Smith says the first grand jury found little, but then "several people" (unnamed) came forward with sworn statements about "crooked deals" [quotation marks in original].[392] He likely refers to C. R. Verry and James Mulloy, both perjurers, the latter by his own admission, and the former described three times by the North Dakota Supreme Court as unworthy of belief. Smith makes the statement that Lanier was Langer's friend and cites Langer's support of Democrats, including Lanier, in 1930.[393] That support, however, was given only after the Leaguers had lost in the primary. Democrats were almost always considered preferable to IVAs by Leaguers. In 1932, when Langer was elected governor, Lanier was running for the Senate as a Democrat and was quoted in the press as being highly critical of Langer. It is obvious from the transcript of the four trials in which Lanier was the prosecutor and Langer a defendant that they were not friendly.

Smith passes lightly over the first trial by saying that much evidence was admitted that would be later "declared inappropriate," and that "an affidavit of prejudice was filed against the rulings of Judge Miller."[394] The latter, of course, is nonsense—affidavits of prejudice are filed against the judge, and before he has made rulings, and before the trial even begins. No affidavit of prejudice was filed in the first trial—the law required that all defendants must sign it and two or three of them declined, so none was filed then. The affidavit of prejudice was filed before the second trial. Evidence in the first trial was not declared "inappropriate" by the Court of Appeals. All the evidence let in, admissible or not, was held insufficient to prove that any federal offense had been committed. The Court of Appeals, after so holding, and ordering a new trial, said that it need not consider the other grounds for appeal, which included a great many examples of erroneous rulings on evidence.

Smith ignores chronology in telling of Langer's victory in the primary, the end of the trial and the disqualification by the Supreme Court, as well as the overwhelming majority he received eleven days after the conviction. He admits that Mrs. Langer, endorsed by the Republican Party when Langer was disqualified, ran "surprisingly well but was defeated by Moody [sic]," a name he consistently misspells.[395] He misrepresents the Gale Wyman–Leedom matter by saying Mulloy was "dispatched by Langer and Frank Vogel" and that "in exchange for certain gratuities both Leedom and Gale Wyman would talk to the judge before and during the trial to make sure Langer got a 'fair break.'"[396] Even Mulloy admitted that he was "dispatched" only to get Leedom to watch the jury, and that Langer and Vogel knew nothing about Gale Wyman's coming to Bismarck until he was there. Wyman talked to his father in advance only about the defense's desire to see the jury panel list in advance, something that had always been allowed in federal court until the first trial under Miller. Both of the Wymans so testified.

Smith says the second trial "was shrouded in controversy."[397] There was nothing shrouded about that trial; it was reported extensively, as few other trials in the history of North Dakota were. He reveals a misunderstanding of jury selection by saying that Henry Charboneau [sic] one of two jurors voting for acquittal, maintained he believed Langer innocent unless more evidence was forthcoming than at the first trial, but "he was placed on the jury anyway."[398] Is he implying that Langer put him on, or Judge Wyman did? Is he implying that jurors should have made up their minds before trial? Or that the United States attorney had no right to challenge jurors for cause or peremptorily? The facts are, of course, is that the government had peremptory challenges to use in jury selection and must have chosen to leave Charbonneau on the jury. Jurors are instructed to consider people innocent until proved guilty, and Charbonneau said he would do just that. It should be remembered that the conviction in the first trial was reversed by the Eighth Circuit Court of Appeals because the evidence was insufficient to prove any violation of federal law, so of course more evidence would have to be forthcoming to justify a conviction. As Charbonneau told the investigators, he heard after the trial that the defense almost struck him from the jury, thinking he was a Lanier "plant," but left him on because they had to use their challenges on jurors they considered more antagonistic than he.

Smith then says that Reich, who he identifies as the other juror voting for acquittal, was from Langer's hometown, as if that were a disqualification or was unknown to the prosecution when it exercised its challenges; and that Reich "later, it was alleged, received a gratuity of nearly one thousand dollars from Frank Vogel in return for his vote of not guilty." He does not say who "alleged" this charge, which he says, "a 1941 congressional investigation could not affirm." This is a very grudging way of admitting it was found to be groundless, and that no evidence was introduced to prove it was in return for a jury action two years earlier.

The testimony in the Senate hearing sheds light on the facts, among which is that the money Reich received more than two years after the trial was over had nothing to do with his service as a juror. Witnesses testified that the money was due to him from an employer, who had a contract with the North Dakota Highway Department headed by Frank Vogel. As to the third trial, Smith implies that the acquittal was due to lack of new evidence, which gave the advantage to the defense. It would be surprising if there were new evidence, and if the prosecution could not convict on admissible evidence after two trials, it should not have brought the third, or, if it did, no one could realistically expect a conviction. But Smith says the outcome did not remove the strong suspicion of wrongdoing in the minds of some voters, and that Langer's political support had eroded considerably. His later elections prove the contary.[399]

In his treatment of the "bond deals," Smith states that people would have expected Langer and Vogel to have the bank bid on bonds at par value and at a lower rate of interest, but "this did not happen. Instead, the V. W. Brewer Company of Des Moines, Iowa, bought the bonds and then resold them to the Bank of North Dakota and other state agencies. In the process the company made a commission of more than a quarter of a million dollars."[400] An accurate figure for **all** sales, most of which were not to the Bank of North Dakota, would be one hundred thousand dollars, as testified to in the Senate by Clyde Duffy, as well as Brewer and Brunk.

Smith's argument assumes a great deal, such as the notion that the Bank of North Dakota had limitless funds and no other commitments. Not even Clyde Duffy, who was hired by the Moses administration to dig into the bond transactions, denied the savings to the taxpayers. Robert Stangler, not a partisan, testified that the Bank of North Dakota overextended itself in supporting the finances of local governments, and still could not buy them all. Nor does Duffy claim that the Bank could have bought all of the bonds that were up for sale or that Langer, or any other North Dakota political figure, profited from Brewer's activities. The Senate investigators, after interviewing a score or more of them, failed to find a single county auditor or commissioner who was critical of the refunding.

Smith criticizes advertising by the state mill in the *Leader* during the second Langer administration, because it advertised where it purchased wheat rather than where it might sell flour.[401] He seems to ignore the fact that North Dakotans buy flour and bake bread. Where better advertise than in North Dakota, where flour buyers could be persuaded that their purchases would help to both reduce their taxes and help the state's distressed farmers? And where better advertise than in a paper that reaches people that other newspapers do not?

Regarding the 1940 campaign, Smith says the League "dutifully" endorsed Langer over Frazier, and says "many believed that Frazier would win handily," but "the Langer organization was now functioning smoothly and Frazier had less political support than he had believed," so Langer won.[402] Smith conveniently ignores the fact that the League precinct and county meetings, operating democratically, sent delegates to the convention, and they chose Langer. He also ignores the fact that Frazier chose not to seek League endorsement, after being specifically asked if he would accept it. Instead he chose the endorsement of League opponents.[403] Leaguers did not appreciate (or vote for) people who refused their endorsements.

Trying to explain Langer's victory in a three-way race for the Senate in 1940, Smith says that the National Democrats put special effort into supporting Charles Vogel and that Langer might have received some Democratic votes because he supported Roosevelt. Langer did support Roosevelt, whom he admired, and probably lost a lot more votes of Republicans by doing so than the votes he gained from Democrats.

When it came to the attempt to unseat Langer in the Senate, Smith says that some of the charges were new, and "took even Langer's most loyal supporters by surprise," and James Mulloy "revealed Langer's dealings with Judge Wyman before the second trial," thus disregarding the testimony in the Senate hearings by even Mulloy and Verry and Clyde Duffy—as well as many others—that all of the charges had been aired in previous campaigns, and that there was never one iota of testimony that Langer ever had any dealings with Judge Wyman. Nor is that all. Smith describes Langer's effort to get Gale Wyman out of Bismarck by saying "Langer admitted giving money to Gale Wyman and to James Mulloy to give to Chet Leedom, Gale Wyman and others," and that he would have given them more had they asked for it. He disregards that Langer gave money to get Gale Wyman back to South Dakota in an effort to remedy Mulloy's stupid behavior. As to Mulloy's admission that he had perjured himself and waited until the statute of limitations had run and other admissions of lying, Smith sanitizes all of this by saying only, "There was considerable testimony that Mulloy was not always honest."[404]

Smith says that "Langer was finally seated in the spring of 1942." In fact, Langer had been acting as senator since the day the new Congress was seated in 1941. While acknowledging that Langer was excellent at helping his constituents, Smith said, in connection with his introduction of private bills to relieve injustices committed by the federal government, that "he was accused by some of introducing private bills and taking up valuable government time and money, but he persisted."[405] Actually, his willingness to take action to correct injustices affecting only one or a few people was one of the endearing things about Langer—and something other legislators might emulate.

A few years ago, the writer's law office handled a case for a Minnesota resident who had been grossly misled by a federal agricultural official and suffered a substantial loss because of it . We sued and lost, the court holding that the employee and the government were immune from suit because the federal government had not consented to be sued. On appeal, the Court of Appeals reluctantly, and by a two-to-one vote, upheld the decision. When the client asked what more could be done, I suggested that she could ask her Congressman (Stangeland) to introduce a private bill for her relief. She did ask him, and Congressman Stangeland's response was to ask what a private bill was, and where was it authorized in the United States Code? Bill Langer would have known, and would have done something about it. He might have achieved justice for her by having Congress make amends for her loss because of the archaic idea, embodied in some laws, that the king can do no wrong. Langer did not believe that the king was always right. Instead his attitude was that injustice might come from anywhere, high or low, and must be opposed wherever it comes from.

Lawrence H. Larsen's Article on the Langer Trials

An article on the Langer trials, written by Lawrence H. Larsen, retired professor of history at the University of Missouri at Kansas City, appeared in *North Dakota History: Journal of the Northern Plains* in 1984. It too has inaccuracies, beginning with a misleading title: "*U.S. v. Langer, et al.*: The U.S. District Attorney's Files."[406] The article includes discussion of the Senate challenge to the seating of Langer, which had little to do with the U.S. attorney's files. The article seems to assume that the result of the first trial was correct and later trials wrong and that the facts can be found only by references to the daily newspapers, such as the *Fargo Forum* and *Bismarck Tribune*, and not the *Leader*, the League weekly newspaper. Nothing is said about the reasons for the reversal by the Court of Appeals after the conviction in the first trial. Despite these problems, however, Larsen's article is generally factual and tends to support the proposition that the prosecutions were, in fact, political, and were pushed by United States Attorney Lanier, even against the advice of the Department of Justice. This writer's opinion is that Lanier, egged on by Judge Miller, was primarily responsible for the continuation of the trials after the reversal of the first verdict, but the first trial was initially incited by disputes between Langer and the Roosevelt Administration, which were seized upon by Lanier and Judge Miller to start a vendetta against Langer. The article presents interesting evidence to show that the main motive of the trials was to get—and keep—Langer out of office.[407] Nevertheless, specific errors include the following:

1) Larsen states that the charge against the defendants was "conspiring to embezzle federal relief funds." There was no suggestion of embezzlement of federal funds in the indictment or the evidence. The charge can best be described as that of conspiracy to defraud the federal government by soliciting political contributions from people who were paid by federal funds, although working in an office labeled as "State Relief Office," thereby somehow interfering with the operation of acts of Congress being administered by those employees.

2) Larsen states that the jury came in at the first trial on June

17, and Langer won a sweeping victory in the primary on June 17. Actually, eleven days intervened between the verdict and the primary election. The verdict was received on June 16, and the election was on June 27, 1934.

3) The author incorrectly states that Thomas Moodie served as governor only four days. According to the 1954 North Dakota Blue Book, Moodie was inaugurated on January 7, 1935, was declared ineligible by the Supreme Court on February 2, and was removed from office on February 16.[408] The Supreme Court decision in the case, *State ex rel Sathre v. Moodie* (258 N.W. 558, 65 N.D. 340, 1935) was released on February 2, 1935, and says that it presumes that the parties will abide by it without a formal writ. If they did, then Moodie was in office twenty-six days, as Langer says in his testimony, but he certainly served more than four days, mainly because the Supreme Court refused to hear the case before he took the oath of office and it took some time thereafter to get a decision.

4) It is inaccurate to say, as the article does, that Moodie "violated a North Dakota residence law by voting in Minnesota." The law in question disqualified from office anyone who had been a resident of the state for less than five years, and the evidence showed that Moodie had voted in Minnesota, and sworn that he was a Minnesota resident, less than five years before assuming the office of governor in North Dakota. Voting in Minnesota was not illegal; it merely made Moodie ineligible to be governor.

5) Along the same line, to say on page seven that North Dakota "had no enforceable law" prohibiting political solicitations is misleading. It had no law at all to that effect. To say, as the author does, that Langer "required" everyone working for the state to give 2 percent of their salary in political donations is false. The number who did not contribute and stayed in office far exceeded those who contributed. The charge that donations were required was echoed in many a political campaign but never proved. Actually, the *Leader* solicitation asked for a 5 percent contribution. The only solicitation for 2 percent was made by a prior (and anti-Langer) League Executive Committee, and at the end of the first trial Judge Miller struck out all references to the 2 percent solicitation and told the jury to disregard it.

6) The article is incorrect in its assertion that "only [Langer] knew about" Langer's loan of $19,000 to the Nonpartisan League. There was testimony offered at the first trial by two of the three members of the former League State Executive Committee that Langer

had financed the League to that extent of that amount and more, and that the executive committee had contracted to repay him for all of his expenditures. Judge Miller excluded this evidence as "immaterial," even though he had allowed the government to present evidence that money was transferred to Langer's account by the executive committee.

7) Errors in attribution of facts diminish the author's credibility. At one point, the editor of the *Bismarck Tribune* is said to be Kenneth Sessions when his name was Kenneth Simons. Similarly, the publisher of the same paper was George D. Mann, not Leo D. Mann, as the author misstates. It was Mann who later made the complaint that resulted in the temporary suspension of the *Leader*'s mailing privileges, which severely handicapped its progress, as Langer testified. It was also the *Tribune* that financed and widely publicized the Johnson case brought against Langer just before the 1934 general election.

8) Larsen's statement that Judge Miller "seemed an unlikely target for the vicious accusations" against him goes too far.[409] Miller was an appointee of President Harding, which, when he was named, caused an outcry that he was a political hack.[410] Even more to the point, he was a long-time personal, political and professional enemy of Langer and should have disqualified himself from trying the case for that reason. The Court of Appeals disqualified him from acting as judge in the second and third trials. He had long been attorney for Alex McKenzie, long-time political boss of North Dakota, who was a paid lobbyist for the Northern Pacific Railway, and had had many confrontations with Langer in court and in politics. He was a likely target for criticism that was scarcely "vicious." The entire affidavit of prejudice filed against him is set out in an appendix to Holzworth's *The Fighting Governor*, and, considering the facts, seems mild rather than vicious.[411] Other authors, including the Robert and Wynona Wilkins and Elwyn Robinson recognized that Miller was "an old enemy" of Langer.[412]

9) To say that Lanier "had no choice" but to reopen the investigation after the verdict was overturned is nonsense. He did not have to reopen it. This writer was United States attorney and knows that a person in that position need not pursue a case he has lost on appeal, regardless of the opinions of the Department of Justice. He certainly need not do so if the Department thinks the case should not be continued—as Professor Larsen says that it did in this case. There is no

indication in Lanier's files that he was ordered to do so, unless it was an order from Judge Miller, who had no authority to make it.

10) To say that Lanier resigned as United States attorney in 1954 "to run unsuccessfully for Congress" ignores the pertinent fact that Eisenhower was elected president in 1952 and it is customary for new presidents to appoint their own U.S. attorneys, especially if the new president belongs to a different party.[413] Lanier certainly knew this—he was appointed U.S. attorney in 1933 when the Democrats elected Roosevelt, as a reward for running for the United States Senate in 1932. The only reason he was not replaced in early 1953, when Eisenhower (Republican) took over from Truman (Democrat) was that Senator Langer was having disagreements with the Department of Justice over who should be appointed to two federal judgeships, and to the offices of U.S. marshal and U.S. attorney. In my own experience, for example, I was appointed to be United States attorney in 1954, after waiting eighteen months for the appointment. Ordinarily Lanier would have been replaced about eighteen months earlier than the date of his actual departure.

11) Finally, it is misleading to use such words as "cunning . . . strategy," admissions of "false information" and trying "to influence a federal judge" against Langer. The testimony in the Senate hearings shows otherwise: Langer's "participation" in the attempt to influence a federal judge was to supply money to get the judge's son back to South Dakota immediately after he found that the young man was in Bismarck.

Governor William Langer

About the Author

Robert Vogel was born December 6, 1918 in Coleharbor, North Dakota where he spent his boyhood. One of five sons born to Frank and Louella Vogel, Bob attended high school in Bismarck where the family moved in 1931. His father was a leader in the Nonpartisan League and supported William Langer's gubernatorial bid in 1932.

Governor Langer appointed Frank Vogel as the state tax commissioner. The senior Vogel then became the state highway commissioner. As one of Langer's closest friends and political advisors, Frank Vogel and his family were close to the Langer family. In high school, Bob Vogel was one of a group of friends, including Emmie Langer, who socialized regularly at the governor's residence on Avenue A and Fourth Street. He graduated from the University of North Dakota in 1939. Following graduation, while working in the trust department of a bank in Minneapolis, he attended the William Mitchell College of Law at night, receiving a juris doctor degree in 1942. Married to Elsa Mork since 1942, the Vogels have four children: Sarah, an attorney and former North Dakota Commissioner of Agriculture; Mary Vogel Carrick, a retired teacher and business owner; Frank, professor of Islamic Law at Harvard Law School; and Bobby, an advocate for the handicapped.

Admitted to the Minnesota bar in 1942 and the North Dakota bar in 1943, Vogel moved his family to Garrison, North Dakota, where he was in private practice from 1943 to 1954. He served as state's attorney for McLean County from 1948 to 1954, and also served on the North Dakota Parole Board, 1949-1954. He was appointed U.S. attorney for the District of North Dakota, in Fargo, North Dakota, 1954 to 1961. He briefly served as special assistant to the U.S. attorney general, 1961-1962, and then entered private law practice in Mandan from 1961 to 1973.

Governor Arthur Link appointed Bob Vogel as a justice to the North Dakota Supreme court in 1973; he was elected the next year to a ten-year term. During his tenure, he wrote more than two hundred opinions for the Court. He resigned in 1978 to become a professor of law at the University of North Dakota Law School. Eventually he reduced his teaching load to part-time and also practiced law in his own office, now Robert Vogel Law Office, P.C. He retired in 1997 after more than fifty years of practicing law.

During his legal career, Vogel lectured at Bar seminars, and once to the National Association of Attorneys General. He is a member of several honorary societies, including the American Law Institute and American Bar Foundation, and has contributed articles to the *Practical Lawyer* and the *North Dakota Law Review*. In addition to being a member of the Minnesota and North Dakota bars, he was also admitted to the Eighth Circuit and United States Supreme Court bars, handling nearly one hundred appeals to various appellate courts. He has represented plaintiffs in cases of medical and legal malpractice and has served as an expert witness in cases of legal malpractice in Canada and the United States, and was named as one of the country's outstanding lawyers in malpractice cases.

Vogel and his wife, Elsa, recently moved to Bismarck, North Dakota, where he continues to write and stays abreast of current legal literature and the political activities in the state.

About the Editor

Janet Daley is a freelance editor and scholar from Bismarck, North Dakota. She served as the editor at at the State Historical Society of North Dakota from 1993 to 2002, editing the state quarterly journal, *North Dakota History*, and publishing fourteen books. Among her many projects, Jan was the managing editor of *A Vast and Open Plain: The Writings of the Lewis and Clark Expedition in North Dakota, 1804-1806* by Clay S. Jenkinson; an editor and contributor to the *Encyclopedia of New York State*; and the indexer and editor for the new *Index to the North Dakota State Historical Quarterly and the State Collections (1906-1944)*. A Phi Beta Kappa graduate of the University of North Dakota (UND) with a B.A. and M.A. in English, Jan received the Maxwell Anderson Alumni Award from the UND Department of English (1997) and was recently named the recipient of the Larry Rowen Remele Award from the Northern Great Plains History Conference Council (2004).

Endnotes

1. Beverly Smith, "The Most Baffling Man in the Senate," *Saturday Evening Post*, Jan. 23, 1954, p. 103.

2. Paul Douglas, *In the Fullness of Time: The Memoirs of Paul H. Douglas* (New York: Harcourt Brace Jovanovich, 1971), p. 178.

3. Theodore B. Pedeliski, "German-Russian Ethnic Factor in William Langer's Campaigns," *North Dakota History* 64.1 (Winter 1997). 2–20.

4. Hereafter, the Nonpartisan League is sometimes called the NPL or the League. For a history of the League, see Robert Morlan's *Political Prairie Fire* (1955; reprint, with a foreword by Larry Remele, St. Paul: Minnesota Historical Society Press, 1985).

5. Smith, "The Most Baffling Man," p. 26.

6. Scott Ellsworth, "Origins of the Nonpartisan League" (Ph.D. diss., Duke University, 1982), iii.

7. Morlan, *Prairie Fire*, p. 214; Elwyn B. Robinson, *History of North Dakota* (Lincoln: University of Nebraska Press, 1966), pp. 327–70.

8. Robinson, *North Dakota*, p. 331; Morlan, *Prairie Fire*, p. 21n.

9. Robinson, *North Dakota*, p. 334; Morlan, *Prairie Fire*, pp. xiv, 47.

10. Larry Remele, "The North Dakota State Library Scandal of 1919," *North Dakota History* 44.1 (Winter 1977): 21–29. No circulation of the offending book had actually taken place in North Dakota schools; see Morlan, *Prairie Fire*, pp. 271–72.

11. Morlan, *Prairie Fire*, pp. 337–38, and Carl H. Chrislock, *Watchdog of Loyalty: The Minnesota Commission of Public Safety During World War I* (St. Paul: Minnesota Historical Society Press, 1991), pp. 166, 273, 318. Townley broke with the NPL in 1922. The contrast between the later careers of Townley and Gilbert is striking.

12. Secretary of State, *North Dakota Centennial Blue Book, 1889-1989* (Bismarck: State Printing Office, 1989).

13. John M. Holzworth, *The Fighting Governor: The Story of William Langer and the State of North Dakota* (Chicago: Pointer Press, 1938), pp. 6–8; *New York Times*, Dec. 4, 1932; Agnes Geelan, *The Dakota Maverick* (Fargo, N.Dak.: Kaye's Printing Co., 1975), p. 18; Robinson, *North Dakota*, p. 335.

14. Robinson, *North Dakota*, pp. 335–36.

15. Robinson, *North Dakota*, p. 336; *Northern Pacific Railway Co v. Morton County*, 32 ND 627, 156 NW 226 (1916); Langer testimony in hearings before the U.S. Senate Committee on Privileges and Elections, pp. 481–82. The Langer hearings before the United States Senate took place during the first and second sessions of the 77th Congress, November 1941–March 1942. Notes on the transcripts of those hearings were taken from the U.S. Congress, Senate Committee on Privileges and Elections, *Senator from North Dakota, Report . . . on the Protest of Various Citizens . . . to the Seating of William Langer*, Senate Report No. 1010, 77th Congress, 2nd Sess., and the U.S. *Congressional Record*, 77th Congress, 1st Sess. 1941. They are part of Record Group 46 and can be found in the Center for Legislative Archives, National Archives and Records Administration (NARA), Washington, D.C. They are cited hereafter as Senate Hearings. In many cases, the author has made extensive notes and transcripts of testimony from the hearings and specific page numbers are not cited in the endnotes. When page numbers are available, they are listed. The seven feet of records includes the testimony taken by the Senate investigators, Elbert Smith and Sam Hood, Jr., which has been typed up and bound into eight Witness Books. Photocopies of the Witness Books were made by the NARA in 1975 and a complete set was deposited with the Langer Papers at the Chester Fritz Library in 1979. They can be found in Boxes 718 and 719 and are paginated consecutively. They are cited hereafter as Witness Books.

16. Ibid.; Holzworth, *Fighting Governor*, pp. 6–8.

17. Pedeliski, "German-Russian Ethnic Factor," pp. 7–11.

18. Pierce Atwater to Harry L. Hopkins, undated, attachment dated Jan. 10, 1935, Box 59, Harry L. Hopkins Papers, Franklin D. Roosevelt Library, Hyde Park, NY, cited hereafter cited as Hopkins Papers. The Hopkins papers for his years in the Department of the Interior were held separately from others in the department in Washington, D.C., apparently because of the predominantly political context of Hopkins's overall relationship to FDR.

19. William Langer Papers, Chester Fritz Library, University of North Dakota, Grand Forks, N. Dak., Collection 19, Boxes 48–54, 64–67, cited hereafter as Langer Papers.

20. Personal communication with the author.

21. Robinson, *North Dakota*, pp. 396–419; D. Jerome Tweton and Daniel F. Rylance, *The Years of Despair: North Dakota in the Depression* (Grand Forks, N.Dak.: The Oxcart Press, 1973, 1974) p. 20; Daniel F. Rylance, "Langer & Themes of North Dakota History," *South Dakota History*, 3 (Winter 1972): 43; Sarah M. Vogel, "The Law of Hard Times: Debtor and Farmer Relief Actions of the 1933 North Dakota Legislative Session," *North Dakota Law Review* 60 (Nov. 3, 1984):489–513; Walter C. Anhalt and Glenn H. Smith, "He Saved the Farm? Governor Langer and the Mortgage Moratoria," *North Dakota Quarterly* 44 (Autumn 1976): 5–17.

22. The acts of Congress allegedly impeded were the Act of July 21, 1932 (Reconstruction Finance Corporation); Act of May 12, 1933 (Federal Emergency Relief Act of 1933); and Act of June 16, 1932 (Industrial Recovery Act). Reconstruction Finance Corporation funding is provided in Sec. 722, Title 15, 1934 Code. Sec. 725 requires that the governor make the applications for funds, and Sec. 726 requires that the governor file monthly reports.

23. Ibid.; Geelan, *Dakota Maverick*, pp. 69–78.

24. Langer Papers, Box 13, Folder 15; Holzworth, *Fighting Governor*, p. 12.

25. S. Vogel, "Law of Hard Times"; Robinson, *North Dakota*, p. 405.

26. Robinson, *North Dakota*, p. 410; Holzworth, *Fighting Governor*, pp. 73–74.

27. Secretary of State, North Dakota, *Election Returns, 1930–1944*; Pedeliski, "German Russian Ethnic Factor," p. 14.

28. Robinson, *North Dakota*, pp. 403–11.

29. Ibid.; Holzworth, *Fighting Governor*, pp. 52–97; Geelan, *Dakota Maverick*, pp. 69–78.

30. Senate Hearings, p. 80.

31. Notes in author's possession.

32. The author has copies of radio speeches given by Frank Vogel during the 1930s, with blue-penciled excisions, made by the attorneys for KFYR Radio (Bismarck), Cox and Cox, who were also attorneys for many large corporations inimical to Langer and the League.

33. Senate Hearings, pp. 505 ff. KFJM, later known as KUND, at the University of North Dakota, has some documents on the attempted buyout by Columbia Broadcasting Company. The radio station has since merged with North Dakota Public Radio.

34. The author has a copy of a form letter from William Langer to Senator W. E. Matthaei, enclosing a refund of a prior contribution for the failed effort.

35. A copy of the proceedings of the North Dakota House of Representatives fact-finding committee, held in August 1934, can be found in the Langer Papers, Box 61, Folder 4, and are numbered pages 1–66; pages 67 and following are missing. Argast's testimony is found on p. 27. Cited hereafter as North Dakota House Committee proceedings.

36. Ibid., pp. 2–6.

37. Ibid., p. 7.

38. Ibid., pp. 7–9.

39. *Bismarck Tribune*, Oct. 29, 1932.

40. Holzworth, *Fighting Governor*, p. 18.

41. In a 1998 interview with K. W. "Bill" Simons, Jr., the son of K. W. "Kenneth" Simons, the editor of the *Bismarck Tribune* in the 1930s, the younger Simons told the author that he had accepted his father's negative portrayal of William Langer until he discovered that many of his college friends admired the former governor/senator. Upon looking into the record of these years, he surmised that he had been "brainwashed" by his father due to some inexplicable hostility between the two. Bill Simons is a distinguished journalist in his own right, and formerly a long-standing, well-respected teacher on the Turtle Mountain Reservation.

42. *Bismarck Tribune*, Oct. 29, 1932. The general election was November 8. The complaint Bradford wrote did not say Langer promised to obtain a pardon, only that he would work to obtain a pardon or other release from the penitentiary.

43. Ibid., Nov. 14, 1932.

44. Ibid., Nov. 20, 1932.

45. Ibid., Dec. 21, 1932.

46. Witness Books, 505ff.; Esther Johnson, starting at p. 532; Ruth Gorman at p.558; Edith Hultin at p. 361 (daughters); O. B. Herigstad at p. 330; Ben Bradford at p. 383; Girdell "Dell" Patterson at p. 1399; Ethel Mills at p. 2473; as well as Langer's testimony at the Senate Committee hearing. Herigstad was the prosecuting attorney, Patterson was a former deputy sheriff and later warden of the state penitentiary, and Mills was Langer's secretary while he was in private practice.

47. Transcripts of the "affidavits" reflect that interviewees were frequently asked to comment on what they knew about several of the more sensational and politically sensitive cases Langer was involved in.

48. Senate Hearings, p. 1987.

49. Edward C. Blackorby, *Prairie Populist: The Life and Times of Usher L. Burdick* (Fargo: North Dakota Institute for Regional Studies and the State Historical Society of North Dakota, 2001), p. 200.

50. *Leader*, July 14, 1933, p. 1.

51. *Bismarck Tribune*, Nov. 7, 1932.

52. Ibid., Nov. 9, 1932.

53. Pedeliski, "German-Russian Ethnic Factor," pp. 13–14.

54. Ibid., p. 14.

55. North Dakota Secretary of State, Compilation of State and National Election Returns, 1930-1944.

56. Hopkins Papers, Box 27. Some of the letters, such as Kinzer's (July 22, 1933) and Anderson's (July 6, 1933), can also be found in RG 118, Records

of the U.S. Attorney, National Archives–Central Plains Region, Kansas City, Mo.

57. Hopkins Papers, Box 27, letter dated July 22, 1933.

58. Ewing testimony at first trial.

59. Robert E. Sherwood, *Roosevelt and Hopkins: An Intimate History* (New York: Harper and Brothers, 1948), p. 77.

60. Hopkins Papers, Box 59, T. J. Edmonds to Aubrey Williams, Jan. 10, 1934; Ibid., Box 74, transcripts of telephone conversations of Apr. 9 and 18, 1934.

61. Ibid., Box 59, letter to Hopkins, May 7, 1935. There are other similar letters.

62. North Dakota House Committee proceedings, pp. 17–34.

63. *Langer v. United States*, 76 F2d 817 (Eighth Circuit, 1935).

64. See *U.S. v. Byers*, 73 F2d (Second Circuit, 1934), and a letter from the U.S. attorney in Cincinnati to Lanier, Apr. 19, 1935, Lanier Papers.

65. Records of the Justice Department, May 19, 1934, National Archives–Central Plains Region, Kansas City, Mo. Cited hereafter as Justice Department Records.

66. Wayne S. Cole, *Senator Gerald P. Nye and American Foreign Relations* (Westport, Conn.: Greenwood Press, 1962), p. 57

67. *Congressional Record-Senate*, Mar.1, 1935.

68. Justice Department Records, mail and files division, nos. 95–56, sub 5, Oct. 9, 1934 to June 29, 1935, pp. 9–10.

69. North Dakota House Committee proceedings, pp. 17–20.

70. Thomas Moodie to James Farley, Hopkins Papers, Box 59.

71. Ibid., Jan. 21, 1936.

72. Ibid., Mar. 10,1936.

73. Ibid., June 17,1936.

74. John C. Eaton to James Farley, July 24, 1936, ibid.

75. Records of the Justice Department, mail and files division, nos. 95–56, sub 5, Oct. 9, 1934 to June 29, 1935, pp. 9–10.

76. Hopkins Papers, Box 59, Dec. 30, 1933; Apr. 18, 1934; Ewing, a witness at the first trial, testified that it was a good committee, and the letters and several transcribed phone calls between him and Hopkins says the same.

77. Correspondence and notes in author's possession.

78. Ibid.

79. Ibid.

80. *Congressional Record-Senate*, v. 88, Part 1, pp. 1350, 1396.

81. Ibid., p. 1396.

82. Notes in author's possession.

83. Ibid.

84. Ibid.; correspondence in author's possession.

85. Notes in author's possession.

86. Langer testimony, Senate Hearings, pp. 481–82; *Northern Pacific v. Morton Co.*, 32 ND 627, 156 NW 226 (1916). The $1.25 million computes to roughly seventeen million dollars in 2003 currency. Comparisons are based on computations of inflation by the Minneapolis Federal Reserve bank and published on its website.

87. Langer Papers, Box 13, folder A-19; Langer testimony, Senate Hearings, pp. 88–89.

88. Langer testimony, Senate Hearings, p. 489.

89. In those days, an attorney general was allowed to also engage in private practice, but then, as now, conflicts of interest were forbidden.

90. Morlan, *Prairie Fire*, p. 342.

91. Collection 968, North Dakota Room, Chester Fritz Library, University of North Dakota. The group included former North Dakota Supreme Court Judge B. F. Spalding, former governor E. J. Sarles, former U.S. senator A. J. Gronna, and many prominent Republican legislators and party officials. Miller became the only federal judge in North Dakota in 1937 when Judge Amidon retired, until his own retirement in 1941. For more on North Dakota's federal judges, see Ardell Tharaldson, *Patronage: Histories and Biographies of North Dakota's Federal Judges* (Bismarck, N.Dak.: North Dakota Branch of the Historical Society of the U.S. Courts in the Eighth Circuit, 2002).

92. Notes in author's possession.

93. Ibid.; see also Robinson, *North Dakota*, pp. 396–419; Geelan, *Dakota Maverick*, pp. 69–78; Holzworth, *Fighting Governor*; Tweton and Rylance, *Years of Despair*, p. 20; Rylance, "William Langer," p. 43; S. Vogel, "The Law of Hard Times,"pp. 489–513; Anhalt and Smith, "He Saved the Farm?" pp. 5–17; Pedeliski, "German-Russian Ethnic Factor," pp. 2–20.

94. Usher Burdick testimony, Senate Hearings, p. 373. Langer testified to the same effect.

95. Since that time in North Dakota, the affidavit has been abolished and each party is entitled to one change of judge, but the Supreme Court names the new judge.

96. Lanier to the Justice Department, Oct. 23, 1935, Justice Department Records.

97. Gale Wyman testimony, Senate Hearings.

98. Report of Don M. Jackson, special assistant to the attorney general, Mar.14, 1936, Justice Department Records.

99. *Scott v. Frazier*, 258 F. 669 (DCND 1919); affd., 253 U.S. 243 (1920), following *Green v. Frazier*, 253 U.S. 233 (1920).

100. Langer testimony, Senate Hearings, p. 526.

101. Usher Burdick, North Dakota House Committee proceedings. See also RG 188, Records of the U.S. Attorney, Boxes 13 and 15, National Archives–Central Plains Region, Kansas City, Missouri.

102. James Hanley testimony, Senate Hearings, p. 361. Hanley, who was one of Langer's defense attorneys, repeated what Judge Miller had told him to Langer before the start of the first trial.

103. District Court of the United States for the District of North Dakota, Southwestern Division, December Term, 1933, p. 1.

104. Ibid., p. 9.

105. Ibid., p. 10.

106. Ibid., p. 11. For more on the repayment to Langer, see Holzworth, *Fighting Governor*, p. 94.

107. Ibid., p. 12.

108. Because the rules are so unfair to defendants, and because of the abuse of the conspiracy laws in the Langer prosecutions in 1934–35, which used and abused the conspiracy laws, and the abuse of the same laws in the persecution of some of the Nonpartisan League organizers in Minnesota during World War I and the Red Scare that followed, during the seven years I was U.S. attorney for the District of North Dakota (1954–61), I never used the conspiracy statutes to prosecute any resident of the United States. I did, however, attempt to use them once to reach a resident of Canada who planned crimes committed in the United States.

109. In the later perjury trial [Dec. 3–6, 1935], Lanier's notes on jurors contain two lists of jurors, each with twenty or more names. One of these lists was headed "Very Bad," with many of those names listed as "Langerite." RG 118, Box 9, Records of the U.S. Attorney, National Archives–Central Plains Region, Kansas City, Mo.

110. When the defense made a motion to "quash" or dismiss the jury panel, they specified that twenty-two of the twenty-three persons on the grand jury that had issued the indictment were opponents of the League, and that twenty of them lived in cities, while 70 percent of North Dakotans lived on farms. Ibid., RG 188, Box 2, Folder 1.

111. Frank Talcott himself, according to Burdick's testimony in the U.S. Senate in 1941, "was pretty bad on jury selection," and at that time was doing nine years in the Leavenworth Penitentiary, convicted of embezzlement of federal funds while he was deputy clerk. Burdick; Senate Hearings.

112. Notes in author's possession. Hooper was later appointed postmaster at Fargo. Montgomery had been clerk since the court was established in 1890, forty-four years earlier, shortly after North Dakota became a state. He remained as clerk until his death in 1942 and was succeeded by Judge Miller's long-time court reporter and secretary, Beatrice A. McMichael.

113. Langer testimony, Senate Hearings, pp. 522–3; Langer testimony, transcript of first trial, pp.19–21, which can be found in *Langer v. United States*, 76 F 2d 817 (Eighth Circuit, 1935), RG 276, Records of the Circuit Court of Appeals, National Archives–Central Plains Region, Kansas City, Mo. Cited hereafter as Trial Transcript. My thanks to Ed Klecker, clerk of courts for the District of North Dakota, Eighth Circuit, Quentin N. Burdick Courthouse, Fargo, who assisted me in finding those records.

114. North Dakota Statutes: Sec. 814, 1925 Supplement, Ch. 81, and 1921 Session Laws, which included women. *Federal Judicial Code* 275,USC Sec.1–28, Sec. 41.

115. Langer Papers, Collection 205, Box 2, Folder 4.

116. Ibid., Box 2, Folder 1.

117. North Dakota House Committee proceedings, p. 42; correspondence in author's possession. For a complete history of Burdick's personal and political life, see Blackorby, *Prairie Populist: The Life and Times of Usher L. Burdick*.

118. The quoted material in this and the two paragraphs below are from Usher Burdick, North Dakota House Committee proceedings, pp. 34–50.

119. Ibid., pp. 51–56; Robinson, *North Dakota*, pp. 415–16.

120. Usher Burdick testimony, Senate Hearings, pp. 353–74; on jury selection, pp. 357–8, 366–9. See also Geelan, *Dakota Maverick*, pp. 91-104.

121. J. M. Hanley testimony, Senate Hearings, pp. 375 ff.

122. Ibid., pp. 375–99; on friendship with Judge Miller, p. 385.

123. Ibid., p. 356.

124. Ibid.

125. Ibid., Gunvaldson papers, Collection 391, Box 1, Folder M, Chester Fritz Library, University of North Dakota, Grand Forks.

126. All quoted material in this paragraph is from Burdick testimony, Senate Hearings, p. 357.

127. Ibid., pp. 46–48.

128. Ibid.

129. Francis Murphy testimony, Senate Hearings, pp. 732ff.

130. A major revision of the Federal Judicial Code in 1948 set up a system of federal random selection of juries, in 28 USC Sec. 1861.

131. 28 USC 276.

132. Murphy testimony, Senate Hearings, pp. 732ff. This is still the practice in federal court in North Dakota and most other federal courts. Most trial lawyers prefer the state system in which the lawyers interrogate the jurors. Many judges prefer the federal system, which takes less time and yields less of the information the lawyer are looking for.

133. Langer testimony, Senate Hearings, pp. 525ff.

134. *Leader*, May 31, 1934.

135. Ibid.

136. Ibid., p. 526.

137. House Concurrent Resolution A-6, 1935 Session Laws, 442. U.S. Senator Schall of Minnesota also introduced a similar resolution in the United States Senate on August 26, 1935, but it was not passed, and reform of the federal justice system did not come until many years later, in 1948, as part of a rewriting of the judicial code.

138. Langer testimony, Senate Hearings, pp. 525ff

139. Ibid.

140. I believe Langer misstated himself or was misquoted here. The Gronna on the Securities Commission was Arthur J. Gronna, a son of Asle J. Gronna, who was both a congressman and a U.S. senator from North Dakota. Another son, James Gronna, was later a state district judge, with chambers in Minot.

141. Geelan, *Dakota Maverick*, pp. 71–72, has a similar report.

142. *Bismarck Tribune*, May 25, 1934, day one of the trial.

143. Trial Transcript.

144. Langer's testimony is from the trial transcript, explained more fully in the Senate Hearings, 1941, and various other places. Langer was recalled several times to accommodate other witnesses.

145. This would be about $700,000 in 2002 dollars. His estimated attorney's income was $25,000 per year, more than $335,000 in 2002. For comparison, his salary as governor in 1935 was $4,000 per year, equal to $52,525 in 2002 dollars.

146. *Bismarck Tribune*, May 28, 1934; Senate Hearings, p. 541.

147. North Dakota House Committee proceedings, 1934.

148. Langer's testimony on the debt of the committee starts at p. 1115, trial transcript.

149. Ibid.

150. Ibid.

151. Senate Hearings, pp. 555–59; Blackorby, *Prairie Populist*, p. 218.

152. Trial transcript.

153. Ibid.

154. Lorena Hickok, *One Third of a Nation: Lorena Hickok Reports on the Great Depression* (1983; new ed.; Urbana: University of Illinois Press, 2000), Richard Lowitt and Maurine Beasley, eds., pp. 58–59. Henry A. Wallace was Roosevelt's secretary of agriculture.

155. Trial transcript, pp. 1115ff.

156. Ann Rathke, *Lady, If You Go Into Politics* (Bismarck, N.Dak.: Sweetgrass Communications, 1992), pp. 52–53.

157. Ibid., pp. 53–54; "Woman's Sagacity Wins Gavel of North Dakota Speakership: Nonpartisan League Honors Mrs. Minnie Craig for Ability," *Christian Science Monitor*, Jan.16, 1933.

158. Hickok, *One Third of a Nation*, p. 56. Lorena Hickok recognized Craig's sensitivity to the serious problems in North Dakota in a letter to Harry Hopkins, written Nov. 3, 1933. See p. 70.

159. The *Leader* did not begin publication until July 14, 1933, so obviously the committee was not appointed to take over as a result of Langer's indictment and removal, as some writers have assumed.

160. This judgment by the FERA man-on-the-spot is in sharp contrast to the impressions related by Lorena Hickok to Harry Hopkins during her brief swing through North Dakota from October 30 to November 6, 1933. See Hickok, *One Third of a Nation*, pp. 55–76.

161. The statutes are cited in the chapter on the inception of the trials.

162. See *Bismarck Tribune*, May 9, 1934, as one example.

163. Trial transcript, p. 1229.

164. Ibid.

165. Pages 21–34, transcript of instructions (Justice files); pp. 1233–46 of trial transcript in Kansas City Archives, Box 2.

166. Ibid., p. 1223.

167. Ibid., p. 1248.

168. Ibid., pp. 1234–35.

169. Ibid., p. 1238.

170. Ibid., p. 1248.

171. Senate Hearings, Burdick testimony begins at page 1 and again at page 353.

172. It does not necessarily always work out that way. When this author was U.S. attorney from 1952 to 1961, I did as much trial work as any of my very good assistants, sometimes more. It is up to the U.S. attorney to decide whether he wants to be a trial lawyer or an administrator, or both.

173. Senate Hearings, p. 361.

174. Ibid.

175. Ibid.

176. Ibid., pp. 375ff.

177. Ibid., p. 361.

178. Trial transcript, pp. 1257–58.

179. Ibid., pp. 1258–59.

180. Ibid., p. 1256.

181. Robinson, *North Dakota*, p. 410. In this author's fifty years of trial work, I have never witnessed such effusive praise given to a jury by any judge.

182. Senate transcript, pp. 536–37.

183. Ibid., pp. 539–42, affidavit in full plus headlines referred to.

184. Any other judge, it can safely be said, would have released all of them on their own recognizance (i.e., a personal bond that they would appear when required to do so), or, at most, a bond signed by the defendant pledging specific real estate as surety for his appearance. This form of bond that guarantees appearance was, and still is, the standard form of bond in use in North Dakota and the federal courts.

185. Langer, Senate hearings.

186. *Harvard Law Review* 48 (Feb. 1935): 687–8, *Illinois Law Review* 229 (Mar. 1935): 945–7, *University of Pennsylvania Law Review* 83 (Jan. 1935): 386–7, and *University of Chicago Law Review* 2 (Feb. 1935): 333–4.

187. *State ex rel Salisbury v. Vogel*, 65 N.D. 137, 256 N.W. 404 (1934).

188. *State ex rel Welford v. Langer*, 65 N.D. 68, 256 N.W.377 (1934).

189. A brief treatment of this tumultuous time in North Dakota's gubernatorial history can be found in Daniel F. Rylance, "The Political Crisis of 1934: William Langer and His Fight for the Governorship," in *North Dakota's Former Governor's Mansion: Its History and Preservation*, ed.

by Virginia L. Heidenreich (Bismarck: State Historical Society of North Dakota, 1992)., pp. 51–62.

190. *Leader*, July 26, 1934, p. 1.

191. North Dakota House Committee proceedings.

192. Ibid., Box 61, Folders 4 and 13.

193. Ibid.

194. Trial transcript.

195. Testimony of Dave Hamilton, Frank Vogel, and Hepner, Witness Books.

196. U.S. Court of Appeals, *Langer v. U.S.*, 76 F 2d 817, p. 826.

197. Langer received 113,027 votes to 37,934 for the IVA (regular Republican) candidate, J. P. Cain, and 47,380 for the anti-Langer League (Rumper) candidate, T. H. H. Thoreson. The term "Rumper" was a term of disparagement used by the majority Nonpartisan Leaguers to describe their dissident opponents when the latter walked out of League conventions or refused to support League candidates.

198. Langer's testimony, Senate Hearings.

199. *Leader*, March 21, 1935.

200. U.S. Court of Appeals, *Langer v. United States*, 76 F 2d 817.

201. Ibid., pp. 826–28.

202. Ibid., p. 828.

203. *Grand Forks Herald*, Dec.15, 1997.

204. *State v. Norton*, 255 NW 787 (ND 1934).

205. Federal law so provided until 1948 when a revision of the Judicial Code set up a system of federal law for random selection among all citizens. See 28 USC Sec.1861.

206. *Duren v. Missouri*, 439 U.S. 357, 58 L. Ed. 579, 99 S. Ct. 664 (1979).

207. Statutes at Large, p. 1147 It has been amended several times since, but it did not ever apply to any of the four Langer trials.

208. *Leader*, May 9, 1935.

209. *Fargo Forum*, May 8, 1935.

210. Ibid.

211. Transcript of the perjury trial, Box 13, p. 60, RG 118, Records of the U.S. Attorney, National Archives–Central Plains Region, Kansas City, Mo.

212. *Congressional Directory*.

213. Murphy testimony, Senate Hearings, pp. 737ff.

214. Senate Hearings, pp. 551–3. The statute at that time was 28 USC 25 (1934).

215. Langer Papers, Collection 205, Box 2, Folder 1, has this and other documents on the perjury trial. Judge Wyman was also appointed to try the retrials of the conspiracy case.

216. See Tharaldson, *Patronage*, pp. 72–77, for information on Davies. I tried cases before Judge Collette, who was a friend of Harry Truman's and very adept at talking lawyers out of making objections.

217. *Bismarck Tribune*, December 2, 1940.

218. Murphy testimony, Senate Hearings, pp. 734–7.

219. Ibid.

220. Murphy testimony, Senate Hearings, p. 741; the indictment is in Langer Papers, Collection 205, Box 2, Folder 1.

221. *Congressional Directory*.

222. *United States v. Berger*, 255 U.S. 34, in which the United States Supreme Court, in a statement not necessary for the decision, mentioned the possibility of a perjury charge based on an affidavit of prejudice, but cited no case law, and indicated that the only function of a judge against whom such an affidavit is filed is to determine whether the allegation, assuming it to be true, would be sufficient to indicate a bias, and if so the judge must withdraw. He must accept the allegation as true in making his determination, and allegations on information and belief are sufficient to raise the issue.

223. Miller's "affidavit," Witness Books, p. 718.

224. Judge A. Lee Wyman testimony, Senate Hearings, p. 151.

225. Langer Papers, Collection 205, Box 2, Folders 1 and 5. A copy of the affidavit is also set out in full in Holzworth, *Fighting Governor*, Appendix A, pp. 123–9.

226. Murphy to Langer, Oct. 17, 1935, Langer Papers, Box 61, Folder 10,

227. Memorandum, Jackson to Department of Justice, Jan.16, 1936, Justice Department Records.

228. Perjury trial transcript, p. 60.

229. Lanier's letters to the Justice Department, Justice Department Records.

230. Ibid., Oct. 19, 1935.

231. Ibid., Oct. 23, 1935.

232. Edward Bushell was one of the four jurors in the William Penn trial of 1670 who refused to agree to the verdict the judge decreed the jury should choose. Though they suffered torture, they were successful in striking down

the "Conventicle Act," which made the Church of England the only legal church in England, leading to freedom of religion, the right to peaceful assembly, freedom of speech, and habeas corpus.

233. Murphy testimony, Senate Hearings.

234. Ibid.

235. Mulloy testimony, Senate Hearings, pp. 546–7; Gale Wyman concurred, Witness Books, pp. 116 and 122.

236. Langer testimony, Senate Hearings, p. 681.

237. Statement of Judge Wyman, Witness Books, p. 151.

238. Langer testimony, Senate Hearings.

239. Bill Langer, in 1936 campaign for governor.

240. Justice Department to Lanier, Oct. 19, 1935, Justice Department Records. Justice papers,

241. Langer testimony, Senate Hearings, p. 636. During the existence of the Langer Defense Fund, one enthusiastic supporter suggested that supporters sell a steer and donate the proceeds. There was no record that anyone ever did, but the suggestion created a storm of disparagement in the daily press.

242. House Concurrent Resolution A-G, 1935 SL, Selection of Unbiased Federal Jurors.

243. Blackorby, *Prairie Populist*, pp. 186–202.

244. Burdick testimony, Senate Hearings, pp. 359–60.

245. Lanier records, Box 13, Folder 3. The legal doctrine of "opening the door" arises when a lawyer asks a witness about part of a subject or transaction, and this permits the opposing lawyer to bring out the rest of the facts of that transaction or subject. Since Langer was present in court, it would otherwise have been improper for his counsel to read his testimony in a prior trial.

246. Murphy testimony, Senate Hearings, pp. 745–6.

247. Senate Hearings, pp. 550–51.

248. Herman Charboneau, in an interview with a University of North Dakota student, Byron Sieber, March 23, 1974; one of a group of Depression interviews, Chester Fritz Library, University of North Dakota, FILE 5.??

249. Charboneau's "affidavit," Witness Books, pp. 1497ff.

250. Senate Hearings, pp. 216 ff. Even if events years later showed gratitude from Langer supporters to Reich, it should be obvious that such gratitude is not proof that a juror was bribed during or before a trial. Lawyers and litigants and judges often thank jurors for a verdict, but that does not necessarily prove the verdict is tainted.

251. Charboneau's "affidavit,"Witness Books, pp. 1497ff.

252. Burdick's "affidavit," Witness Books, pp. 360, 368; Langer, pp. 536, 671; Murphy, p. 748.

253. Murphy, Witness Books, p. 748.

254. Charboneau's "affidavit," Witness Books, pp.1497ff.

255. Ibid.

256. Senate Hearings, p. 766, where attorneys for the protesters, Verry and others, denied any intention to impugn Judge Wyman. Judge Wyman's own statement to Hood and Smith can be found on p. 151 of the Witness Books.

257. Murphy to the Justice Department, Justice Department Records.

258. Usher L. Burdick and George Wallace letters to the Justice Department, Justice Department Records.

259. Dan M. Jackson, special assistant to the Attorney General, to Attorney General Cummings, Jan. 16, 1936, Justice Department Records.

260. *Fargo Forum,* Morning Edition, Dec. 20, 1935.

261. *Leader*, Dec. 26, 1935.

262. P. W. Lanier to Attorney General Cummings, Apr. 3, 1936, Justice Department Records.

263. Jackson to Attorney General Cummings, Mar. 14, 1936, Justice Department Records.

264. *Langer v. United States*, 76 F 2d 817 (Eighth Circuit, 1935), RG 276, Records of the Circuit Court of Appeals. National Archives–Central Plains Region, Kansas City, Mo.

265. Rylance, "The Political Crisis of 1934."

266. North Dakota Supreme Court, *Sathre v. Moodie*, 258 NW 558, 65 ND 340 (1935).

267. Pedeliski, "German-Russian Ethnic Factor," pp. 14–16.

268. Amick was a member of Verry's committee working to unseat Langer. His testimony starts at p. 427, Witness Books.

269. Blackorby, *Prairie Populist*, p. 227.

270. Ibid., pp. 227–28.

271. Langer received 61,533 votes to Frazier's 48,441 and Whelan's 42,271 in the primary.

272. Geelan, *Dakota Maverick*, p. 91.

273. Ethel Mills's "affidavit," Witness Books, starts at p. 2473. She was Langer's long-time secretary in private practice.

274. Ibid.

275. Senate Hearings, p. 731.

276. Mulloy testimony, Senate Hearings, p. 50. He worked from April or May 1940, and was then friendly to Langer. After being fired, he ran against Erickson for the position of insurance commissioner and was critical of his former boss, but not of Langer.

277. *Bismarck Tribune*, Jan. 14, 1939.

278. For evidence, consult the following statements in the Witness Books: Pat Wood, p. 104 (womanizer, drinker, bad checks); Gale Wyman, beginning at p. 22 (alcoholic, womanizer); J. D. Evans, pp. 166, 194, 239 (owes him money, drinks a lot, "mysterious women"); C. G. Byerly, mayor of Mandan, p. 2125 (double crosser, drunk, bum checks); P. G. Miller, p. 1583, ("rotten, darn outlaw," drunk on job, padded expenses); Ethel Mills, p. 2473 (had affair with a woman in Chicago, got paid two salaries from state, drunkard); C. J. Myers, p. 2751 (listed as "Meyers" by investigators; bad checks, jumped hotel bills, drunk); Dr. M. W. Roan, p. 2931 (most disreputable man in North Dakota, drunkard, owes bills); Alvin C. Strutz, p. 3068 (rewrote bills to get double salary, fired him for not working); Oscar E. Erickson, pp. 3360, 3466 (still owes on fifty dollar note; hired because of his family and fired for not working); C. J. Murphy, p. 3927, of Grand Forks, attorney for Great Northern railway; C. P. Stone, p. 746, former brother-in-law; J. A. Hagarty. There is considerable testimony to the same effect in the trial transcripts. Mulloy himself admits lying to a political friend (Art Bonzer) and accepting $275 from him in return for a false promise to tell the inside story of his break with Langer, which had not happened (p. 75), lying to his former brother-in-law that he was getting five thousand dollars from Senator Nye to expose Langer (p. 75), and that he was a criminal (p. 77). This all contrasts to the investigators' failure to mention any problems with Mulloy's credibility. Instead they called him "the star witness for the protestants" (p. 17 of the "List of Persons" in their report).

279. Langer testified Mrs. Mulloy told him this and there was no attorney-client relation between them.

280. Mulloy testimony, Senate Hearings, pp. 76, 77, and 80.

281. Ibid., pp. 65 and 67.

282. Fuller, Witness Books, starting at p. 888. Mulloy admitted the contact and he also admitted that his trip to see Fuller was partly paid for by Senator Nye, who told Fuller to pay for it, as will appear later.

283. *North Dakota Centennial Blue Book, 1989-1999*, pp. 273, 277, 280, 283, and 299.

284. Strutz's "affidavit," Witness Books, beginning at p. 3068, and C. J. "Red" Myers's "affidavit," beginning at p. 2751, Witness Books.

285. Senate Hearings, p, 106.

286. The fourth time was *Verry v. Yule*, 15 NW 2d 210 (ND 1944) in which the Supreme Court reversed a decision in his wife's favor in the District Court.

287. 42 ND 264, 172 NW 867 (1919).

288. *NW Reporter*, p. 868.

289. 163 NW 2d 721 (ND 1969), p. 735.

290. 191 NW 2d 798 (ND 1971).

291. Witness Books in the Langer Papers.

292. If any reader believes the author has overstated or misstated the actions of the Senate investigators, that reader should read the report of the minority members of the Senate Committee, which contains more vitriolic descriptions of those actions than this chapter does. The minority report is Document 11, part two, Senate Reports, 77th Congress, 2nd Session, No. 19556, Government Reports Section, Chester Fritz Library, University of North Dakota, and other federal depositories. The majority report is part one of the same document 11 and was obviously much influenced by the Witness Books prepared by the investigators. It contains some indications that it may have been written, at least in part, by the investigators themselves.

293. Two examples include promises made to J. K. Murray and John Fleck during their "affidavits" in the Witness Books. There were many others.

294. A search of the Burleigh County records was made for cases filed there, but most of the records had been destroyed pursuant to a law that specifies a time after which records can be destroyed unless the State Historical Society decides they should be preserved. Some brief document entries were found. None indicated a judgment against Langer. The information given here is largely from Langer's Senate testimony and the Senate investigators' Witness Books.

295. See Langer testimony, Senate Hearings, pp. 444–45, and the "affidavit" of J. P. Newton, clerk of the North Dakota Supreme Court, Witness Books, p. 2725.

296. Newton interview, Witness Books, p. 3725.

297. Langer testimony, Senate Hearings.

298. Ibid.

299. Smith, "The Most Baffling Man," p. 102.

300. Sources for this section are Langer's testimony, Senate Hearings, and the "affidavit" of Andrew Feist, Witness Books, p. 3264, who acted as intermediary between Langer and the friend who talked to the divorced woman when Langer was not allowed to talk to her.

301. Swain's "affidavit," Witness Books, p. 2262. Scores of other people were asked the same question.

302. Langer testimony, Senate Hearings.

303. *Bismarck Tribune*, Feb. 2–3, 1934.

304. The facts stated in this discussion are based largely on the testimonies of Langer, Brunk, Brewer, and Sullivan, given as witnesses before to the Senate Committee, much of it undisputed. Testimony to the contrary, if there was any, will be discussed. Some came from three out-of-state appraisers, chosen by the Senate Committee: Ellis Southworth, Ersel Walley, and True D. Morse.

305. Testimony of Brunk, Brewer, and Sullivan, Senate Hearings; Sullivan's "affidavit," Witness Books, p. 3956 ff.

306. Brunk testimony, Senate Hearings.

307. This discussion is based largely on the "affidavits" of Thomas V. Sullivan (more than 100 pages but barely mentioned by the investigators in their report), Congressman Lemke, Tax Commissioner John Gray, Witness Books; Langer testimony, Senate Hearings.

308. James Manahan, *Trials of a Lawyer* (Minneapolis: Franham Printing Co., 1933).

309. This writer has a photocopy of a political poster advertising an NPL meeting at Pembina, N. Dak., on March 22, 1920, at which "Attorney Thomas Sullivan of Saint Paul" was to speak.

310. *Gilbert v. Minnesota*, 254 U.S. 325 (1920).

311. The story of the origin in Mexico of the animosity of the two is set forth in, of all places, the Senate's memorial volume after Langer's death, in an appendix by Usher L. Burdick, a long-time friend of both. Langer and Lemke had many disagreements in later years, political and otherwise, as biographies of each make clear.

312. 297 U.S. 135, 56 S. Ct. 426, 80 L. Ed. 532 (1936).

313. Senator Tom Connally, Senate committee member, Senate Hearings, p. 617.

314. Geelan, *Dakota Maverick*, 92–104; Blackorby, *Prairie Populist*, pp. 242–47.

315. Geelan, *Dakota Maverick*, p. 103.

316. Ibid.

317. Ibid.

318. Robert M. Horne, "The Controversy over the Seating of William Langer, 1940–1942" (master's thesis, University of North Dakota, 1964).

319. Howard Fuller "affidavit," Witness Books, p. 888ff.

320. Senate Hearings, p. 798, where it is quoted from the Lemke "affidavit" given to the Senate investigators.

321. This admission of lack of the basis for charges he had publicly made for many campaigns, as well as the well-known fact that he had violated the regulations of the North Dakota Homebuilders Association law by borrowing money from it to build in Fargo a large house costing many times the five-thousand-dollar maximum amount permitted, makes it puzzling to figure out why he is recognized by historians, such as Robinson, as thoroughly honest.

322. *Leader*, July 4, 1940.

323. Senate Hearings, p. 85. E. J. Klaudt, who had been working with Mulloy and Clyde Duffy, testified to some accounting records in the Senate hearings and said that that he was then employed then as "special examining commissioner," but did not name Governor Moses specifically, although it appears that he was the governor's employee, Senate Hearings, p. 313. Duffy did not offer specific testimony as to his own role, see Senate Hearings, p. 131.

324. *Bismarck Tribune*, Feb. 17, 1939.

325. Edward C. Blackorby, *Prairie Rebel: The Public Life of William Lemke* (Lincoln: University of Nebraska Press, 1963), p. 244.

326. E. J. Klaudt had brought the action against Insurance Commissioner Oscar E. Erickson. See *Leader*, July 23, 1942.

327. Hopkins Papers.

328. Having been, after a short interval of a year, Lanier's successor, I can state with assurance that the decision to prosecute rests fully in the hands of the U.S. attorney or his assistant to whom he delegates the authority. Various federal investigative agencies investigate allegations of crime and report to the U.S. attorney, but he decides whether to proceed. (The Justice Department may have the authority to order a prosecution dropped but it never did during my seven years in that position.)

329. Lanier letter to Attorney General, Oct. 23, 1935. Later, in a request for extra funds for a court reporter to record the proceedings of the grand jury, Lanier stated that Judge Miller had ordered the presentation to the grand jury. In my experience, grand juries (which only hear one side of the case) almost invariably indict if the prosecuting attorney wants an indictment.

330. Ibid.

331. Justice papers, Oct. 19, 1034.

332. *Graves v. New York ex rel. O'Keefe*, 306 U.S. 486 (1939).

333. Feb. 15, 1935.

334. *Leader*, Oct. 22, 1942.

335. Robert Vogel papers.

336. 395 US 486 (1969); see also Justice William Douglas's "The Court Years," pp. 150–51.

337. Senator Green, reported a Resolution (S. Res. 220) accompanied by a report (#1010). The resolution, reads in part: "Resolved, That the case of William Langer does not fall within the constitutional provisions for expulsion or any punishment by a two-thirds vote, because Senator Langer is neither charged with nor proven to have committed disorderly behavior during his membership in the Senate (emphasis added), *Congressional Record*, Jan. 29, 1942 (77th Congress, Second Session, Vol. 88, Part l, p. 822.

338. Presidential records, Hyde Park, Aug. 4, 1943.

339. One example among many: *Congressional Record*, Vol. 105, part 3, p. 3529, shows that on March 9, 1959, the year he died, he introduced S. J. Resolution 69, a "Joint Resolution proposing an amendment to the Constitution of the United States Relative to the Equal Rights for men and women," on behalf of himself and Senator Dodd.

340. Vogel source.

341. Arthur John Keeffe, July 1959.

342. *New York Times*, Jan. 1, 1952, p. 6.

343. Robert Vogel recollection.

344. In the early Nonpartisan League years, membership dues were either six dollars, or later sixteen dollars for two years. League enemies called the members "sixteen-dollar suckers." Sixteen dollars in 1928 would be equivalent to about $150 in 2002.

345. *Grand Forks Herald*, Nov. 9, 1959, reporting speech at New England, N. Dak.

346. *Leader*, May 4, 1918.

347. Langer testimony, Senate Hearings, pp. 622–3; Nelson, *Land of the Dacotahs*, p. 309, estimates the saving at $400,000, equivalent to more than ten million dollars in 2000.

348. Langer testimony, Senate Hearings, pp. 654 ff.

349. Dubious then, but not so dubious later, after the United States Supreme Court upheld a Minnesota statutory moratorium in *Home Building and Loan Association v. Blaisdell*, 290 U.S. 398 (1934). Langer declared the moratorium 1n 1933 after it was authorized by the 1933 Legislature, Ch. 145 1933 Session Laws, and the Legislature made it statutory as Ch. 161, 1937 Session Laws. For more detail on the moratorium and embargo see S. Vogel, "Law of Hard Times," p. 489.

350. John L. Shover, *The Cornbelt Rebellion: The Farmers' Holiday Association* (Urbana: University of Illinois Press, 1965), p. 77.

351. Ibid., p. 81.

352. For more detail on this very tense era, see Shover, *Cornbelt Rebellion*, generally, but especially pp. 77–97. Usher Burdick of North Dakota, later a longtime congressman, was very active in the movement.

353. See Langer testimony, Senate Hearings, 515 ff. Later, the United States Supreme Court upheld a moratorium in Minnesota.

354. Wilkins and Wilkins, *North Dakota*, p. 116; Langer testimony, Senate Hearings, pp. 610–11.

355. *Congressional Record*, Vol. 88, part 1, p. 1350.

356. Ibid., p. 1396.

357. Conrad W. Leifur, *Our State, North Dakota* (New York, Cincinnati: American Book Co., 1942).

358. Larry Remele, "North Dakota's Changing History," *North Dakota Quarterly* 56, no. 4 (Fall 1988), p. 358.

359. Leifur, pp. 304–7.

360. Hatch Act, 53 Stat. 1147, adopted August 2, 1939, and much amended later.

361. See, for example, the *Leader*, Oct. 11, 1934, in which a letter of the Democratic state chairman to federal employees, asking for money, is set out.

362. Ibid. The *Leader* listed the names of nine people who were fired by the Ole H. Olson administration, and saying there were hundreds more.

363. Vogel, "Sources of the North Dakota Constitution," *North Dakota Law Review* 65 (1959):3.

364. Robinson, *North Dakota*, pp. 403–19.

365. Ibid., p. 403. I have been told that Langer spoke German with an Austrian dialect, which many of the Volga-area Germans from Russia found odd. His parents came from the Austro-Hungarian Empire, in what is now the Czech Republic.

366. Ibid., pp. 404–9. This was, after all, long before the adoption of the Hatch Act in 1939 and every administration used its power of patronage to put its people into office. This includes not only the Nonpartisan League, but the prior and subsequent Republican administrations and all Democratic administrations. And it includes many administrations after passage of the Hatch Act.

367. Ibid., p. 410.

368. Ibid., p. 412.

369. In addition, the source citations given for the statements as to the "bond deals" are to wrong pages of the Senate Report.

370. Ibid., p. 412, fn. 14.

371. Ibid., p. 416.

372. Wilkins and Wilkins, *North Dakota*.

373. Ibid., pp. 116-17.

374. Ibid., p. 117.

375. Senate Hearings, p.72; Thomas W. Howard, ed., *The North Dakota Political Tradition* (Ames: Iowa State University Press, 1981).

376. Wilkins and Wilkins, *North Dakota*, pp. 120–21, 119, and 151.

377. Ibid., p. 149.

378. The house still stands and was valued in 1993 by the City Assessor at $107,000, letter to the author from Cass County Auditor, in response to a request.

379. August 7, 1957.

380. Howard, ed., *North Dakota Political Tradition*.

381. Ibid., p. 64.

382. Ibid., p. 92.

383. Ibid., p. 124.

384. Geelan, *Dakota Maverick*, p. 18.

385. Glenn Smith, "William Langer and the Art of Personal Politics," in *North Dakota Political Tradition*, Thomas Howard, ed., p. 126.

386. Ibid., p. 132.

387. Ibid., p. 133.

388. Ibid., p. 134.

389. Ibid. The embargo was held constitutional in *Farmers Grain Co. of Embden v U.S.*, 273 F. 635, but reversed by the United States Supreme Court, 258 U.S. 50. It was in effect from the time it was declared, Oct. 16, 1933, to the time it was declared unconstitutional, January 1934.

390. Smith, "William Langer," p. 134.

391. Ibid., p. 135.

392. Ibid., p. 136.

393. Ibid.

394. Ibid.

395. Ibid., p. 137. The correct spelling is Moodie.

396. Ibid.

397. Ibid.

398. The juror's name was Hermistos or Herman Charbonneau.

399. Ibid., p. 138.

400. Ibid., p. 140.

401. Ibid., p. 141.

402. Ibid., p. 142.

403. The author has copies of the original telegrams from Frank Vogel to Frazier and Lemke, and their replies.

404. Smith, "William Langer," p. 144.

405. Ibid., pp. 145–46. Presumably, this is a reference to the last gasp of Langer's enemies when a committee headed by his longtime antagonist, state Senator Joe Bridston, and including C. R. Verry, tried to unseat him once again. The Senate committee listened to Bridston and his attorney, concluded that they had no proof that Langer's private bills had any improper motive, and dismissed the petitions. Private bills are bills to recompense or assist individuals in some way; in this case to keep immigrants facing deportation from being deported until their cases could be heard. Langer at the time was chairman the Senate Judiciary Committee' subcommittee on Immigration, and there was no showing whatever that he received any money or benefit for introducing the bills. Practically all the people involved were living in other states. See Don Eppler, "Langer Accused Again: Joseph Bridston's Attempt to Unseat William Langer From the Senate" (master's thesis, University of North Dakota, 1978).

406. Lawrence Larsen, "*U.S. v. Langer, et al*: The U.S. District Attorney's Files," *North Dakota History: Journal of the Northern Plains*, 51, no. 2 (Spring 1984): 4–13.

407. See statement of Lanier to the Department of Justice, pp. 5–6, after the hung jury in the second conspiracy trial, that "the result is undoubtedly a victory for the government," which can only mean that the government succeeded in its purpose of removing Langer from office in 1934 and keeping him out to the date of the quoted letter, Nov. 19, 1935, and thereafter. The victory, of course, was only temporary. Langer was reelected governor a year later, and United States Senate from 1941 until his death in 1959.

408. *North Dakota Blue Book, 1954*, pp. 149, 307.

409. Ibid., p. 10.

410. See Morlan, *Prairie Fire*, p. 342.

411. Holzworth, *Fighting Governor*, pp. 123–29.

412. Wilkins and Wilkins, *North Dakota*, and Robinson, *History of North Dakota*, recognize that Miller was "an old enemy" of Langer.

413. Larsen, "*U.S. v. Langer, et al*," p. 13.

Index

Aarhus, P. J., 55-56
Affidavit of prejudice: 34, 80-89
Affidavits: collected by Smith and Hood, 17, 132
Alex Johnson Hotel (Rapid City, S.Dak.), 106
Amick, I. N., 102
Amidon, Charles, 32, 35, 42, 43, 45
Anderson, A. M., 21, 109, 139
Anderson, Carl, 12, 54-55
Argast, Fred J., 12, 54, 68
Atwater, Pierce, 5, 24, 27
Baker, Berta, 118, 130
Bank of North Dakota, 5, 23, 24, 38, 132-133, 137, 152, 159, 163, 170
Barkley, Alben, 103
Bismarck Capital, 21
Bismarck Tribune, 3, 13, 15, 19-21, 29, 60, 81, 136, 150
Bismarck: typhoid fever epidemic in, 31-32
Bismarck Water Supply Co.: lawsuit against, 7, 31-32
Blackorby, Edward, 102
Boise, Charlie, 19
Bradford, Ben, 17-18
Brady, J. T., 50
Brandby, Stella, 38
Brant, E. H., 52, 56, 92
Brewer, V. W., 120-125, 132
Brunk, Gregory, 120-125
Buckley case: Langer's involvement in, 119
Burdick, Usher, 19, 20, 28, 36, 69, 86, 90, 91, 94, 132; on jury selection, 42-46; on Judge Miller, 63
Burleigh County, 19
Burton, Harold, 109
Butler, Pierce, 129
Buttz, Judge, 120

Capitol building (Bismarck), **6** burned down, 24
Cardozo, Benjamin, 126
Carmody, John, 113
Casselton, 3, 11, 66, 67
Censorship: of political campaigns, 11
Chaput, Oscar J., 7, 25, 52, 60, 62, 64, 66, 92
Charboneau, Herman, 92, 93, 95
Christianson, Adolph M., 5, 23, 24, 27, 52, 53; testimony of, 56-57
Churchill, Winston, 147
Citizens Clean Courts Committee, 32
Collette, Caskie, 81
Columbia Broadcasting Co., 11
Columbia University (N.Y.), 3
Congressional Record, 82, 134, 144
Connally, Tom, 104, 111, 131, 133
Conspiracy: definition of, 38-39, 64-65
Craig, Minnie D., 23, 24, 52, 54, 56, 68; testimony of, 57-58
Crockett, William, 101
Dakota Maverick (Geelan), 133
Dakota National Bank and Trust Co., 38
Dalstad, G. Leonard, 124
Davies, Ronald N., 81
Deadwood, S.Dak., 87
Debs, Eugene, 39
Deis case: Langer's involvement in, 114-118
Dell, Richard, 148-149
DePuy, H. C., 21
Dietz Lumber Co.: lawsuit involving, 30-31
Donnybrook, 14
Dorety, attorney, 152
Douglas, Paul, 1
Doyle, S. J., 24
Duffy, Clyde, 104, 124, 132, 137
Eaton, John C., 27

Edmonds, T. J., 23, 27
Eisenhower Administration, 28
Elections in N.Dak.: 5
Ellsworth, Scott, 1
Embargo: on wheat exports, 5
Equal Rights Amendment, 146
Erickson, Oscar E., 7, 25, 49, 51, 55, 81, **91**, 92, 93, **103**, 106, 107
Evidence: admission of, 75, 76
Ewing, Sherrard, 22, 24, 27, 52, 53, 57; testimony of, 58
Falconer, William, 68
Fargo Forum, 3, 13, 78, 95, 97, 150
Farley, James, 26, 78
Farmers Holiday Association, 120-121
Farmers Security Bank of Park River v. Verry, 108
Federal Emergency Relief Act, 36-37
Federal Emergency Relief Administration, 5, 22, 58
Federal Land Bank, 27, 152
Federal Trade Commission, 147
Feist, Andrew R., 132
Forde, O. T., 38
Fort Yates: Langer's jail break-in at, 118-119
Frahm, H. C., 92
Frazier, Lynn J., 25, 32, 102, **119**, 128
Frazier, Roy, 12, 54, 68
French, L. M., 38
Fruh, Al, 50
Fuller, Howard, 107, 135
Garberg, Peter B., 42
Gardner, A. K., 73
Garrison, 72
Geelan, Agnes, 103, 165
Gilbert, Joseph, 2, 126
Godwin, William, 68, **103**
Governor's mansion (Bismarck): **98**, 102
Grand Forks Herald, 3, 13, 32
Gray, John, **103**, 118, 130
Great Depression, 5

Great Northern Railroad: 120, 151; tax reductions of, 128-130
Great Northern v. Weeks, 129
Green, Theodore, 132
Green v. Frazier, 35
Grimson, Gudmunder, 17
Gronna, Arthur J., 51
Gunvaldson, Ole, 44, 46, 69, 70, 78, 139
Gurney, John, 132
Hagan, John N., 106, 117, 130, 164
Hamilton, Dave, 52
Hample, Gideon A., 7, 25, 60
Hanley, James M., 32, 43, 45, 46, 47, 63, 64, 132
Harding, William, 7
Hatch Act, 77
Hedging: in grain market, 54
Hepner, George, 69
Herigstad, O. B., 19
Hermann v. Ramadan, 109
Hickok, Lorena, 56-57, 150
Hilton, Clifford L., 126
History of North Dakota (Robinson): on Langer, 160-162
Hood, ____, South Dakota deputy marshal, 87
Hood and Smith, Senate investigators: 17, 93, 95, 109, 110-112, 144
Hood, Sam, Jr. *See* Hood and Smith, Senate investigators
Hooper, Wynn, 41, 42, 47
Hoover case: Langer's involvement in, 114
Hoover, Charlie, 114
Hopkins, Harry, 5, 22, 23, 26, 29, 56-57, 78, 79, 140
Horne, Robert, 134
Howard, Thomas, 164
Howe, Louis McHenry, 22, 26
Hulett, Lester, 47, 50
Hultin, Clarence, 17
Hultin, Edith, 17

204

Hung jury: in Langer trial, 92
Hyland, Frank, 13
Ickes, Harold, 25, 29, 140
Independent Voters Association, 13, 32, 52, 78
Ingstad, Fred B., 132
Internal Revenue Service, 29, 97
Jackson County, Minn., 126
Jackson, Dan, 84, 85, 95, 96
Janke, ____, juror, 92
Jansonius, Fred, 116, 120, 138
Johnson case: Langer's involvement in, 14-19
Johnson, Esther, 14, 17, 18
Johnson, Floyd, 14, 18
Journal of the American Bar Association, 147
Joyce, Charlie, 135
Judicial Code (28 USC), 90
Junge, Phrene, 38
Jury: judge's instructions to, 60-65, 77; random selection requirements of, 76; selection in Langer trials, 36, 40-51; selection of in federal court, 75-76
Keenan, Joseph, 24, 25, 86, 141
KFJM Radio, 11
Kinzer, Joseph, 7, 25, 52, 54
Kinzer, R. A., 7, 22, 23, 25, 38, 52, 56, 57, 59, 60, 62, 66, 81, 92
Klaudt, A. J., 124, 132, 137
Krueger, Otto, 28
Krulewitch v. United States, 39
La Follette, Robert M., 103
Land Finance Co., 127
Langer Defense Fund, 90
Langer, Lydia Cady, **99**, 100, 102, **104**, **105**, 114
Langer v. United States, 24
Langer, William: as asst. state's attorney, **3**, 30-31; budget cuts by, 9, 13; campaign style of, **33**, 10-11, 154; charges of income tax violations of, 141-142; conspiracy charges against, 25, 37-38; during appeal process, 71; early history of, 4; and his enemies, 139-155; first conspiracy trial of, 7, 36, 52-67; as governor, 5, 9, 23, **119**, **176**; and Johnson case, 14-19; and Nonpartisan League, 32-33; perjury trial of, 80-88; second conspiracy trial of, 89-96; Senate hearings on, 131-138; Senate investigation of, 104-130; third conspiracy trial of, 96-101; as U.S. senator, 8, 102-138
Lanier, Powless W. ("Pete"), 23, 24, 26, 27, 28, 29, 37, 40, 42, 43, 70, 78, 79, 139, 140
Larsen, Lawrence H.: on Langer trials, 172-175
Lashkowitz, Harry, 28
Leader (Nonpartisan League paper), 6, 20, **37**, 37, 40, 52, 73, 76, 77, 97, 138, 140
Leavenworth Penitentiary, 67
Leedom, Chet, 87, 94, 105
Lehmann Brothers, 123
Leifur, Conrad: on Langer, 156-160
Lemke, William, 12, 45, 78, 111, **111**, 163, 164; on kickbacks, 136; and Mexican land deal, 127-130
Lewis, C. L., 123
Little, C. B., 31
Lucas, Scott W., 49-50, 109
Maloney, Francis, 103
Manahan, James, 125-126
Mann, George D., 19
McCarthy, Joseph, 112
McCue, Thomas F., 32
McCulloch, Hugh, 123
McCumber, Porter J., 32
McCurdy, ____, attorney, 120
McDonald, Harold, 7, 25, 37, 38, 52, 57, 58, 73, 92; testimony of, 59-60, 64, 66, 69
McDonald, S. S., 13

McFarland, Ernest, 103
McFarland, R. G., 16
McGurren, James, 138
McKenna, George, 16
McKenzie, Alexander, 7, 14, 30, 32, 35, 164-165, 174
McLachlan, Alden, 150
McLean County Nonpartisan League, 72
Mexico: purchase of land by Langer and Lemke, 127-132
Miller, Andrew A., **4**, 29, 30, 33, 34, 35, 36, **41**; and jury selection, 40-51; conduct of first conspiracy trial, 51-67, 70; appeal ruling, 70-79; perjury charges by, 80-88, 89, 139, 140
Miller, P. H., 117
Mills, Ethel, 12, 15
Milo, Joe, 14
Minnesota Commission on Public Safety, 126
Minot Daily News, 3, 13, 150
Montgomery, J. A., 41, 42, 47
Moodie, Thomas, 26, 100-101, 157, 173
Moratorium: on farm foreclosures, 5, 7, 21, 34, 109, 152-153, 157, 159, 163, 166-167
Morse, True D., 123, 132
Morton County: Langer as assistant state's attorney for, 3, 30
Moses, John, 101, 102, 106, 108, 124, 136-138, 144, 158
Mulholland, Matt, 19
Mulloy, James, 50-51, 87, 94, 102, **103**, 104 111, 118, 124, 131, 132, 135 137, 162, 167, 168, 171
Murdock, Orrice ("Abe"), 109, 133
Murphy, Francis, 30, 45, 47-50, 63, 72, 73; and perjury trial, 80-88; and second conspiracy trial, 89-96; and third conspiracy trial, 96-101, 110, 118; and Senate hearings, 131-138
Murphy, R. B., 25, 27, 95

Murray, J. K., 81, 97, 141
Myers, C. J. ("Red"), 106, 112
National Industrial Recovery Act, 36-37
National Women's Party, 146
Newton, J. H., 113
Nichols, Lee, 23, 24, 26, 52, 53, 68
nolle prosse, 95-96
Nonpartisan Leader. See Leader
Nonpartisan League: early history of, 1 3; Executive Committee of, 54-55, 68; Langer's split with, 32-33
Normanden (newspaper), 44
North Dakota: A Centennial History (Wilkins and Wilkins): on Langer, 162-164
North Dakota Agricultural College, 153
North Dakota Highway Department, 40, 59, 60, 69
North Dakota House of Representatives: fact-finding committee of, 12, 42
North Dakota National Guard, 7, 33, 153
North Dakota Political Tradition (Howard, ed.): on Langer, 164-171
North Dakota Railroad Commission, 13
North Dakota Securities Commission, 51
North Dakota State Bar Board, 16
North Dakota State Board of Equalization, 129
North Dakota State Board of Health, 31-33
North Dakota State Industrial Commission, 106
North Dakota State Mill and Elevator, 5, 153
North Dakota Supreme Court, 4, 8, 15, 17, 23, 31, 53, 67-68, 71, 75, 96, 108, 113, 114, 131, 135. *See also* individual cases
Northern Pacific Railway Co.: 129, 174; lawsuit involving, 30-31
Nye, Gerald P., 25, 27, 29, 54, 78, 97, 102, 114, 117, **119**, 128, 131, 135-136

Occident Elevator Co.: lawsuit involving, 30-31
Offer of proof: in Langer trial, 55
Olson, Ole, 68, 100, 157
Omland, John R., 106
One Third of a Nation (Hickok), 140
Oster, Emma, 114-117
Oster, Jacob, 115-117
Our State, North Dakota (Leifur), on Langer, 156-160
Owen, O. T., 118, 130
Pardon Board, 14
Patronage: complaints about, 23, 26
Patronage: political, 76-77
Patterson, Dell, 15
Patterson Hotel, 44
Paulson, Happy, 95
Pearl Harbor: attack on, 134
Pennsylvania v. Nelson, 126
Peterson, ___, murder victim, 115
Pfenning, W. J., 38
Phelps case: Langer's involvement in, 113-114
Postal Inspectors, 147
Powell v. McCormack, 145
"Power to the People: The Nonpartisan League," 165
Prejudice. *See* Affidavit of prejudice
Reconstruction Finance Corp., 36-37
Regional Agricultural Credit Corporation, 27
Reich, Ernie, 92, 93
Remele, Larry, 156, 165
Reno, Milo, 120-121
Republican Organizing Committee, 149
Republican party in N.Dak., 3
Richland County, 34
Riley, D. D., 15
Roan and Strauss, physicians, 106-107
Robinson, Elwyn B.: 3; on Langer, 160-162
Roder, Otto, 51, 65

Roosevelt, Franklin Delano, 21, 22, 23, 26, 27
Rumpers, 101
Runck, Joe, 66-67
Rural Electrification Administration, 148-149
Ryckman, Ed., 38
Rylance, Dan, 68
Sathre, P. O., 51, 130
State ex rel Sathre v. Moodie, 173
Saturday Evening Post, 1, 114
Schumacher, H. C., 44, 69
Scott, Archie, 118
Scott, Edith, 38, 52; testimony of, 58-59
Shafer, George, 13, 27, 52, 78
Shall, Thomas D., 90
Shaw, B. C., 114
Simons, Kenneth, 13, 15, 19
Sinkler, Ed, 18, 63, 65, 90
Slovarp, Emma Oster. *See* Oster, Emma.
Smith, Beverly, 114
Smith, Elbert. *See* Hood and Smith, Senate investigators.
Smith, Ellison DuRant, 114
Smith, Glenn: on Langer, 165-172
Southworth, Ellis B., 123, 132
Standard Oil Co.: lawsuit involving, 30-31
Stangler, Robert, 23, 24, 52, 54, 132-133
State Emergency Relief Office, 40, 58, 73, 140
State printing office: proposal of, 13
State Relief Committee, 52-54, 56-59, 92. *See also* names of individual members.
State v. Norton, 75
Stone, C. P., 136
Strack, Howard, 65, 87, 94, 92, 95
Strutz, Alvin C., 28, 106, 107, 117, 130
Sullivan, John, 92, 123

Sullivan, Thomas V., 120-125, 127-130
Swain, C. C., 118
Talcott, Frank, 41, 84
Thompson, Arthur E., 23, 24, 52, 53
Thoreson, T. H. H., 20, 101
Thorp, George, 63, 90
Townley, A. C., 2, **119**, 126, 164
Trials of a Lawyer (Manahan), 126
Typhoid fever: and lawsuit, 31
"*U.S. v. Langer, et al.*: The U.S. District Attorney's Files," 172-175
United States Court of Appeals for the Eighth Circuit, 34, 66-70; ruling of, 71, 79, 81, 97-98
United States Department of Interior, 29
United States Department of Justice, 25, 84, 86: Fraud Section, 147
United States Securities and Exchange Commission, 147
United States Senate Post Office Committee, 147
United States Senate Judiciary Committee, 147
United States Senate Committee on Privileges and Elections: 8, 17; Burdick's testimony to, 45-56, 63; Langer's case to, 104-138
United States Supreme Court, 35, 37, 39, 76, 82, 112, 126, 129, 130, 142, 145
United States v. Berger, 82, 86
United States v. Byers, 24
University of North Dakota School of Law, 3
Valley City, 21
Van Horne, Clarence, 138
Verry, C. R., 15, 93, 102, 104, 108-109, 131, 132
Verry v. Murphy, 109
Vogel, Charles, 45, 60, 81, 102, 103, 154
Vogel, Frank, 5, 7, 11, 14, 25, 40, 52, 59-60, 62, 66, 67, 69, 72, 81, 93, **103**, 144-145, 152, 161, 169

Vogel, Robert, 72, 91
Wagner Act, 39
Walkenburg, A. B., 73
Wallace, George, 52, 95
Wallace, Henry, 57
Walley, Ersel, 123, 132
Ward County Courthouse, 14
Ward County Independent, 123
Warner Agency, 66
Water: contamination of in Bismarck, 31
Welford, Walter, 68, 97, **101**, 106
Welk, Lawrence, 29
Whelan, Thomas J., 102, 103, 154
Wicks, Marcella, 121
Wilkins, Robert P.: on Langer, 162-164
Wilkins, Wynona: on Langer, 162-164
"William Langer and the Art of Personal Politics," 165-172
Williams, Aubrey, 27
Williams, John E., 54, 56, 57, 59, 92
Williams County, 42
Williston Chamber of Commerce, 151
Wishek, John, 106
Wood, F. B., 164, 165
Woorough, J. W., 73
Works Progress Administration, 26, 27
World War I: and the Nonpartisan League, 2
Wyman, A. Lee, 34, 39-40, 79, 88; judge of second conspiracy trial, 91-96; judge of third conspiracy trial, 96-101, 108; written statement of, 132
Wyman, Gale, 86, 87, 88, 94, 105, 108, 132
Yeater, Paul J., 7, 25
Young, Clyde, 113
Zlevor, Rose, 38
Zuger and Miller Law Firm, 30

To order additional copies of

Unequal Contest
Bill Langer and His Political Enemies
by Robert Vogel
Edited by Janet Daley

send check for $17.95
for each copy ordered to:

Crain Grosinger Publishing
P.O. Box 55
Mandan, ND 58554

includes sales tax and standard shipping.
if you prefer priority shipping send $20.00/book.

To pay by credit card call:

701-663-0846; 877-566-2665 (toll-free)

If ordering six or more copies call for discount.

Be sure to visit
www.wmlanger.com
and take the "What Would Wm. Langer Do?" quiz.

Crain Grosinger Publishing *is located at 210 Collins Avenue in Mandan, North Dakota. The business was founded in 1993 by Paula Crain Grosinger and Brian Grosinger. Crain Grosinger Publishing is an independent book publisher dedicated to providing a voice for those who should be a part of serious public discourse in the upper Midwest and beyond.*

Member of the Small Publishers Association of North America and the North Dakota Newspaper Association.